EDUCATION AND NATION-BUILDING
IN THE THIRD WORLD

EDUCATION
AND
NATION-BUILDING
in the Third World

Edited by

J. LOWE
N. GRANT
T. D. WILLIAMS

BARNES & NOBLE, Inc.

NEW YORK

PUBLISHERS & BOOKSELLERS SINCE 1837

Published by
Scottish Academic Press Ltd.
25 Perth Street, Edinburgh 3
First Published in the United States of America, 1971
by Barnes and Noble Inc.

ISBN 389 04167 X

Printed in Great Britain

PREFACE

Within recent years increasing attention has been paid to the contribution that education can make to the goals of national development, especially in the so-called developing countries. The present survey of some of the key aspects of the relationship arose from a seminar on Education and Nation-Building, held at Edinburgh University in 1969. The papers presented at that seminar have been modified for the purposes of publication.

The survey is divided into four parts. It begins with a critical examination of the current scope and rationale of international aid programmes. There follow three chapters on the relationship between economic planning and education, two couched in global terms and one dealing specifically with African development. The next two chapters are concerned with the sociological and political context. Succeeding chapters then consider three topics of central importance: the role of adult education; the education of women; and the language problem. Two concluding chapters draw parallels, first, between the Cuban and African approaches to educational planning and, secondly, between the Soviet experience and that of the developing countries in general.

CONTENTS

CHAPTER I

WORLD RE-APPRAISALS

H. L. ELVIN*

The establishment of the United Nations after the Second World War gave renewed hope for the institutional embodiment of the idea of a world community. Its major purpose was to keep the peace, indeed to build a permanent structure for peace-keeping. This hope, in spite of a few successes, has so far been disappointed. But there was a second purpose: through international action to promote human welfare so that the advantages of modern life could be enjoyed by the many low-income countries as well as by those that were more advanced. The incipient world community recognised an obligation, as did the richer countries on their own account, to assist in the economic and social development of the under-developed parts of the world. This marked a major advance in the sense of the moral solidarity of mankind.

A series of Specialised Agencies soon flanked the main United Nations Organisation to help forward this work in education, food and agriculture, health and labour, and after a period of conservative reluctance the World Bank also became heavily involved. The United States as the most affluent country of all set a generous example with its programmes, official and private, of international aid. Britain and France, whose colonial empires were in these years giving way to numerous independent states, recognised a special continuing obligation to the peoples they had formerly ruled. Other countries, such as the Soviet Union, the Federal Republic of Germany and the Scandinavians, developed their own programmes of bilateral aid as well as contributing to the work of the UN Agencies.

---

* I should like to thank my friend, Mr Raymond Lyons, who does not agree with all the views I have expressed in this paper, for reading it in draft and making a number of suggestions that I have incorporated.

Even countries that were in receipt of aid began to assist one another. Most important of all, the low-income countries themselves set out to raise standards of living by planning more modern economies and societies. The intolerable gap between the richer and the poorer countries has in these two decades hit the conscience of mankind.[1]

It is now twenty years or more since this promising assumption of responsibility began. Dr Mukherjee quotes the words with which President Truman launched his Point Four Programme on 20 January 1949:

We must embark on a bold new program for making the benefits of our scientific advances and industrial progress available for the improvement and growth of underdeveloped areas. More than half the people of the world are living in conditions approaching misery. Their food is inadequate. They are victims of disease. Their economic life is primitive and stagnant. For the first time in history, humanity possesses the knowledge and skill to relieve the suffering of these people.[2]

This was a moment of great hope. Should not the determination these words expressed have led by now to a great leap forward in the welfare of mankind? Can we really say that this has happened? Have we gone forward or even, relatively, back?

The answer depends on the way the question is spelled out. If one asks whether the economies of the less developed countries are somewhat more advanced than they were, the answer is yes. There has certainly been growth in terms of real gross national product per head (on average for the low-income countries of perhaps 15 per cent between 1960 and 1966). And there has undoubtedly been development, especially in the social welfare services (sometimes, it may be, at the expense of investment that would have led to economic growth). To the simple, unqualified question as to whether there has been both growth and development, the short answer is yes. In education, specifically, if one asks the straight question whether there are more children in school than there were twenty years ago, the answer is again yes.

But put the question in other terms. Is the gap between the

2

richer and the poorer countries beginning to close? The answer, everyone seems to agree, is no: it is widening. This is because there has been more investment, and a greater growth in GNP per head, in the developed countries, and because the rise in population has been greater in the 'developing' ones. What is no less serious is the fact that the terms of trade have been swinging against the low-income countries, largely off-setting the effect of external aid. Trade, as has been said for many years now, is as important as aid. And trade is failing to bring surplus enough at the same time that the total or external debt is increasing and the cost of its annual servicing becoming very serious indeed. There is even evidence to suggest that the countries with the lowest GNP per head are the ones getting the least external aid per head.

In education, the statement that there are more children in school now than there were twenty years ago ignores the fantastic rate at which the world's population is increasing. Mr Philip Coombs wrote a most useful study for the Conference on the World Crisis in Education that met at Williamsburg, Virginia, in October 1967. In the revised edition, published in 1968, he says, 'Despite this great educational expansion a parallel population growth has led to an increase in the aggregate number of adult illiterates in the world. The figure for UNESCO's member states currently exceeds 460 million illiterate adults, or almost 60 per cent of their active population.'[3] Professor George Bereday, editing a series of papers prepared for this same Conference, says, 'It has been estimated that one quarter of the world's population will not attend any school in this century. In many of the less developed countries that figure may be 50 per cent. When compared with previous centuries this still represents an advance, but in an age committed to the concept of universal education this is a calamity.'[4] One must remember that in these last twenty years there has been an immense upsurge in the popular demand for education as a human right, apart altogether from the realisation that it is indispensable for economic and social development. This is only one facet of the 'revolution in rising expectations' the

3

world over. Absolutely we may be making small advances. Relatively the sad truth may be that we are falling back. Professor Gunnar Myrdal has written a magisterial work about the problems of development in the countries of South-East Asia. His sub-title is significant: 'An Inquiry into the *Poverty of Nations*', an ironic echo, nearly two hundred years later, of the title of Adam Smith's great book.[5]

These are the questions that are puzzling people. We are at a moment when re-appraisal is in the air. It would be wrong to discourage it for fear of playing into the hands of those who really want to contract out of our obligations to mankind. The questions must be faced; and they are of two broad kinds. First, are the concepts with which we have been working appropriate to the real problems? This is only another way of saying, have we understood clearly enough what the problems of economic and social development are, so that we can attack them in the right places and in the right way? Secondly, have our machinery and procedures been right, both internationally and within each country's own planning? In this paper I wish to review the experience that leads to the putting of these questions and to indicate the suggestions that are being made for improving our concepts and our procedures.

President Truman saw the problem as passing on to the less developed countries the benefits that the more advanced countries enjoyed. This means giving them some of the products of the advanced countries, both capital and consumer goods. It implies also investment and loans. More importantly it implies the transmission of knowledge and skill, by sending them expert advisers and receiving their younger people into education and training courses of all kinds. By any reasonable standard a great deal has been given in these various ways during the succeeding twenty years. But one is tempted to ask: has this been enough?

Unfortunately 'enough' is a rather empty word. One must go on to ask, enough to do what? The economist might say that enough help should be given to enable an under-developed country to reach what Professor Rostow described in a now

4

famous phrase as the 'take-off point' for a modern economy. This means the point at which an economy can go ahead under its own impetus, with the ability to grow its own capital or to borrow on a sound business basis.

Or a value judgment may be implied in the word 'enough'. How much ought Dives to have given Lazarus beyond the crumbs that fell from his table? The United Nations target for the donor countries was set in 1964 at 1 per cent of national income, and in 1968 this was raised to 1 per cent of gross national product. In 1967 the net flow of financial resources from Britain was 0·97 per cent of national income, or 0·77 per cent of gross national product. This includes both official and private flows.* The British official aid programme in 1967-8 amounted to nearly £208 millions, or 1·5 per cent of public expenditure (on defence we spent 15·1 per cent and on our own education 12 per cent).[6] Education has now overtaken Defence.

The fact that this level is what it is, higher than it might have been, lower than many would wish it to be, must be taken in some degree as reflecting priorities in the minds of the peoples of the advanced countries. It might be thought that as the rich countries are getting richer, and as they are not too far now from that 1 per cent target, we ought to be able to reach it soon by a kind of natural increase. Unhappily there is no certainty of that at all. The richer countries as a whole prefer to spend their money on defence. This is not a case of simple wickedness. The reason is that there is too little assurance of world order for them to feel they can do anything else. Or they prefer to spend their money on landing men on the moon and suchlike things. This is partly because these bring indirect benefits to defence and partly for prestige. It has even been said—though I cannot give the reference—that the change-over from black and white to colour television will cost the British viewing public something like £300 millions. The

* Later Note: In 1969 the total flow of funds, official and private, counting towards the UNCTAD target of 1 per cent of GNP came to 0·97 per cent of GNP (Ministry of Overseas Development figures), but official aid was far below the proportion of the total that it should have reached.

difference between black and white and colour television would seem to be marginal. But such is our sense of relative values. Colour television is 'progress'. Feeding starving people is not.

We have reached a level of international aid beyond which it is unlikely that governments will go in the near future. There is even a danger that it may fall. This is a very real danger with American aid, the biggest of all. Countries like Britain that are in trouble with their balance of payments will have difficulty in keeping their contributions up. Mr Andrew Shonfield pointed out nearly ten years ago that the deficit on the balance of payments in 1958-9 gave a great shock to the United States and made it realise that however rich it was there might be limits on what it could spend abroad.[7] The huge cost of the war in Vietnam has accentuated these fears. We indeed cannot count on any increase in the volume of international aid in the immediate future.

The proportion of international aid that goes to education, like the proportion in national budgets, may be taken as a rough indication of the importance people give to it in economic and social development (though it must be remembered that part of the pressure is for education as good in itself). Mr Coombs in his Williamsburg study gives some figures, though these, as he says, must be read as extremely approximate. He says that the 'developing' countries as a whole are spending about ten billion dollars annually on education, or some 4 per cent of their gross national product. (When one remembers that they must give priority to the bare necessities of life, such as food, this does not compare badly with our own figure of 5·03 per cent in 1965 or 6·3 per cent in 1966.) Some 10 per cent of their educational expenditure comes from external sources (so that, for all our aid, they are doing 90 per cent of the job themselves). Of this external aid between 10 and 20 per cent comes through the United Nations or other multilateral agencies, 80 or 90 per cent coming through private or public bilateral arrangements. The share of education in all international aid Mr Coombs estimates at around 10 per cent.[8]

There will be some commentators who feel that the share of

education in national budgets and in international aid cannot be appreciably higher while there are so many other insistent needs. There will be others who feel that if the perpetual speeches about the cardinal importance of education in development mean anything then the share of education should be markedly higher. Argument about this at the present time does not seem likely to be fruitful. There has been quite enough competition among the UN Agencies and it militates against the combined attack on the problems of development that is needed. It would be better to enquire whether what is being done across the board could be better done, and if such enquiries themselves suggest that relatively greater effort should go into education then will be the time to press for that. Meanwhile, since total resources nationally and internationally will continue to be limited, let us see whether the resources we can command might be deployed to better advantage.

Arguments are being put forward that the total problem of economic and social development has not been well understood, and more particularly it has been said that the kinds of thing we have been trying to do in education have not been related to economic and social development as they should have been. Let us look at these two questions, the broader and the more specific one, and after that consider the further question as to whether the machinery and the procedures we have been using have been as effective as they might be.

The first discovery leading to a modification of the idea that international assistance was a matter of passing on benefits was that in order to utilise what was given a receiving country had to be ready to do so. This in turn led to the belief that a receiving country must be helped to proceed through a preparatory stage before it could hope to go forward by itself. Early in the days of technical assistance stories were told of machines that were unused because those to whom they had been given did not know how to maintain them, and indeed of equipment still rusting in store because administrative arrangements had gone wrong. There was in many countries a perpetual headache for resident advisers because of rapid

7

changes of government, or even of régimes. The paradox was that the countries against which such charges were privately made were almost always the ones that needed help most.

People drew a comparison between the great success of Marshall Aid in Europe, which really did help the war-devastated countries to get on their feet, and the aid to the low-income countries of Africa, Asia and Latin America which did not seem to be having anything like a similar effect. What were the differentiating factors in these two cases? The countries of Western Europe that were given Marshall Aid were, as the jargon goes, 'achievement motivated'. They wanted very much indeed to restore their economic and social life. Their peoples were not being asked to change century-old ways, as a Latin America peasant or an Indian craftsman might be; they simply needed help in bringing back a way of life they knew, and knew how to make profitable and rewarding. Their public services were basically there; they needed only to be got going again. They had technically trained labour forces, disorganised and dispersed temporarily, but no more. They had all enjoyed universal primary education, and a fair degree of secondary and higher education, for a long time. Once immediate post-war questions were settled they were likely to have stable political régimes.

In the under-developed countries these things were either not true at all or were much less so. Whereas what the countries of Europe needed was mostly an injection of capital and a renewal of equipment, what was needed in the under-developed countries was something more like an economic revolution, in the extreme case a transformation of a subsistence into a cash economy or of a mediaeval into a modern agriculture. Nor was it a matter of economics only. There were factors that were social as well as economic, such as the system of land-tenure. And there were political clashes that had to be resolved after independence, such as the role of tribal affiliations in a new nation. Above all there was the revolution in ideas that was needed, often from a past that was dominated by custom and magic to an acceptance of the working hypothesis of cause and

8

effect and of readiness for rational change—and this at a time when new nations were most anxious to realise their identity to themselves by affirming their sense of a past which under colonial rule they felt to have been brushed aside. Was it any cause for surprise that technical assistance to the low-income countries failed to have the quick revitalising effect that Marshall Aid had had for Europe?

Early in the life of the United Nations it was realised that a special effort must be made for development, beyond the scope of the ordinary programmes and budgets of the Specialised Agencies. So what was at first called Technical Assistance was launched, financed from a fund that was contributed annually, to which the low-income countries could make requests, and with a vague kind of co-ordination in New York and in the field. Much particular good work was done, but this machinery proved far from satisfactory, and for reasons that it was never difficult to state: the uncertainty of what funds would be available from year to year (and therefore the tendency to limit advisers' contracts to a year or at most two), the dispersal in different places of the various Specialised Agencies and their rivalry with each other, the lack of power either of the United Nations or of the receiving countries to plan really sustained combined attacks with a perspective of a decade rather than a year or so. Since those days the machinery has been somewhat improved, and there are current investigations that ought to lead to further improvement. But the root trouble has been less in the machinery than in the very concepts involved, in understanding the problem and the kinds of action needed to deal with it. The one thing that can be said with certainty about the members of a United Nations or Agency Secretariat is that they are too driven to have time for fundamental thinking; and the one thing that can be said with certainty about the average governmental representative at UN meetings where these problems are discussed is that they are the spokesmen of their own countries, not world statesmen thinking of the world and of the work of the UN as a whole. (There are a few shining exceptions to those generalisations; but very few.)

It was the economists who first called for a modification of the simple notion of the passing on of benefits. They insisted that a country could not be expected to modernise itself until the economy had a reasonably satisfactory 'infra-structure'. This was thought of at first as primarily an economic infra-structure, but it was obvious that it must also include an at least moderately satisfactory administration, a certain general level of education and some provision of specific training, as well as ports, railways, roads and the like. But it was some time, thanks to the conservatism of the World Bank, before the concept of 'pre-investment' became familiar, that is the making of funds available to create the conditions in which ordinary investment would be attractive. Increasingly it was seen that there must be 'soft loans', as well as hard loans with the normal conditions and interest rates. Meanwhile education especially suffered. Only 16 per cent of a technical assistance grant could be spent on equipment, and it was often what was needed most. And how could building schools be thought of as investment, except metaphorically? What was the rate of return on education?

The next extension of thinking came with the idea of investing in human resources as well as in physical plant. Whether the word investment was a metaphor need not concern us very much here. If it was, it was a metaphor with some justice in it. The pressure for the acceptance of this idea came largely from Professor Theodore Schultz of Chicago and his associates. He had argued that you could not explain the greater prosperity of the United States merely by its natural resources and its physical capital. The money and effort that had been put into education over so long a time must explain a large part of the otherwise inexplicable gap between the United States and other countries. It was a natural extension of this concept to argue that a plan for economic development must consider available resources of manpower trained to different needed levels and must make provision for such education and training. The first striking embodiment of this idea was the contribution of Professor Harbison to the Ashby Report on educational development in Nigeria.[9]

Professor Schultz and his colleagues have come in for a good deal of criticism on this point or that since he began to put forward his ideas. The claims for the advantages of manpower planning have also fallen somewhat out of favour, for the simple reason that they were often far more precise than good sense could warrant. But both these concepts have contributed to an advance in thinking. Those who are involved in planning the economic development of a country now automatically recognise the importance both of general education and of more specific kinds of training, whereas some of them might have been tempted previously to under-estimate these. And although manpower forecasting, and relating educational and training provision to such forecasting, is now seen to be a more hazardous game than it at first looked, the general (as distinct from the detailed) case for it has been widely accepted.

The real defects of such otherwise welcome developments in thinking have been pointed out very cogently by Professor Myrdal. They were only extensions of an approach that was still basically economic. The economics must be there; but economics alone is not enough. A Western economist who addresses himself to the problems of development only as an economist is much exposed to the danger of generalising about non-Western economies as if they were the economies with which he is familiar. It is the questions prompted by other disciplines, above all comparative sociology, that will be most likely to shake him out of his first assumptions. But Myrdal's criticism goes beyond this. An exclusively economic framework of discourse leaves out social, and especially institutional, factors that we cannot possibly afford to ignore.

Take India as an example. If you want to come to grips with the forces that are holding India back it is not enough to think of injecting capital, sending surplus grain, or making gifts of equipment, and of deploying foreign advisers on agriculture and industry (any more, one might add, than it is enough to help with the expansion of education, if by that you mean only supplying more of the same kind of thing that India has had till now). You have to deal with the role of the money-lender.

And with caste. Caste originally had an economic basis, and the legacy of caste still has to be dealt with. (One may say that if a high-caste Congressman would take off his shoes and get into the paddy-fields it would have more effect than speeches about the hand going along with the head and the heart, but it is psychologically easy for an American in India, or even now an Englishman, to take his coat off: do we realise what it would mean to a high-caste Indian?) How can India develop a rational nutrition policy while cows remain sacred and monkeys consume food that could nourish millions of human beings? Yet are we to attack religion? Why is it that some local communities in India respond to the opportunity to improve their standard of living while it seems that nothing can raise others out of the torpor of ages?[10] As Dr Rao, now Minister of Education, has said,[11] the root of the problem of India's economic development is not in economics at all: it is in the psychology of the people. The contribution of the economist, indispensable as it is, must be supplemented, and attention paid to institutions, social structures and ways of life.

People professionally concerned with education have come into these discussions rather more in recent years. Though very happy to welcome colleagues who told governments that education was investment, they have been by no means happy with some of the economists' terms and ideas: these left out too much of what teachers and educational administrators knew from their experience and that seemed to them important. Dr C. E. Beeby of New Zealand (and formerly of UNESCO) argues[12] that what you can do in a school system depends first and foremost on the quality of your teachers. It takes some time for any country to move from the stage in which schoolteachers are barely educated and rarely trained to one in which they are both trained and educated. These stages may be speeded up; they cannot be avoided. What you can do with educated and trained teachers is quite different from what you should attempt with teachers who are uneducated and untrained. In the first situation you should give great initiative and independence to your professionals; in the second, central leadership and even detailed control may be your only hope of progress.

Dr Beeby has also brought some balance into the notion of planning. Educational administrators who suppose themselves to have been planning educational development all their lives have got a bit restive with the idea that there should be a new race of people, called *planners*, trained as such. Planning is a function of all good administration, not a separate mystique. It may be sensible to have a Planning Department within a Ministry of Education, to give special attention to the way the different factors in the 'system' inter-operate, to ascertain the statistical facts, to forecast the effects of a proposed policy; and it may be reasonable to recruit appropriate specialists (statisticians, for instance) who will serve under—not on top of—the administrator who is head of such a Department. It may be sensible to have a National Plan; though within, not outside, the administration. Planning has in recent years rightly become respectable, even though the Russians do it. But the professional planner—usually an enthusiastic and gifted young man whose qualities will only come to fruition after some years of experience, during which he can develop a 'sense' for administration in a given field—is another matter. If he is planning education he must know what education, not merely statistics, is about.

The interplay between the economists and the educationists has brought into the foreground the idea that the *kind* of education you engage in may be even more important than the quantity of it. The economists have pointed out that much of the education given in low-income countries seems to have little relevance to their economic needs. Educationists have also often said that the kind of education given has little apparent relevance to the individual's needs. India is a glaring example of the justice of both these criticisms. Independent India inherited from the British Raj a system of education that was sadly inadequate in scope, intended for the most part to train clerks for the administration, but with the saving grace of good quality in the higher reaches. Independent India has striven heroically to extend education quantitatively, but it has not re-shaped the whole system with new attention to the kind of education given, which is what the country needs. It was the great virtue of the recent Education Commission[13] that it saw this and insisted on it. Professor Myrdal makes the same point. But, as the reception of the Indian Report already shows, it will not be easy to turn these ideas into effect. The trouble is not merely lack of money, but a thousand inbred conservatisms and vested interests.

It would seem then as if more recent evaluation of experience over these last two decades is beginning to lead to a better understanding of the problems of economic and social development and of the relation of education to it. Concepts are being re-examined and are getting more relevant. But it would be foolish to be very optimistic. The establishment of inter-disciplinary concepts, like the establishment of inter-ministerial co-operation, is a very difficult thing.

Every discipline has its own framework of discourse. This is a necessary instrument for work within the discipline, but it can be a prison when a wider view must be taken. In Bernard Shaw's play, *The Doctor's Dilemma*, Sir Colenso Ridgeon confesses to some of his colleagues that he has been feeling out of sorts. Cutler Walpole, the surgeon, sees at once what is wrong: it is blood-poisoning and he must be allowed to cut out the 'nuciform sac' (whether there is such an organ is open to doubt). On the other hand, Sir Ralph Bloomfield Bonnington, the consultant physician, proud of his scientific basis, thinks this is nonsense. The trouble is that the white corpuscles aren't doing their work. The remedy? To 'stimulate the phagocytes'. The only general practitioner in the party begs leave to suggest something much simpler: a pound of ripe greengages, taken daily half an hour before lunch. When a country is not functioning properly the economist sees the trouble in economic terms, the sociologist in inappropriate institutions and social attitudes, and the educationist (who may know ordinary human situations a little better) is regarded by both as much less 'scientific' than they are.

Shaw shows his consultants as honourable professional men, but so self-confident within the terms of their own experience that they are unconsciously perhaps just a trifle arrogant. They are, of course, agreed about one thing: that it really is a menace to medicine to have these general practitioners around (though their friend Blenkinsop is a decent chap and has had bad luck). Similarly there is a tendency in some quarters to concede that education ought to be studied, though of course in Departments of Economics and Sociology—people in Departments of Education are decent enough chaps, but awful fuddy-duddies. It is not surprising that some of those concerned with education in their daily work have begun to detect a note of arrogance in some of the statements made by some economists about what should be done to make education play its part in economic development. Those economists against whom such a charge cannot be made in their turn feel that this is unreasonable. And so tempers get a little frayed. The moral is as simple as it sounds sententious: that if educationists should realise that what can be measured without distortion should not be ignored, so economists should realise that not everything in education can be measured, or measured without damage to factors that involve value judgments more than statistics.

The difficulties are in large degree in terms and concepts with which exponents of different disciplines work. It is surprising that so many economists cannot see what to the educationist is obvious: that the concept of 'efficiency' as applied to education is really a metaphor, drawn from the world of factories and physical production, and that the word 'effectiveness' would be much less distorting. The concept of 'efficiency' at least tempts one to suppose that a class of eighty children taken by one teacher is twice as efficient as a class of forty, because the staff input is only half as much for the same output. If the word 'effectiveness' were used one would at least enquire into the relative chances of educating well with large and small classes, with less risk of jumping to foolish conclusions. It has similarly been suggested that the distorting word 'output' should be dropped, and the word 'outcomes' used instead. Why not?

The economists would be unhappy about these changes, because the substituted terms are less cut and dried. Precisely:
that is their virtue. In human situations it is of the greatest
importance not to measure the wrong things.

If we move from the realm of concepts to the middle ground,
as one might call it, between theory and practice, we find that
a great deal of research and policy consideration remains to
be done. Let us take two or three examples.

How important is general literacy in the movement from a
pre-technical to a modern economy? It seems almost frivolous
to raise this question without going into it at much greater
length than this paper can permit. However, one may note
three stages in the argument during these two decades. At first
there was a belief in mass campaigns to persuade people to
learn to read and write. It had not been noted, however, that
where these had been successful, as in the Soviet Union, two
factors were present: first, a genuinely revolutionary mood;
and second, economic development that gave expanding opportunities for work in which reading and writing could be put
to use. The second stage of thinking came when the results of
mass campaigns without these factors were seen to be disappointing. The ordinary rural worker did not seem to have
much desire to learn to read and write. He could be stimulated
for a while, but a year later (after the missionaries of literacy
had departed) he was probably reading nothing at all. What
he wanted, it was argued, was to improve his yields, or to have
a link road with the highway for getting to his market, or
perhaps to have a village school. Then let us start there, and
en route to getting all these things he will find increasingly that
to be able to read and write is useful too. This view was not
all foolishness. But it was based on putting things the wrong
way round, as Professor Myrdal says: literacy is to a large
extent the pre-requisite for entering modern life, not a mere
incidental. In many cases the merging of literacy work in
'social education' or 'community development' led to its
neglect.

The third stage in the discussion is more balanced. While

general literacy is not necessary to reach the 'take-off point' (it is commonly said that England had about 40 per cent literacy round the year 1800) a fairly high level of literacy is needed at first and thereafter it must spread quickly if economic and social development is to be maintained (Myrdal has a good point when he notes that English industrial achievement was rapidly overtaken in the second half of the nineteenth century by Germany and the United States where general systems of public education came into being earlier than they did in England). Two things seem tolerably clear. First, that for a country like India to aim at a mass movement that would make everybody literate in, say, five to ten years, is not realistic. To some extent the effort must be made where the relevance and usefulness of reading and writing are—or can be shown to be —clear. This is the way, as M. Roger Thabault has shown, that learning to read and write came to make sense to the peasants in nineteenth-century France.[14] Secondly, it is indeed intolerable that in India there should have been thirty-six million more illiterates in the course of only ten years. A great effort could be made to show that reading and writing are relevant and useful if literacy were fused with programmes of economic and social development as it has not been. (I was once speaking in a meeting about literacy in an Indian village and found that I had been preceded by an agricultural extension officer. I asked if he had told them that there were many things in print that would help them to improve the yields from their crops and their stock. The answer I got was that he had said nothing about this.) There is no doubt that the request transmitted to UNESCO by the United Nations two years ago (roughly speaking to work out the cost of making the whole world literate and to prepare a programme for doing so) was too vague and wide. UNESCO offered as a first stage a number of pilot projects to show what connection there was between readiness to learn to read and write and prospects of economic and social betterment. That was no doubt good sense. But the lessons of the pilot projects must be acted on, and in a large way. Literacy may have been under-valued, but it is still part of the greater whole, the complex of bringing the mass of people technically and culturally into the modern world.

If one is supinely selective in literacy work then one almost confines it to urban centres, where the prospects are best; and this would merely perpetuate the neglect of rural betterment, which, it is widely felt, has been the most neglected sector yet in plans for economic and social development. This is the second area we might note where much more positive thinking is necessary in the middle ground between theory and policy. There have been great efforts to improve agricultural practice the world over. Many things have been found out and much knowledge and skill taken from one area to another. But it has to be admitted that the problem goes beyond economics, and beyond the point where the United Nations writ runs. In Latin America nothing radical is likely to happen till there is a change in the class structure of society, and that is the last thing that their ruling groups intend to have happen. Can the change come the other way round? Could the pressure for a better life from the peasants and the labourers, or even the attraction of more profitable agriculture, lead through success to perceptible modifications of the class structure? That, after all, was the way it happened in most Western countries. But such a process would take a very long time.

There has been much discussion about the role of schools in rural betterment, and there are no agreed answers. Some voices, like that of President Julius Nyerere of Tanzania,[15] say that the future of their country is bound to be largely agricultural and that the rural schools must orient themselves to this. Others, with jaded memories of the sad school gardens that have made so little difference in the African bush, feel that this is asking too much of the schools: the problem is one of rural betterment as such. But it does seem to be an advance that some national leaders no longer look just to technology in industry for their progress, that they are thinking of a kind of orientation of their schools to contemporary rural life, and a better orientation than Gandhian 'basic education' (which, for all its central rightness in wanting the hand, the head and the

heart to be educated together, was essentially backward-looking).
It is not without interest that the next technical conference
in education called by the Commonwealth is to be on this
subject.*

There are other problems of educational policy in which we
are far from agreement, and some of these have an important
bearing on economic and social development. One might
instance the difficulty in deciding how much relative effort
should go into primary education in comparison with secondary
and higher education. Here even political factors may be
important. The head of a Ministry of Education said to me
once that his country could afford primary schools for only 50
per cent of the children if they were to develop secondary and
higher education to the bare minimum that the need for
educated manpower dictated. People would accept this, making the tacit assumption that their children would be in the
fortunate 50 per cent. But what would happen when they
found their children were not? They all had votes!

Perhaps the most difficult area of decision relates to vocational education. Here it is only too easy for educationists who
are unrealistic to get into disagreement with economists who
take too short a view. Education that is in a broad sense more
vocationally oriented has to have a larger place. Chairs of
Latin in African universities have been an absurdity when
there have been no Chairs of Agriculture or Veterinary Science.
As secondary schools become more general in formerly dependent countries they will have to get right away from the
imitation of English grammar schools or French lycées. The
primary schools must be more vitally related to the communities they are in, including their working life. On the other hand
to set the children spinning for hours on end, or to give them
narrow vocational training before they can read and write, is
economic as well as educational nonsense. As Professor Mark
Blaug and others have pointed out, if you are preparing children
for a swiftly changing economy they need more general

* Later Note: This Conference took place at the University of Ghana, 23
March–2 April 1970.

19

education, giving them basic skills and a grasp of basic principles that they can later apply in a succession of jobs.

As these examples show, if the answers are not always clear at least the right questions are now being asked, and there is better understanding of the concepts that are relevant. But a much stronger consensus is needed, so that there can be a firm base for effective policy decisions. Progress is being made. But world population is threatening to double every thirty or forty years, and the gap between the richer and the poorer nations is increasing while we wait.

This leads us to our last major topic. Could we at least improve the methods of planning for economic and social development, education included? And could we improve the procedures and machinery for international aid?

Whatever the shortcomings of planning in the low-income countries, one thing is certain: planning there must be. Time is too short to permit the slow evolution through *laisser faire* that the Western countries enjoyed. Resources are too short to permit any misuse of them that can possibly be foreseen and avoided. The dilemma of the under-developed countries is cruel: they must save in order to form the capital they need, and they cannot save except by keeping down a level of consumption that is already much too low. M. André Philip pointed out many years ago that this is why the under-developed countries are often driven to personal, or at least one-party rule. The alternative is the 'soft state' that, as Professor Myrdal says, does not have power enough to carry drastic reforms through. Perhaps the most important service that the developed countries can do for the under-developed is to send them people who will help them to plan with expertness and wisdom. UNESCO, as such and through IIEP, has played an increasing part in helping low-income countries to improve their educational planning, and OECD has been active, though chiefly in relation to its own member countries. But the planning advisers must understand that theirs is a many-sided task, with a necessary preparation in more than one discipline. It is of no use to send planning advisers, especially in education, who are mere economists, or mere sociologists, or mere teachers or educational administrators. They must at least be multi-disciplined enough in mind to be fully co-operating members of mixed teams. Those engaged in education, whether foreign advisers, administrators or teachers, have a special responsibility. If there is a possibility that, say, 10 per cent of the available funds may be devoted to new developments it is not too difficult to insist that these developments be planned. But what of the need for planned reform in the remaining 90 per cent of necessarily committed expenditures? It is in the existing structure and practices that we are almost certain to find the greatest misuse of resources, the most serious sacrifice of quality, the most entrenched conservatism of practice. The educationist planner of education, external or internal, has to think radically, as well as in terms of a country's own needs and values.

The machinery and procedures for international aid would seem to be very much in need of improvement. The responsibility for the welfare side of the work of the United Nations has been placed with its Economic and Social Council. It is difficult not to agree with Mr Andrew Shonfield that this Council has failed to fulfil a useful function and should be discarded. It is not an expert but a governmental body, yet it consists of representatives of only a small number of the members of the United Nations. Naturally the General Assembly and its Committees tend to go over the same ground again. Then there are the Specialised Agencies, each with its own General Conference, programme and budget and Executive Board or Governing Body. But worse, the United Nations Organisation has its own social programme and is a kind of half-Agency on its own account. This is foolish, for if more power goes to the UN the Agencies feel that it is going to a rival Agency. The UN should not have particular programmes. It should be referee when necessary, but above all 'animateur' and co-ordinator, with real powers of decision and command. The structure of the Agencies is also very imperfect. UNESCO, which I know best, has its General Conference (a body that in fact makes little change in the draft programme presented to it

21

but that generally permits such a multiplicity of demands from member states that coherence and concentration are almost impossible to achieve: the Secretariat tries to respond to what member states have indicated they would separately like at the previous Conference and the result is a bit of everything with little chance for a genuine, as distinct from a verbal, directive conception). It also has its Executive Board, which is not executive but deliberative, and a place for speech-making rather than short business-like discussion. The General Conference and the Board meet for so much of the time that the Secretariat is hard put to it to get on with its job. Shonfield is right when he says that the World Bank has the right sort of structure for the Agencies also: a very independent expert management, with an Annual General Meeting at which the member states express their views (as they should and must) but without getting involved in technical matters on which they are most unlikely to be expert.

In the early days of the Specialised Agencies a Committee was established consisting of their Heads, under UN Chairmanship. It was called the Administrative Committee on Co-ordination. It was undoubtedly a committee. But it administered nothing, and did precious little co-ordination. It is said that it now does co-ordinate rather more. Whether it yet feels itself a body with a unified purpose and an identity of its own, as distinct from its parts, one cannot be sure. Relations have often been bad between the Agencies. Those between UNESCO and FAO were disastrously so for a long time, but happily they have now very much improved. An agreement has been drawn up between UNESCO, FAO and ILO concerning education in rural areas, science and training. This is very welcome. There have also been attempts to improve co-ordination among the representatives of the different Agencies in the field, but they do not seem to have amounted to a great deal. Obviously the Resident Representative of the UN should be the unchallenged head of a co-operating team, co-operating on an agreed joint programme. If one looks at the Programme of the different Agencies one is struck by the fact that most of the activities might have been proposed had there been only this one Agency at work. Occasionally the help of some other Agency is needed, and then this is noted and quite often the help is readily given. But if the Agencies really accepted the idea that the attack on the problems of economic and social development must be many-sided yet properly combined, and that this was their main task, the programmes would be transformed. They should be.

A more emphatic status for the Resident Representative would help to put the planning focus where it should be, on the country, not the region. UNESCO has called a series of large regional conferences to draw up regional 'plans' for regions as large as Africa south of the Sahara and Southern Asia. These 'plans' have been drawn up in a considerable hurry. Yet after each conference it has been hoped that realistic national plans would conform to them. This is putting things the wrong way round. Regional conferences can be useful (as these have been) for comparison and stimulating discussion, but for serious planning the country must be the effective unit.

Some light is breaking in. The Secretary-General of the United Nations, opening the 45th Session of ECOSOC in July 1968, said that 'new efforts should be made to streamline our machinery, our procedures, and perhaps some of our activities'. This is hardly a clarion call, but it is a useful whistle. U Thant went on to explain the task given to the Enlarged Committee for Programme and Co-ordination by the General Assembly. (It is difficult for those not in the midst of the verbal fight to keep track of these committees and organisations and their initials, but this apparently is a committee consisting of sixteen members of ECOSOC plus five members appointed by the President of the General Assembly; why it should be so constituted I do not know.) The Secretary-General also noted with pleasure the assignment given to Sir Robert Jackson to report on the effectiveness of present arrangements for aid. This has been given him by the Governing Council of the United Nations Development Programme (that—UNDP for short—is the former Technical Assistance Programme merged with the Special Fund).[16] There is also a committee under Mr Lester Pearson, the former Prime Minister of Canada (with one British member, Sir Edward Boyle), to examine the effectiveness of international aid. The Jackson Report will deal with the effectiveness of present UN machinery and methods and the capacity of the UN to discharge these duties. The Enlarged Committee will enable governments to exercise a watching brief over the operation rather than doing work of its own. The Pearson Committee will report to the World Bank (which is not a Specialised Agency of the UN) and will especially consider the needs of aided countries and their capacity to receive and absorb aid. These are signs that all those concerned are anxious to see if procedures can be improved. One hopes that the Reports will be practical, even if astringent; and that they will be acted on.*

Let me now sum up this necessarily far from profound review and consider in brief terms what the present position is.

The assumption of an obligation by the community of nations to aid the economic and social development of the low-income countries did mark a step forward towards a world order. The decision of these countries to plan their development was right. Yet it is true that the planning has been inadequate and that international aid has been less in quantity than it could have been without the threat of war; and it has sometimes been misdirected. These things have been due partly to concepts that have not been properly thought out or based on enough knowledge, and partly to poor machinery, national and international. So after two decades of effort, we are at a moment of re-appraisal. If this re-appraisal is well and truly carried out we can make real progress in the post-Development Decade towards a more effective educational contribution to economic and social development. But will we? It would be a matter of great shame to all of us if we did not.

* Later Note: The Pearson and Jackson Reports have now been published. The Jackson Report recommends radical reorganisation of Aid machinery along the general lines recommended here, except that it would make ECOSOC—but a reconstituted and better equipped ECOSOC—the world 'Parliament' for aid.

NOTES AND REFERENCES

1 Dr K. C. Mukherjee notes that the average income per head in the United States is $2,500 as compared with something like $150 per head for the two thirds of the world's population in the under-developed countries (*Under-Development, Educational Policy and Planning*, Asia Publishing House, 1968, p. 16).
2 ibid., p. 8.
3 Philip H. Coombs, *The World Educational Crisis* (OUP, 1968), p. 3.
4 *Essays on World Education* (OUP, 1969), p. vii.
5 Gunnar Myrdal, *Asian Drama: An Inquiry into the Poverty of Nations* (Penguin Books, 1969).
6 Ministry of Overseas Development, *Aid for Development Fact Sheet, New Series No. 2* (December 1968).
7 Andrew Shonfield, *The Attack on World Poverty* (London, 1960).
8 Philip H. Coombs, op. cit. (OUP, 1968), p. 150.
9 *Investment in Education* (Government Printer, Lagos, 1960).
10 See Kusum Nair, *Blossoms in the Dust* (London, 1962).
11 V. K. R. V. Rao, *Education and Human Resource Development* (Allied Publishers, 1966).
12 C. E. Beeby, *The Quality of Education in Developing Countries* (Harvard, 1966).
13 *Report of the Education Commission* (Government of India, 1966).
14 Roger Thabault, *Mon Village* (Paris, 1943).
15 Julius K. Nyerere, *Education for Self-Reliance* (Government Printer, Dar es Salaam, 1967).
16 See *International Development Review*, December 1968.

CHAPTER 2

THE DEMAND FOR EDUCATION

T. DAVID WILLIAMS

INTRODUCTION

Analysis of the part played by education in increasing the productive capacity of the individual or of the economy is a relatively recent phenomenon (i.e. it has largely been confined to the last fifteen years[1]) although the practice of providing an education that 'fits' a person for the role he is expected to play in society and in the economy is much older. The principal differences between the 'economics of education' and the traditional practice are: first, the new approach makes explicit and assigns weight to some factors (i.e. those affecting 'productivity') which were previously implicit in broad judgments about the effectiveness of rival schemes for education; second, it tends to ignore (and implicitly assign a zero weight) to aspects of the educational process which do not have a *direct* economic significance.

There are considerable benefits to be gained from making one's assumptions explicit: a causal relationship between factors may be assumed and remain unexamined and unchallenged, until one attempts to spell out the logical connection between them or to specify the evidence that supports the practical significance of the connection, but specification of the linkage may show that the assumed relationship is logically unsound or empirically insubstantial.

On the other hand, the formulation of models—and their use for practical purposes—may also have drawbacks. The number of variables has to be kept small and has to be limited to those for which a weight can be assigned, and as a consequence important matters may be left out of consideration. Model-builders are, of course, aware of this, and frequently in deference to their less sophisticated readers, draw attention to the limitations of their models. There may be a tendency, however—among the users if not the builders of the model—to proceed as if the model alone provides a sufficient basis for policy-making, with the result that decisions may be based on a much narrower range of considerations than would be the case in the best types of 'intuitive' judgment.

Failure to appreciate the limitations of either implicit theorising or model building is responsible for much of the lack of communication between economists and educators. When the economist talks of the occupational competence or of the additional income consequent on a given type of education, the educator frequently reacts in horror, protesting that education is not just a matter of improving one's material well-being, tending to forget that for most people this was an important function of education long before the economist came on the scene, and that a common method for assessing the relative desirability of different schools is their success in providing access to good jobs: in this sense, the economist is simply making explicit a set of criteria that are already present, but his assessment of the factors making for success may sometimes be inadequate. The economist tends, moreover, to feel that his professional competence is more suitable for designing the model than for evaluating its assumptions; this would not matter if *someone* was seen to be responsible for laying the foundations upon which the superstructure is to rest, but not infrequently the educator—and the policy-maker—is left with the feeling that the economist has assumed away the most important parts of the problem.

Most of the work on education done by economists has been concerned with the improvement of the productive capacity of society, but there is no reason why demand for education for other purposes—for personal enjoyment, for social integration or for political understanding—should not be treated by economists (and others) as having a valid claim on national resources. It is true that in the present state of knowledge the nature of these demands and the way to satisfy them cannot be specified with precision, and policies to deal with them rest largely on subjective judgment or guesses. The same is, however, true of many of the policy decisions affecting potential productive capacity. All the economist can expect to do at present is to clarify the nature of some of the decisions that are made about educational expenditures and to distinguish them from the decisions which still rest on 'judgment'. As the state of knowledge improves, so the range of decisions dependent on guesswork can be narrowed.

This chapter is primarily concerned with the demand for education to improve productive capacity. There is an extensive literature on the relation between educational expenditures and the production frontier and it is not possible in the space available to follow in detail the arguments in support of various models, but the assumptions and logical structure of the principal models will be described and special attention will be paid to their applicability to the circumstances of the less developed countries. The chapter also includes a discussion of some aspects of the social demand for education, though this section is very brief and is intended merely to point out some of the issues on which decisions have to be made.

EDUCATION AND THE PRODUCTION FRONTIER:
THE RATE-OF-RETURN APPROACH

Estimates of the rate of return are based on the costs of acquiring some additional education and the extra income which is earned as a result of it. Most estimates that have been made have been related to the effects of formal education but if data were available it could be used for examining the effects of on-the-job training.

An early variant of this approach was to estimate the difference in life income associated with different levels of education. The average lifetime earnings of people with eight years of education, for example, would be compared with those of people with twelve years of education. Apart from questions involving the validity of the data or the imputation of a causal relationship between education and income, this method suffered from the fact that it made no distinction between income now and income in the future. One hundred pounds today is worth more than a hundred pounds next year: for one thing, if one had the hundred pounds now one could invest it and earn the interest, and, for another, if one is due to receive a hundred pounds in a year's time one may die in the meantime and never enjoy it.

The person with more education may make a great deal more money in the future but while he is undergoing his education he earns less, typically much less, than the person who has immediately become a full-time member of the labour force, and in some countries—though often not in the less developed countries—he may earn less in the early years after graduation while he is undergoing some form of either formal or informal apprenticeship.

To meet this problem, incomes were estimated in terms of their present discounted value:

$$\text{Income in Year } 1 + \frac{\text{Income in Year } 2}{(1+i)} + \frac{\text{Income in Year } 3}{(1+i)^2}$$
$$\ldots \text{ etc.}$$

where Income in Year 1 refers to income earned in the first year after the base year and where i represents the rate of interest. On this basis, one could compare the present value of the life income of people with x years of education and those with $x+y$ years.

An alternative would be to take the 'additional income'—that is, the difference in each year between the income of those with x and those with $x+y$ years. In the early years—after those with x years had graduated and were working while the others were continuing their education—the 'additional income' would be negative. The present value of additional income can then be compared with the present value of the additional costs of education.

The rate of return brings together the stream of costs and stream of additional income in a slightly different way.[2] To simplify notation, costs and additional income in the first year may be described as C_0 and AI_0, costs and additional income in the following year as C_1 and AI_1, and so on to the final year of the average working life as C_n and AI_n. In the example being used—the difference between eight and twelve years of education—C would be zero after C_3, and AI would be negative at least until AI_4.

$$C_0 + \frac{C_1}{(1+r)} + \frac{C_2}{(1+r)^2} \cdots + \frac{C_n}{(1+r)}$$
$$= AI_0 + \frac{AI_1}{(1+r)} + \frac{AI_2}{(1+r)^2} \cdots + \frac{AI_n}{(1+r)^n}$$

where r is the value that brings both sides of the equation to equality: r is the rate of return.

Data on the present pattern of income broken down by the age and educational level of the recipients are available in some of the developed countries, and one can derive from them an approximation to relative income stream which shows what is being earned on average by 50-year-olds with twelve and eight years of education, what is being earned by 45-year-olds . . . and so on back to entry to the labour force. Cross section data of this sort may, however, provide a significantly different picture from the sort of thing one would get if one were able to obtain proper life-income streams, which would show, for example, the comparative incomes of 50-year-olds now, of 45-year-olds five years ago and so on. These data unfortunately are rarely available. The figures that are used give a different picture to the 'real' one since the income of people who entered the labour force 30 years ago, for example, depends to some extent on the relation between their level of education and that prevailing in the labour market when they entered it: people who entered the labour force a long time ago may have been relatively well educated, and thus had access to good jobs, though the level of education they achieved may be below the average achieved more recently. On the other hand there is a tendency for new entrants to the labour force to benefit more from salary increases than do long-service employees who are wedded to a particular job or employer.

The problem caused by lack of the appropriate data is perhaps less serious than it might appear, providing that one does have data for the past ten or fifteen years. Discounting of future income means that unless differentials become very great after twenty years or so the most important data are those which are relevant to the relatively near future. But for countries which can only provide present cross section data, particularly when there have been great changes in educational output, the limitations are severe.

Rate of return analysis may be used either to evaluate the advisability of an individual seeking more education or of society deciding that more resources should be devoted to education. In estimating the pay-off for the individual, the relevant returns are those that he actually receives—so that one needs post-tax incomes; the relevant costs in this case are those incurred by the student—his fees together with other expenses due to his education (and less anything saved due to education —if, for example, costs include meals a deduction should be made for the meals that he would, in any case, have eaten). In estimating the social pay-off, one would be interested in the pre-tax income and costs should include any subsidies paid by the government or other agencies which supplement fees.

There have been several objections raised against rate of return calculations. Though this is not the place for a comprehensive review of the literature[3] it will be useful to summarise the most important ones and indicate the answers provided by the proponents of the approach.

The most fundamental objections are those which suggest that the correlation between additional education and additional income is probably due to their both being consequences of other factors which cannot be significantly affected by education. There are three principal groups of 'other factors'. First a person's access to positions of power and affluence is very much influenced by the social and economic circumstances of his or her relatives. Someone who comes from a family that has good connections is likely to get a good job even if he or she has relatively weak educational qualifications; at the same time, well-connected families tend to provide their children with an extensive education for a variety of reasons that are only tenuously related to occupational competence—to put it briefly, and not entirely accurately, because a certain type of education is part of the experience appropriate to members of their class.

Second, in a society in which the educational system is seen as one of the avenues of social and economic mobility, intelligence and motivation are significant factors in determining both educational success (and the amount of education) and occupational success. The correlation between education and income may be because a high level of education and a high level of income are both more likely to be achieved by people with ability, ambition and determination. Employers may, indeed, put a value on a given level of education not because it has any direct significance for occupational competence but because they believe it defines a man who is in the top 5, 10 or 20 per cent of his age group and that it is a proxy for connection, motivation or ability.

Protagonists of the rate or return argue that detailed studies carried out in the United States, the place for which most of the relevant studies are available, using data on age, race, intelligence, motivation, parental occupation and other key factors as well as education and income, show that education is 'the single most powerful determinant of family income'[4] and that 'objections to the use of simple average earnings of different age and education groups on the grounds of spurious correlation are correct but qualitatively not terribly important'.[5]

This brings us to the third set of 'other factors': those which cannot in present circumstances be adequately measured (for example, important aspects of 'intelligence' and 'motivation' may be missed by the usual tests of intelligence and need-achievement; the significance of family connection may not be reflected by data about parents' occupation and education) and in some cases cannot be specified in a precise way, because they arise from the complex web of social relations.[6]

32

It is difficult to evaluate the strength of this argument. On the one hand, there are 'unknowns' and 'unknowables' involved in every decision that people make and one cannot prevaricate endlessly merely because information which is not presently available might, if it were available, indicate that a different decision would be the appropriate one. On the other hand, it would be most unwise to dismiss the reservations of knowledgeable people merely because these reservations cannot be expressed in simple quantitative or algebraic form. A 'solution' arrived at by disregarding these reservations may exacerbate the problems for which one is seeking a solution.

Both the critics and the protagonists of that rate of return appear, however, to be agreed that a not insubstantial part of the return as conventionally measured is due to 'other factors',[7] and if one is comparing the returns to education with some other type of investment the difference between the real return and the measured return may be critical. Whether or not 'other factors' are equally important in determining the relative return on alternative forms of educational expenditure is a matter for which there are, at present, no reliable data.

There are other objections which do not challenge the conceptual structure of the rate-of-return analysis but which question the relevance of the aggregate data available. Aggregate data do not differentiate among the graduates of different schools or universities, although the average incomes may be heavily influenced by the performance of graduates from élite institutions, and their relevance to the prospects of a marginal college is doubtful. Rate-of-return analysis is entirely appropriate to disaggregated data but even in the most developed countries it has not yet proved practicable to analyse data in these terms.

The rate of return may provide a better basis for individual than for collective decision-making. One of the functions of the educational system is to act as a selective device for the labour market: it provides employers with a means of discriminating among potential employees. If only 10 per cent of the age group graduate from secondary school the graduates may be

33

treated as the 'top 10 per cent' of their age group, their level of education being used as a proxy for intelligence, motivation, adaptability and so on. Employers may be more interested in getting someone from the 'top 10 per cent', for example, than in particular academic qualifications. As the general level of education increases, the relevant qualification moves from primary completion to secondary then university graduation, and perhaps then to some form of post-graduate training. For the individual, it remains true that some extra education pays off, but the community does not benefit from the escalation of standards unless the education leads directly to greater occupational competence, which is much more difficult to measure.

Finally, it has been pointed out by many writers that rate-of-return estimates neglect both the personal satisfaction one may derive from education—the consumption effect—and its external effects. As long as it is clearly understood that the value of education as a consumption good is not included in the estimate, the matter can be handled quite simply. Decisions about expenditure on education as an investment could be handled on the basis of the rate of return, and an estimate of any additional education required because of its intrinsic value should be made on the same basis that one makes any other decision about consumption.[8]

By external effects in this context we mean the benefits or losses incurred by the community which are not adequately reflected by income payments.[9] Research work carried on as part of the educational system may produce substantial benefits which are difficult to measure and to relate to the return on specific inputs: a major technical breakthrough or the nurturing of a genius may significantly alter the options facing society; improvements in the stock of knowledge and the capacity of people to deal systematically with complex ideas may create an environment in which invention and innovation are stimulated and widespread literacy may be a predisposing, and perhaps necessary, condition of sustained economic growth. It would be very difficult to find any reliable quantitative estimate of the likely significance of these effects in particular circumstances,

34

though they may be far more important than any of the things that one can measure. One should, however, insist that anyone who is arguing that their effect is likely to be significant should provide strong circumstantial evidence in support of his contention.

In so far as incomes provide a reasonable guide to productivity they do so in the context of a given set of options. The effect of structural changes cannot be handled on this basis. But neither can they be handled by any other method of analysis. Estimates—or guesses—about the probability of structural change being effected could be made independently, and decisions about the educational expenditure should be made on the most appropriate assumptions with respect to structural change.

The usefulness of the rate of return approach is limited in the less developed countries by sparseness of data; by the degree of likelihood that many of the countries are on the verge of significant structural change; by the fact that the annual flow of graduates is high relative to the stock and by the social divide between urban and rural workers, between 'modern' and 'traditional' activities and between the élite (with its strong bureaucratic element) and the masses.

It has already been suggested that the rate-of-return approach is not very helpful in differentiating between educational and other forms of expenditure because it cannot take into account many of the issues which are critical for that decision and this is at least as true in the less developed countries as in the more developed countries. There may, however, be a substantial advantage to be gained from comparing the rate of return on different types of educational investment.

Since data are sparse, an approximation could be arrived at by using current wages and salaries for jobs requiring various types and levels of educational attainment and, where practicable, adjusting these to allow for expected changes in the near future. One should make allowance for the possibility of unemployment as well as for the salaries or wages earned by graduates who obtain employment: if, for example, the graduates of a particular type of training (type A) are more likely to find employment than the graduates of an alternative type (type B), A may be more attractive than B even if the average salaries of *employed* graduates are higher for B than for A.

The rate of return could then be used as a check on proposed educational outputs: if the proposed distribution of expenditure differs significantly from the pattern which would be suggested by the rate of return one should treat it as a warning signal that the matter should be examined more closely. One may find, for example, that people are trained to become middle-level technicians—because they are allegedly in short supply—but that the rate of return for people who use their training to do that kind of work is relatively low. In this case one is likely to find either that few people will go in for that kind of training or, perhaps more likely, that most graduates will use it as a bridge to something else. It should also lead one to look carefully at the reality of 'shortages', as defined by planners, which do not affect employers enough to make them feel that it is in their interest to offer a higher price.

It is a particular merit of the rate of return approach that it concentrates attention upon the linkages between the educational system and the labour market, which is the point at which many forms of educational planning are especially weak. There may be 'shortages' which are not reflected in the price offered for the relevant types of manpower, but where there are severe distortions due to institutional or cultural factors it is unlikely that simply increasing the supply of manpower will resolve the problems.

MANPOWER PLANNING

(a) *Employers' Estimates*
The simplest type of manpower estimate is based on questionnaires delivered to, or interviews with, owners, managers or personnel officers. Typically all establishments with more than some minimal number of employees are covered, and the respondent is provided with a list of occupations and asked how

many people the establishment needs in each category at present and at some time in the future.

The defects of the method are widely acknowledged: it is not always clear whether a stated 'demand' for skilled workers means that the respondent is unable to find skilled workers at a salary appropriate to skilled workers or merely that he would like to have better trained workers for unskilled rates; few respondents are in a position to make a serious assessment of their future demand for manpower; moreover, since respondents have nothing to gain from devoting much time to the questionnaire many will either ignore it or deal with it casually, and in the less developed countries a significant portion of the demand for manpower in ten—or even five—years' time might come from establishments not presently covered by the survey.

There are three principal reasons why the method is so frequently used despite its obvious limitations.[10] First, it is relatively easy to carry out and the manpower planner who is hard pressed for data can be sure of getting something even if it is not very accurate; second, other methods which have greater respectability also rest on a series of questionable assumptions and while more elegant they are not necessarily more accurate or relevant, and third, this method may uncover genuine shortages before they would otherwise become obvious. It is, moreover, possible to undertake surveys on a continuing basis with relatively little additional expense.

While it is relatively easy to get an estimate of occupational needs, determination of the level and type of education required to produce or stimulate occupational competence is a more complex matter—though this problem is not peculiar to this method. In some cases the matching of education and occupation has suffered from attempts to provide a greater degree of precision than is practicable. The objective should be to determine the range of types and levels of education that would be suitable for each occupation, allowing for the effects of relative wages and prices in establishing specific points within the range.

Perhaps the greatest danger involved in 'matching' man-

37

power needs with educational pre-requisites (though, again, this is not peculiar to this technique of estimating manpower needs) is that it will owe less to evidence that there is a significant relationship between certain kinds of education and effective occupational performance than to 'contemporary wisdom' about what the relationship ought to be. For example, it is frequently supposed, and often asserted, that people trained in the natural sciences or the social sciences are better equipped to deal with the 'modern world' than people trained in, for example, law or classics. The argument has some appeal to 'common sense', and it is very probably true that there are some important administrative jobs which call for specialised knowledge of 'modern' techniques, but it should be recognised that there is as yet very little hard evidence that either the physical or social sciences provide a more suitable training for administrators and executives than more traditional subjects. Since in some cases proposals for changing the type of education being offered in higher-level institutions in order to make it more relevant involve substantial additional costs, proposals of this sort may retard rather than stimulate the process of modernisation.[11]

There are different views about the comprehensiveness that should be attempted in enquiries of this sort. One view is that the coverage of establishments should be as wide as possible in order to give a picture of total labour market needs. This means, however, that many questionnaires will be distributed to small-scale employers who lack the information and perhaps the ability to provide meaningful answers, while the survey staff will lack the resources to do any adequate checking on respondents, far less to follow up the implications of their answers. The probable result is that there will be a large but indeterminate proportion of the answers which may represent nothing more than figures that were thought up on the spur of the moment.

In most of the less developed countries a relatively small number of employers, including the government, account for a substantial proportion of high-level manpower (secondary and higher-level graduates). By concentrating attention on major employers it is possible to conduct a survey which covers a wide range of information and to provide an adequate follow-up service to obtain any clarification or simplification that may be desirable. It is desirable to ascertain employers' views on the most appropriate forms of education or training for various occupations, since this will be an important factor in hiring practices regardless of the actual merit of the programmes, and where possible information should be obtained about other criteria used in hiring since there is little point in providing training for people who will fail to qualify on other counts.[12]

This type of enquiry may, in short, be seen as providing an important channel of communication between the planning board and key figures in the economy, but if one tries to use it beyond its capacity—by seeking a comprehensiveness of coverage or precision of expectation that the instruments cannot provide—it is likely to degenerate into a barren exercise that wastes the scarce resources embodied in the survey staff providing 'data' that are too vague to be used as guide-posts and which may be pointing in the wrong direction altogether.

(b) *Technological Requirements*

The basic assumptions on which this method is based are that levels of economic growth are closely related to certain kinds of technology and that a given form of technology requires fairly specific types of manpower.[13] The purpose is to estimate the manpower structure that is implied in the over-all economic target set up by the planning agency. One starts with the estimate of national income in the target year or years (five years, ten years, twenty years hence) and the way in which it is broken down among the sectors (manufacturing, services, agriculture etc., or a more detailed breakdown if considered practicable and desirable)[14] and then one estimates the size of the labour force required in each sector by dividing the income expected to be generated in the sector by the productivity of labour expected in that sector.

The next step is to distribute the labour force in each sector into major occupational groups.[15] This may be done either by using the occupational breakdown that presently characterises the country and making any adjustments that seem to be indicated by trends in the country or by reference to the experience of similar but slightly more developed countries—one may take the average from a group of similar countries or a particular country which seems to be particularly appropriate.[16]

Occupational requirements are then translated into educational requirements by specifying the range of educational levels appropriate to each occupation. In so far as there is believed to be a close relationship between income levels, technology, occupational mix and appropriate levels of education, one should refer to the experience of economies similar to the economy planned for the target year. The leading exponent of this method has emphasised that what is needed is not the average level of education of people in each occupational group but the range and the appropriate weights. For example, in 1959 clerical workers in Japan were distributed as follows: 29% had completed elementary education, 56% had completed secondary education and 15% had completed higher education.[17]

After completing these steps one gets the total number of primary, secondary and higher-level graduates that will be required in the target year if the planned level of national income is to be achieved. Comparing this with the presently available stock of graduates and allowing for (a) the flow of graduates already planned and (b) the wastage rate between the present and the target year, one can determine the changes that should be made in the annual flow if the stock is to reach the appropriate level in the target year.

The value of international comparison is of course open to question on a number of counts. First, there is the problem of finding 'similar' countries—even though two countries have similar levels of per capita income and similar sectoral contributions to national income the structure of the sectors may be radically different; second, the occupational compositions of each sector in the chosen country and the educational mix in occupational groups may be different from what 'they should be' in that country, in which case one is embodying their mistakes when one uses their data as a guide; third, the relationship may be appropriate to highly specific circumstances in that country but not appropriate to other countries, and fourth, there may be significant differences among countries in standards of classification: this may be the case with respect to occupational groups, with terms like 'professional' and 'clerk' having very different connotations, but it is particularly likely to create problems when comparing educational levels since there are significant differences among countries in the standards required for entry to or graduation from high school and university.

Attempts to use the relationships existing in one country as a guide to the appropriate relations in another raise both theoretical and practical difficulties. If country A decides that the appropriate pattern is that which existed in country B ten or fifteen years (or more) before the target date and it follows from this that there must be a large increase in the number of university graduates, for example, it must be sure that the quality of the graduates, as well as their numbers, matches that of country B.[18] Reference to the experience of the United States is perhaps instructive on this point. One often hears comment to the effect that American universities provide a better model for the less developed countries than do British universities, because the Americans have catered to a broader section of the population and have provided for more vocationally oriented courses. It may be the case that universities in less developed countries should be less concerned with 'academic standards' than many of them—especially in Africa—have been, but the argument is not supported by American experience. The educational system in the United States has had for a long time a very considerable élite component, where standards are at least as high as in British universities; it has also catered to people who could not find, or did not wish to find, a place in this section of the academic establishment and many of these people have done work of great practical—and not infrequently, academic—value. This experience does not demonstrate that concern with 'standards' is unimportant: it demonstrates that when a country is wealthy enough to provide experiments in mass education while also building up an élite sector, the experiments sometimes pay off handsomely.

The usefulness of this method depends to a large extent on the feasibility of establishing appropriate comparisons and limits of variability. Adequate information about many of the critical factors is very hard to come by in many of the less developed countries and there is very little historical data available. One may, perhaps, exaggerate the dimensions of the problem: any set of assumptions about future demands for manpower and about the matching between manpower requirements and the education or training that will facilitate adequate levels o competence rests implicitly on ideas about the transferability of experience. On the other hand, the usefulness of comparisons between different time-periods is open to question: it is possible that levels of education which would have been entirely adequate fifteen years ago may be insufficient for dealing with the technological changes which have taken place since then.

Nonetheless, data from similar countries, even for different periods and allowing for the crudeness of comparison, classification and implied causation provide a set of norms against which planners may compare their own estimates or guesses. A substantial discrepancy should be treated as a warning signal and planners should either satisfy themselves that the comparisons really are invalid or be prepared to make adjustments in the plan.

(c) *National Income-Education Ratios*

Many of the less developed countries will be unable to make much use of the method just described because there is insufficient information about the sectoral-occupational breakdowns in their own and similar countries. To get around this problem, and also reduce the time and resources that have to be devoted to working out the arithmetic of the estimates, several people have suggested a rule-of-thumb approach relating the educational stock directly to the level of income or changes in the stock and income.

The most well-known of these is the Harbison estimate (to be considered in more detail in the next section), which says that an increase of 1 per cent in national income should be accompanied by an increase of 2 per cent in the stock of university graduates. There does not appear to be any publicly available information about how this figure was arrived at,[19] and since the ratio between educational stock and national income at the beginning of the period will vary substantially from country to country, there is no sound theoretical reason why there should be a simple rule about the rates of change. But Harbison has had a great deal of experience as a manpower planner and his 'hunches' may be worth a lot more than most people's logic. On the other hand, other rule-of-thumb estimates suggest radically different relationships and one that appeared in a book of which Harbison was a co-editor suggested a relationship between high-level manpower and national income, which, depending on circumstances, could give a desired change in the number of graduates either very much lower or very much higher than that indicated by Harbison himself.[20]

More sophisticated models have been developed relating the required levels of educational output to per capita levels of national income without the need to work through sectoral occupational data. The 'econometric models' of Tinbergen, Bos and Correa[21] can be looked at from two perspectives: first, as a theoretical system which draws attention to the significance of certain key relationships and second, as a statement about the empirical values of these relationships 'in the real world'.

In the simplest form of theoretical model, the demand for secondary graduates is assumed to bear a constant relationship to the level of income: for example $N^2 = \alpha^2 Y_t$, where Y_t is the national income at time t, N^2 is the labour force with a secondary education and α^2 is the factor which shows the desired relationship between Y and N^2. In the simple example we are discussing, its value was given as 0·20, with Y being measured in billions of dollars and N in millions of people, so that when the volume of production was '100' (billion) the required manpower with secondary education was '20' (million). Once the appropriate relationship had been reached, an increase in national income would require an equal proportional increase in the stock of secondary graduates, so that an increase of 5 per cent per year in national income would require an increase in the secondary stock at the rate of 5 per cent per year.

The model also makes assumptions about the wastage rate among secondary graduates. The simplest assumption is that this is a constant proportion of the stock: if in the example already given, the wastage rate factor was 0·10, then additions to the stock of secondary graduates (assuming the right rates at the start of the process) appropriate to an increase of national income by 15 per cent would be composed of two factors: (a) the stock would have to increase by 15 per cent—from 20 to 23; (b) 10 per cent of the stock would be lost through wastage —2 out of 20—and they would have to be replaced, so that new recruits would have to be $3 + 2 = 5$ per cent.

In the same model an assumption is made that only university graduates are required in teaching. The demand for university graduates is thus composed of two elements: one is the demand for non-teaching members of the labour force and is related to the level of income, and the other is the demand for teachers, based on the numbers of students required to meet the target output of graduates and the student-teacher ratio.

Using these very simple relationships the model can show what is implied for the educational system by various rates of growth. The model can be modified to include a larger number of variables and greater 'realism' in the basic relationships. In more complex models the need for manpower is seen to depend not only on expected increases in national income but also on changes in productivity. When productivity is improved the number of workers required to produce a given output is reduced, and the model reflects this by introducing a negative productivity effect on the demand for labour[22]; more accurate estimates of wastage can be made; the education-income ratios can be worked out on a sectoral level and other modifications introduced.

Greater realism—in the sense that the model reflects the complexities of the 'real world'—is not necessarily an advantage. Greater sophistication may make heavy demands on the time and ingenuity of the planner without appreciably affecting the results, and where data are scarce 'there is no point in introducing theoretically refined concepts and relationships if they cannot be translated into numerical estimates'.[23]

These models have been criticised on the grounds that their authors, so far from answering any relevant questions, 'assume the answers and put them into a simple mathematical form'.[24] The significance of this criticism depends to a large extent on what one expects, or thinks other people expect, from these models. A useful model is one which helps one to appreciate the consequences or implications of one's assumptions and to check the internal consistency of one's argument, but the planner who has no idea either what the teacher-student ratio, for example, is likely to be in ten years' time or what it ought to be is not going to find any help here. The question of whether a specific country is likely to have or to need the same education-income ratio as an average of 'similar' countries cannot be answered simply by reference to a model: but if one has some idea of what the ratios ought to be or will be, one can see what this implies for various parts of the system. What worries the critics is that once assumptions have been made and used in the model, there may be a tendency to treat the assumptions as though their validity was established.

Some work has been done, however, on the estimation of appropriate relationships on the basis of data from several of the less developed countries. The results obtained are useful in so far as they give planners an idea of experience elsewhere, but their application to a particular country should be clearly established and not simply assumed to hold good.

A simple application of the model has been tried with East African data.[25] A regression equation, based on data from twenty countries (some developed, some less developed) gave the relationship between the number of graduates and national income (measured in 1957 US dollars) and this could be expressed in the form $G = 5 \cdot 2 Y^{1 \cdot 038} P^{0 \cdot 164}$ where P = population. If the relationships between the stock of graduates and national income was the 'right one' in the base year, this would mean that the numbers of graduates should increase at a slightly faster rate than the increase in national income and there should be a small additional increase as population grows.

For most of the East African countries the stock in the base year was of approximately the right size, and this meant that, as income rose, the addition to the stock of graduates should rise at a slightly faster rate. The Uganda plan envisioned an increase in national income of $8\frac{1}{2}$ per cent a year and the indicated increase in the number of graduates was 9·3 per cent. In a nineteen-year period this would mean an increase of 550 per cent. Moreover, if Ugandanisation were to be fully carried out the stock of graduates would have to increase twenty fold.

The educational task imposed is obviously a formidable one. Awareness of the costs involved may concentrate attention on ways of reducing the costs without lowering the contribution to the economy: more efficient methods of education may be feasible and more effective use made of skilled manpower so that not so much would be needed.[26]

The use of the model draws attention to problems that might not otherwise be so obvious. In much the same way that estimates of the manpower requirements of specific projects[27] may alert the planner to something that he has neglected to consider with sufficient care, estimates of the education-income relationship may indicate deficiencies in the plan before they have become obvious through inadequate performance.

(d) *The Stages of Educational Development*

The methods described above start with data on output in the labour force and work back to the educational system. Another approach is to start with data on the educational system and work out appropriate strategies on the assumption that the stage of educational development provides a useful first approximation to manpower needs.

Harbison and Myers,[28] who pioneered this approach, begin by suggesting various 'indicators of human resource development'; they then point out that information on the stocks of various types of high level manpower is only rarely available in the less developed countries and suggest some 'second-best' measures which include data on enrolment ratios at various levels of education; finally, they state that 'after a number of trials with some of the indicators just discussed, we developed a fairly simple composite index to distinguish among countries'.[29] Countries are grouped into four categories and manpower 'strategies' are suggested for moving the countries in one category to a higher one.

Countries are grouped according to their score on a composite index in which primary education is not counted at all, secondary education scores according to the percentage of the appropriate age group attending secondary school and higher level education is scored by taking the percentage and multiplying it by five.

The advantage of using educational enrolments as a proxy for the supply of manpower, and the supply of manpower as a proxy for demand for manpower, is that data are available for many countries for which information about either the total numbers of graduates of various types or the demand for manpower would be difficult if not impossible to obtain. Since there is a fairly close correlation between enrolment indices— or at least the composite index—and national income it may appear that there ought to be a causal link between them.

Harbison and Myers are careful to point out that cross section data such as they use, which give both enrolment ratios and national income at a point of time, do not establish that there is any causal relationship, though they tend to argue as though such a relationship existed; it is possible that a causal relationship does exist but that it is one in which high income makes it possible to spend more on education and not the other way around: indeed, if there *is* a causal relationship, the movement from income to enrolment is far more plausible than one from enrolment to income since presently enrolled students make very little contribution to national income.

Enrolment levels may change substantially in short periods of time and the relative position of countries according to the composite index may go through significant changes in a few years; since there is likely to be a lag between the time when a survey is carried out and the results collated and analysed, policy decisions may be based on data which are no longer relevant.[30]

The heavy weighting attached to 'high-level' manpower-training follows earlier work in which Harbison and Myers participated, which has emphasised the role of élites in the process of industrialisation[31] and, moreover, reflects a judgment shared by many manpower experts. It is not, however, a judgment which should be accepted without question.

There is perhaps a tendency to underestimate the usefulness of primary education—except as a bridge to secondary education—in developing countries. The reasons given for attaching a low priority to primary education usually fall into one of the following categories: first, primary education is often of very low quality and likely to have little permanent effect unless reinforced by some post-primary education; second, even if the quality is reasonably good it does not take the student far enough with the skills required in the modern sector; third, formal education is a significant asset only in the modern sector and since this sector (represented approximately by wage and salary earners in establishments with more than ten employees) is frequently unable to absorb the present numbers of primary school graduates it would be wasteful to devote resources to increasing their numbers; and, finally, there is a belief in some quarters that formal education—or at least the type of education a student is likely to receive in many of the less developed countries—reduces the willingness, and perhaps even the ability, of the student to take up rural or other manual work.

Each of these points may be valid in certain circumstances but they can be seriously misleading in others. Primary edu-

48

cation is often of low quality and in many cases expansion of secondary school output is necessary to provide the teachers who will be able to improve the standards. But extending the length of schooling considered necessary for the acquisition of basic skills may be a self-defeating exercise: insufficient attention is paid to the lower forms because it is supposed that their deficiencies will be made up in the higher forms and because a low priority is attached to primary education, educational resources are concentrated elsewhere and many primary schools have grossly inadequate facilities.

The value of good primary schooling lies not only in what is directly taught in the school but in providing the ground-work which enables an ambitious person to acquire more complex skills through self-education. Moreover, functional literacy and numeracy may prove very useful in many occupations outside the modern sector. There is, it is true, little hard evidence presently available about the value of basic education to farmers, craftsmen, traders and others seeking to adapt traditional methods to contemporary needs but it is reasonable to suppose that while literacy and numeracy will not necessarily induce people to change their style of life they may well be predisposing factors since they increase contact with and perhaps also sensitivity to new ideas.

Data on unemployment in most of the less developed countries are usually unreliable but there appears to be general agreement that the numbers of unemployed are increasing rapidly in less developed countries where a substantial proportion of the relevant age group is attending primary school. However, movement from the rural to urban areas and willingness to accept periods of unemployment while seeking a job in the modern sector is also found in countries where only a small proportion of the age group graduate from primary school. Whatever the level of enrolment in the primary schools the urban-modern sector is very attractive because the returns for those who are able to get jobs are often much greater than the candidate could earn elsewhere.

Historical experience is not always a sound guide to contemporary needs, for reasons that have been mentioned above, but there does appear to be strong circumstantial evidence that a substantial level of primary education was a predisposing factor if not a precondition for the 'take-off' into sustained economic growth of the presently developed countries. Anderson has suggested than an adult male literacy rate of about 40 per cent constitutes a sort of development threshold.[32] The balance between primary and secondary education during and after the 'take-off' period was more favourable to primary education than is the case in many of the less developed economies today: Britain, the United States and Japan, for example, had universal primary education by or shortly after 1900, and about the same time the ratio or primary to post-primary students was between 32:1 and 35:1; in Ghana in 1960, even if one were to include all middle-school students in the 'primary' category, the ratio of primary to post-primary students was 31:1.[33]

THE SOCIAL DEMAND FOR EDUCATION

The expression 'social demand for education' has been used to explain the community's interest in providing education for all people who 'want' an education and who are able to satisfy the minimum academic entrance requirements. Popular demand for widespread education has four components: everyone has a 'right' to the opportunity to benefit from the economic advantages conferred by education; everyone has a 'right' to the personal satisfaction derived from education; education enables one the better to fulfil one's duties as a citizen; and widespread education reduces the social and cultural divide between rulers and ruled, between managers and workers.

This is not the place to analyse these objectives, but a few points should be made. If the purpose of the scheme is to provide personal benefit to people who receive the education, one may ask why they should not be expected to pay for the education themselves; their willingness to do so would be a test of whether or not they really wanted an education rather than a concealed specific subsidy which could only be obtained if one undertook the education—since a person starting or continuing an education for which neither he nor his family are paying the full cost is being subsidised. It might be argued that because of inequality of income, many people would be denied the opportunity of getting an education if it was not subsidised; this is true, but the same can be said of alternative ways of spending the money: if one's principal concern is that people with incomes below a certain level are unduly handicapped, it would be possible to provide a guaranteed income up to a certain level or subsidies which could be spent either on education or on other things. There is, however, a major problem with proposals for providing education only on an optional basis: most education is undertaken by children and adolescents, and the cost would have to be borne by the parents; those who reap the benefit and those who pay the cost are different parties, and it may be felt that there would be too great a temptation to parents to use a non-specific subsidy for their own ends, to the great loss of their children.

The proposition that education enhances the quality of the civic contribution rests more on faith than evidence, but one might argue that it gives people the technical capacity to deal with a wider range of ideas. It might reduce social and cultural distinctions if everyone were to receive a similar type of education, but even in the most developed countries the disparities in quality among institutions at an equal level of education are enormous. Moreover, when the general level of education is increased, the level required for entry to the better positions also increases; and there is little evidence that massive public expenditure on education has much effect on aggregate social mobility.

There is another, though related, argument advanced with respect to the less developed countries, an argument which is perhaps implicit in much discussion in the more developed countries, to support expansion of secondary education: if 'qualified' primary graduates are unable to find places in secondary schools they will be a source of political trouble. But if more students are taken into the secondary system than can later be effectively absorbed either in the labour market or in higher education, *they* will be a potential source of political trouble, and unemployed secondary leavers are more likely to be a significant political force than unemployed primary leavers: they and their relatives will have invested a great deal more in education than will primary leavers, their expectations will be more exalted and they will be more articulate.

Though 'non-economic' arguments for increasing educational expenditures have less force than is sometimes supposed, there may be substantial social and political benefits to be derived from serious attempts to reduce the inequalities of access to education among different regions or different groups. It is possible that, at least in the short run, the greatest output of graduates from a given level of investment would be achieved by improving facilities in areas which already have a favourable record of educational achievement,[34] but the advantages of this sort of policy may be outweighed by the benefits of achieving a greater degree of parity even if at the cost of fewer graduates.

First, even in areas where there has in the past been little manifest enthusiasm for education, it is very likely that there will be a substantial number of young people who have the potential to make an important contribution to the welfare of the community, and even if most students fail to complete primary school the pay-off on the few who are able to realise their potential may be considerable. In many cases there is no straightforward way to measure this in advance, and provision for education in relatively deprived areas has to rest on the common-sense assumption that talent can only be developed and recognised where there is a reasonable degree of opportunity.

Second, the educational system provides, or is widely believed to provide, a major avenue of social mobility for the individual. This does not mean that widespread education necessarily reduces the gap between the élite and the rest of society; it does mean that one of the important means of access to the élite is believed to be through the educational system. A region which has a relatively backward educational system is liable to find not only that it has fewer graduates but that it has fewer senior and middle-rank civil servants, unless it is sufficiently powerful to insist that appointments be made on a quota system or according to some other criteria which override 'objective qualification'. In either case there are likely to be severe problems relating to political cohesion, administrative efficiency and attitudes towards modernisation.

Third, the extent to which a government can command the positive allegiance of its people rather than their mere acquiescence depends to some extent on the degree to which people feel that they are sharing in the fruits of development. Access to positions of power on the part of sons and kinsmen is one manifestation of this and many people in the rural areas who may not experience much material improvement in their own lives may feel that things are changing for the better when a young man or woman from their own or a neighbouring village gets the sort of job that used to be the preserve of strangers, and when they can feel that their own child may, if he is both clever and lucky, have the same good fortune. The extent to which the educational system provides opportunity for the sons or daughters of the average man can be greatly exaggerated, but as long as it provides *some* opportunity, and is perceived to do so, the provision of educational facilities could have a substantial political effect.

SUMMARY AND CONCLUSION

Decisions about the type and amount of education provided in a society depend on assumptions that are often implicit about various sources of demand for education: for trained manpower (the appropriate 'training' may be specified in many different ways; it need not be narrowly vocational), for improved awareness of social, civic or religious duties and for personal development and satisfaction.

Discussion of the economic aspects of demand for education has usually been concentrated on education which is believed to increase the material well-being of the individual or society, but as long as policy-makers are prepared to specify the weight they attach to other objectives there is no reason why these should not be included in an economic analysis of educational and manpower planning: economists *qua* economists are agnostic about goals, but there must be *something* to be maximised.

There are many aspects of education about which many reasonable and well-informed people might agree but which are not susceptible to precise specification. In these cases, judgment had to be exercised and it cannot be replaced by purely quantitative or logical analysis.

It is useful, however, to seek to define the limits within which analysis can effectively supplement judgment, to examine the internal consistency of arguments and the extent to which assumptions about matters of fact are supported by evidence.

The methods described in this chapter for estimating the investment demand for education (i.e. for things which will, hopefully, increase income) suffer from a number of deficiencies, but for the most part they are deficiencies in knowledge of facts and relationships which the models might help to expose but for which their progenitors are not responsible. The models, used sensibly, narrow the range in which guesswork, prejudice and misinformation are significant factors in policy decisions and provide useful cross-checks on decisions arrived at by other means.

To expect more of them or to imagine that they have greater validity than the data and assumptions which they embody would be to invite disaster. They cannot provide the 'right' answer but they may help in avoiding some bad answers, and the resources not wasted on misguided projects may prove critical in determining whether or not an economy is able to achieve sustained economic growth.

NOTES AND REFERENCES

1 The treatment of economics of education appears to have had a much longer tradition in Russia than in other European countries. See e.g. Kahan, A., 'Russian Scholars and Statesmen on Education as an Investment' in Anderson, C. A., and Bowman, M. J. (eds.), *Education and Economic Development* (Aldine Publishing Company, Chicago, 1965);

see also the reprint of the 1925 paper of Shumlins, S. C., 'The Economic Significance of National Education' in Robinson, E. A. G., and Vaizey, J. E. (eds.), in *The Economics of Education* (published for the International Economics Association by Macmillan and Co. Ltd., 1966).

2 A lucid treatment of the difference between present value and rate of return methods may be found in Dryden, M. M., 'Capital Budgeting: Treatment of Uncertainty and Investment Criteria' in *Scottish Journal of Political Economy*, vol. ix, pp. 235-59.

3 See e.g. Blaug, M., 'The Rate of Return on Investment in Education' in *The Manchester School*, vol. 33 (1965), no. 3, for a thorough, though polemical, discussion of objections raised to the rate of return analysis. The article is reprinted in Blaug, M. (ed.), *Economics of Education 1* (Penguin Modern Economics).

4 Blaug, ibid., p. 224.

5 Morgan, J. N., and David, M. H., 'Education and Income' in *Quarterly Journal of Economics*, August 1963, pp. 436-7.

6 cf. Hoselitz, B. F., '. . . investment in man is a joint product attributable not only to the educational process as such, but also to the cultural, social and material environment in which this new and larger amount of education is acquired'; Coleman, J. S. (ed.), *Education and Political Development* (Princeton University Press, 1965).

7 Blaug, op. cit., argues that the usual tests overstate the effects of 'other factors' on income, but notes that other factors may be held to 'explain' 40 per cent of the correlation between length of education and income; this means that the return could be almost doubled or halved depending on the operation of other factors. A more critical view is taken by Stephen Merrett, who argues that the usual tests under-state the effects of other factors ('The Rate of Return to Education: a Critique' in *Oxford Economic Papers*, vol. 18, no. 3, November 1966).

8 If the present value of the cost of a given amount of education is £5,000 and the present value of additional income is £4,500, one would then have to decide whether the consumption value of the education is worth at least £500—in which case, the education would be a good buy.

9 For a more comprehensive treatment of external effects, see Weisbrod, B. A., *External Benefits of Public Education: An Economic Analysis* (Princeton, 1964).

10 As Davis remarks of a more sophisticated method: 'Almost everyone can see the holes in the scheme and that is one of its chief virtues.' Davis, R. C., *Planning Human Resource Development* (Rand McNally and Co., Chicago, 1966), p. 36.

11 An additional problem in that some types of education may be more difficult to transfer than others; it may be the case that more 'modern' subjects, with less formalised didactic techniques, make greater demands on the teachers, lecturers or demonstrators than can, in general, be met except in very favourable circumstances.

12 For example, it has been suggested that 'Puerto Rican managers prefer to hire relatives and are unwilling to pay an attractive salary to trainees' (Knowles, N. H., 'Manpower and Education in Puerto Rico' in Harbison, F., and Myers, C. A. (eds.), *Manpower and Education* (McGraw-Hill, New York, 1965)). In the same book Horowitz, M. A., and Whyte, W. F., discuss the significance of social and cultural factors in the allocation of high-level manpower in, respectively, the Argentine and Peru. Robert I. Crane has argued that Indian technical graduates found it difficult to obtain employment in India before the First World War because the principal employers were prejudiced against Indian technicians ('Technical Education and Economic Development in India before World War I' in Anderson, C. A., and Bowman, M. J. (eds.), op. cit.).

13 '. . . the idea of manpower requirements as used here relates to the functional (or occupational) composition of employment that will be necessary if certain social and/or economic targets are to be achieved. The concept, in other words, is more a technological than economic one' (Parnes, H. S., 'Manpower Analysis and Educational Planning' in *Planning Education for Economic and Social Development* (OECD), p. 76). A clear exposition of this method is given in Davis, op. cit. See also Anderson, C. A., and Bowman, M. J., 'Theoretical Considerations in Functional Planning' in Bereday, G. Z. F., Lauerys, J. A., and Blaug, M. (eds.), *Educational Planning* (Evans Brothers Ltd., London, 1967).

14 For example, Parnes gives the United States breakdown for 1950: agriculture 12%; mining and quarrying 1·7%; manufacturing 27·4%; construction 6·1%; electricity, gas, water and sanitary services 1·4%; commerce 22%; transport, storage and communication 7·2%; services 20%; and activities not adequately described 1·4%; op. cit., table 4.

15 See Parnes, H. S., *Forecasting Educational Needs for Economic and Social Development* (OECD, October 1962). In appendix C table 4 he shows occupational breakdowns in various industrial groups and the following example is taken from the table. The percentage of all workers who were in the professional, technical and kindred groups were: all industries 8·7%; agriculture 0·6%; manufacturing 4·6%; construction 3·7%; services 31·7% . . . etc.

16 For example, the manpower plan for Puerto Rico was based on the assumption that the education mix required in 1975 would be similar to that achieved in the United States in 1950.

17 Parnes, H. S., op. cit., appendix D, table 2.

18 There is not infrequently an inconsistency in the work of manpower planners on this point. Knowles, for example, argues that in order to achieve an educational flow in Puerto Rico in 1975 similar to that in the United States in 1950, it would be necessary to accept a (presumably short-run) situation in which 'standards' would be low. But unless the standards were similar to those in the United States the point of relating

the output of graduates would be lost. The technique can be reduced to an absurdity in which the appropriate 'outputs' could be achieved by, for example, declaring that henceforth everyone who graduates from secondary school will receive a university degree.

19 Guy Hunter wrote, '. . . on the basis of history in other countries, Professor Harbison and I agree to use a factor of two times the rate of growth of GDP . . .' ('Issues in Manpower Policy: Some Contrasts from East Africa and South-east Asia' in Harbison, F., and Myers, C. A. (eds.), op. cit., p. 336).

20 'It seems plausible to suggest, as a first approximation, that the ratio of high-level manpower in the total labour force should be raised by 1 per cent for each increase in the national output growth rate of 1 per cent' (Glassburner, B., 'High-level Manpower for Economic Development: The Indonesia Experience' in Harbison and Myers, op. cit., p. 198). To illustrate the point, Glassburner says that since the ratio in Indonesia in the early 1960's was 1·8 per cent an increase in the per capita growth rate of 1 per cent would require raising the ratio to 2·8 per cent which would require 'an immediate expansion or an increase of efficiency at higher levels of education of approximately 55 per cent'. On the other hand, a growth rate which may be large but which is no greater than that presently attained in a given country would require no more than that the total number of graduates should increase at the same rate as the increase in the labour force.

21 See *Econometric Models of Education* (OECD, 1965), which contains chapters by Tinbergen, J., and Bos, H. C. (describing and explaining the 'basic model' and applications to various countries by L. J. Emery, J. Blum and G. Williams). The chapter by Williams and a concluding chapter by Tinbergen and Bos contain a good discussion of the limitations of the models. See also Correa, H., and Tinbergen, J., 'Quantitative Adaptation of Education to Accelerated Growth' in *Kyklos*, vol. xv, 1962, and comments on that paper by Bombach, G., Balogh, T., and Sen, A. K., in Vaizey, J. E. (ed.), *The Residual Factor and Economic Growth* (OECD, 1964). Useful discussion may be conveniently found in Davis, op. cit., and Anderson and Bowman, 'Theoretical considerations in Educational Planning' in Bereday et al., op. cit.

22 According to Tinbergen and Bos the productivity factor 'measures approximately the (negative) influence of increasing labour productivity on the demand for manpower' (op. cit., p. 222). An alternative explanation is that population increase, even without any increase in income, will increase the demand for high-level manpower because some elements in the demand, such as health and education are in part a function of population (Rado, E. R., and Jolly, J. R., 'The demand for manpower: An East African Case Study' in *Journal of Development Studies*, vol. 1, no. 3, April 1965).

23 Tinbergen, J., and Bos, H. C., op. cit., p. 10.

E 57

24 Balogh, T., in *The Residual Factor and Economic Growth*, p. 180.

25 Rado, E. R., and Jolly, J. R., op. cit.

26 In a later paper Rado suggested that estimates of the required number of highest-level manpower in Uganda had been overstated because several of the jobs to which they had been assigned could be done by people with lower-level training. This may well have been a sound point, but if estimates made on the basis of international comparisons can be adjusted in this way it calls into question the use of the technique at all, since it rests on the assumption that actual experience, which presumably includes some wastage of resources, is a more useful guide than *a priori* reasoning (Rado, E. R., 'The 1966-71 Uganda Manpower Plan: a note' in *Journal of Development Studies*, vol. 3, no. 4, July 1967, pp. 451-6).

27 See, for example, Hanson, W. L., 'Human Capital Requirements for Educational Expansion' in Anderson, C. A., and Bowman, M. J. (eds.), *Education and Economic Development*, and the estimate by Rudolph C. Blitz of the numbers of doctors and nurses implicitly required by plans to improve medical facilities in Chile ('The Role of High-Level Manpower in the Economic Development in Chile' in Harbison, F., and Myers, C. A. (eds.), op. cit.).

28 Harbison, F., and Myers, C. A., *Education, Manpower and Economic Growth*, (McGraw Hill, 1964.) See also the reviews by Bowman, M. J., and Sen, A. K., in, respectively, *The Journal of Political Economy*, vol. 73 (1966), and the *Indian Economic Review*, vol. 1 (1966), both reprinted in Blaug, M., op. cit., 2.

29 op. cit., p. 31.

30 Williams, T. D., 'Educational Development in Ghana and Guatemala: Some Problems in Estimating Levels of Educational Growth' in *Comparative Education Review*, October 1966.

31 See for example, Kerr, C., Dunlop, J. T., Harbison, F., and Myers, C. A., *Industrialism and Industrial Man* (Harvard University Press, 1960).

32 Anderson, C. A., 'Literacy and Schooling on the Development Threshold and Some Historical Cases' in Anderson and Bowman (eds.), op. cit. See also Passin, H., 'Portents of Modernity and the Meiji Emergence' in the same book.

33 Ratio of primary to post-primary students:

United States, 1890	35:1
Japan, 1900	32:1
England and Wales, 1910	32:1

(Source *Japan's Growth and Education* (Ministry of Education, Japan, 1963), pp. 214-15.) Similar, but not identical, data are given in Kaser, M. C., 'Education and Economic Progress: Experience in Industrialised Market Economies' in Robinson, E. A. G., and Vaizey, J. E. (eds.), op. cit. The Ghana figures for primary and middle-school students, students in secondary school, teacher training and University are based on

58

tables 167, 168, 169, 171, 172 and 173 of the *1962 Statistical Year Book* (Central Bureau of Statistics, Accra, 1964).

34 See the discussion of 'equity versus efficiency' in Anderson, C. A., and Bowman, M. J., 'Theoretical Considerations in Educational Planning' in Bereday et al., op. cit.

CHAPTER 3

THE EFFICIENCY OF EDUCATION

T. DAVID WILLIAMS

Some of the problems involved in trying to identify and measure the outputs of the educational system have been discussed in Chapter Two. Additional difficulties arise when one attempts to compare the costs and returns from alternative educational programmes: the nature of the outputs and the types of by-products have to be specified carefully and there are also several problems connected with estimation of the actual and potential inputs to the educational system.

Even when output is clearly identifiable and measurable in unambiguous terms and when there is a common range of inputs among the units whose efficiency[1] is being compared, there may be significant differences in the way in which factors are combined and there are some factors that cannot be accurately measured. One may vary the rates of capital to labour and of skilled to unskilled labour on the one hand, and on the other, managerial flair, labour morale and even sheer luck may account for significant variations in output and destroy the validity of conclusions drawn on the basis of standard measurements of input. All sophisticated measurements of productivity identify certain quantifiable inputs and recognise that there is a residual element which is due to factors that either have not been identified or for which no adequate weighting can be established.

Measurements of efficiency are based entirely on factors which are susceptible to measurement and about which data are available; automatic use of efficiency criteria may thus lead to serious errors in formulation of policy. The difficulties involved in the application of the concept of efficiency to education appear to some to be quite insuperable; they fear that the introduction of efficiency concepts will lead to crude mechanical responses to 'statistics' which tell only part of the story: that aspects which cannot be easily measured will be left out of account and in effect treated as if they should be assigned a zero weight. But even those whose sensibilities are most deeply offended by discussion of efficiency do make judgments which imply assumptions about relative efficiency: School A is better than School B; there is a minimal level of qualification required to teach in such or such a school; it is better to spend money on this than on that . . . and so on. Implicit judgments about goals and the ways to achieve them have sometimes turned out to be most acute but unless one is prepared to trust to luck or rare genius, there is a good deal to be said for trying to make one's judgments explicit.

Measurement may lead to careful consideration of the circumstances which distinguish relatively efficient situations from relatively inefficient ones: the explanation may be the simple one suggested by differences in the easily quantifiable inputs or it may be more complex, but the attempt to measure inputs should help to focus attention on the critical variables and may provide objective evidence about matters which would otherwise be the subject of guess work. Moreover, the attempt to apply a logic, the logic of efficiency, obliges one to think carefully about the connections between what one wants done and the way one is trying to do it.

When one attempts to establish efficiency tests for education, the issue is further complicated by the difficulty of establishing appropriate indices of output. The use of examination results as a measure of output suffers not only from the fact that they are relevant only to part of the activities of a school or university but that they may be deficient measures even of the things that they are supposed to measure.[2]

Perhaps the most formidable problem encountered in making efficiency estimates is that students are both an input and an output. The proportion of students passing examinations of a given standard, or meeting other tests required for graduation, depends to a large extent on the ability and circumstances of the students themselves. If there were accurate objective measures of the abilities of students before and after they had

61

attended a school or university one would be able to estimate the 'value added' by the institution; in the absence of such a measure the best available indices of ability should be used.[3]

Even if it were possible to provide an adequate measure of 'student output' from various levels of the academic system, which should include an estimate of the value of partial completion of a stage as well as graduation, there would still be the problem of evaluating joint products and by-products.[4] To give one example, universities are often responsible for a great deal of research work and this function is perhaps especially important in the less developed countries since there are very few other agencies which are in a position to carry out research.[5]

The main part of this chapter deals with the data required if one is to evaluate the efficiency of basic policy decisions about educational matters. The 'profile' that is suggested is one that should, with respect to its principal elements, be feasible for most of the less developed countries in which there is a serious commitment to educational progress.

Much of this chapter will be concerned with physical inputs and outputs: the numbers of teachers with varying levels of qualification and the standards of plant and equipment on the one hand and the numbers of students or graduates on the other. Policy decisions cannot be made on the basis of physical input-output relationships alone—one needs to know the cost of various inputs before one can decide which combination of factors is most efficient from an economic point of view, but it is very important to obtain data on the physical relationships: at present one has very little idea of the extent to which effective substitution among factors can take place and until one knows more about this one knows very little of the effective options facing the policy-maker.

PROFILE OF AN EDUCATIONAL SYSTEM

I *The Students*

(a) *The Flow:* The simplest element in the profile is the movement of students through and out of the system. Even this, however, presents several conceptual and practical difficulties which are not always recognised.[6]

Data are often presented in the form of numbers of students in each class in a given year. If, for example, the primary cycle consists of six classes, each of which is supposed to be completed in one year, and the number of students in the first class is 100 while the number in the sixth is 20, the wastage rate is said to be 80. A small though significant step in the right direction is to analyse the progress of cohorts: the numbers of students in class 6 in year X is compared with the numbers in class 5 in year $X - 1$ and so on back to the number in class 1 in year $X - 5$.

This eliminates the effect of changes in initial enrolment, but one may still get a seriously misleading impression of the rate of drop-out and one will know nothing about the time it takes for students to complete the cycle: to begin to deal with these problems one needs to know how many students are repeating a year. It may be worthwhile to labour the point by giving a simple example: if the data show that there are 100 students in class 1 in year X and 50 in class 2 in year $X + 1$ we may conclude that the drop-out rate is 50 per cent; but if—for reasons which need not presently detain us—students usually repeat class 1 but not class 2, the situation may be that in year $X + 1$ there are 50 new students in class 2 and 50 repeaters in class 1, so the drop-out rate would have been zero, not 50 per cent; if on the other hand there were 25 new students in class 2 (the other 25 being repeaters) and no repeaters in class 1, the drop-out rate would have been 75 per cent. Information about repeaters does not enable us to distinguish between students who drop out after failing to gain promotion to a higher class and those who drop out after successfully completing the year's work: for this, one needs data showing the numbers of students eligible to move to a higher class.[7]

It is more difficult to estimate the average length of time taken by those students who pass through the cycle. If students typically remain in the same school the records would be available at source, and data could be provided for all school leavers showing how long they had been in the system. In some countries, however, students frequently move from one school to another and it may be necessary to undertake sample surveys to obtain the data.

Every educational system should have recognised exit points and bridge points. At exit points students may move into the labour force with some meaningful level of qualification; at bridge points students may move from one stage of the system to another. Sometimes exit points and bridge points coincide, as when primary school completion provides both a labour market qualification and a pre-requisite for secondary education. In many cases, exit points are determined by chance factors and are a residual of decisions about bridge points. Exit points *should* follow completion of a 'stage' of learning—the acquisition of functional literacy or functional numeracy, for example.

It may be the case that at some periods an extra year would yield very high dividends in consolidating a 'stage of knowledge' while at others it would do no more than provide an introduction to a higher stage which would only be useful if the student was to be committed to several years of work. A great deal of research needs to be done on this, and a high priority in educational budgets should be devoted to getting it started.

The determination of bridge points might appear to be a simple matter: students either move from primary to secondary school or they do not. A slightly more complex matter is which stream or type of post-primary education they enter: some streams provide 'academic' training and are themselves designed to provide a channel to higher education, and others offer programmes more directly oriented to vocational work of one kind or another.

If one could assume that evaluations of the capacity and orientation of students after six years of primary schooling were not only objectively valid at the time but also prognostically valid, one could be reasonably sure that decisions as to whether or not students continued their education—and which type of education they should undertake—had been appropriate ones and that the great majority of students 'ought' to continue along the path to which they had been assigned. But neither assumption is justified even in the most developed countries. It is, therefore, very important that there be some form of 'second chance': whether they have temporarily left the educational system altogether or have got into the 'wrong' stream, students should have an opportunity to re-enter at the appropriate point. This is not simply a matter of equity; when a community is making great sacrifices to provide training for its people but its selection procedures are unavoidably crude, it cannot afford to be lavish with the 'wrong' people.

Few countries afford second chances to those who fail to enter the secondary system at all, but in many there are very strong pressures to allow several chances to those who enter the 'wrong' stream. That the reason for this is often political rather than educational need not detain us here. There is substantial evidence that streams designed to offer terminal vocational courses become instead a widely recognised and widely used bridge to academic courses or to more prestigious types of vocational course.[8]

The problems this situation creates are twofold. First, courses designed for, and perhaps admirably suited for, one type of programme become instead feeder courses for institutions which would be much better approached through a different programme. Second, since many vocational courses require scarce equipment and capable technicians who might be even scarcer, the training may not only be irrelevant but also very expensive.

Wherever possible, data should be presented in disaggregated form because national or regional data may conceal very large variations around the mean and be profoundly misleading. There should be no technical difficulty about this since the data are collected from small units and built up, though the preparation and printing of additional tables may put a heavy burden on available manpower.

Disaggregation does, however, add one difficulty to analysis, though probably a minor one. If there is an asymmetrical mobility within the system, wastage rates in some areas may be either over-stated or under-stated. For example, Guatemalan urban schools have a negative wastage rate: there are more new students in class 2 of a given urban system than have passed the class 1 examinations the year before in the same urban area; evidently because students come in from the rural areas—or in some places from night schools. If it were felt that inter-regional mobility of this sort seriously affected the data, sample surveys could be undertaken to estimate the significance of inter-area movements and appropriate allowances could be made.

(b) *The Catchment Area:* Analysis of flow data often rests on one of two implicit assumptions: first, that all students are of approximately equal capacity or, second, that students are the most academically gifted of their age group so that wastage is due either to some generalised, though perhaps temporary, incapacity to profit from education or to inadequacy of the schools to tap the students' potential.

In many parts of the world access to any form of education is limited to a minority of the age group, but we have little information about the relative abilities of children who attend school and those who do not. In some of the more developed countries where primary education is universal it has become apparent that access to secondary and higher education depends to a significant extent on factors which are not directly related to measurable indicators of intelligence.[9]

This presents two problems in estimating the efficiency of the educational system. The first is that the efficiency of the system as a whole may be profoundly influenced by the relative quality of its recruits, and this in turn may be determined by circumstances remote from the internal structure of the educational system. The second is that comparisons among segments of the system may be misleading because, for various reasons, one segment attracts students with a greater potential than do others: in this case performance may bear little relation to the more easily measured inputs.

Even though standard intelligence tests may provide only a crude approximation to natural abilities—perhaps severely dis-

66

counting some aspects of intelligence—there is a great deal to be said for conducting such tests in all schools. There would be two advantages to this: first, it might be possible to make judgments, even though tentative ones, about the disparity between potential and achievement and to see to what extent failure was due to lack of ability rather than to other factors; second, it might be possible to find patterns of test scores which would have a reasonably high prognostic value.

There is the problem that scores on tests may be significantly affected by cultural factors which have little to do with innate mental ability. Since most tests have been developed in industrial countries, students from less developed countries may obtain lower scores than they 'should' in terms of their ability, simply because they are not sufficiently familiar with the implicit context which gives meaning to some of the questions. The problem is not that students in some of the less developed countries may appear to show up poorly in international comparisons but that it is difficult to interpret the results in the context of the less developed countries themselves, since one does not know what would be the average score within the country on that type of test—and so one has little idea of how the student population compares with the non-student population in terms of ability. One would need to carry out further tests on the population as a whole to assess the extent to which the student population was tapping the best talent, but tests in schools would at least enable one to group schools with matching student abilities and thus isolate the effect of other factors.

British evidence shows that, except for the highest levels of ability, access to secondary and higher education is significantly affected by the socio-economic status of the student's parents and other factors: within the public system, students who attend the 'better' primary schools not only do better in examinations but improve their measured intelligence as compared with those in other schools—and the children of non-manual workers are more likely to attend such schools than the children of manual workers; among the children of non-manual parents a higher proportion at each level of ability stay at school than among the children of manual workers and among the 'low' manual group the majority of students even of very high ability drop out of school. There are in addition great disparities, which bear little relationship to measured ability,[10] in the proportion of an age group attending school in different geographical areas.

Part of the discrepancy may be due less to the difference in facilities provided than to the supporting influence of parents with a positive and discriminating approach to education and to the advantages, in the better schools, of a stimulating peer group. The issue is further complicated, for Britain at least, by the fact that many of the 'better' secondary schools, even in the public sector, appear to be committed to a style of life from which many working-class students feel alienated and which is sometimes actively hostile to them.[11]

Despite the greater proportion of students who undergo higher education in the United States, the evidence is clear that there, too, one finds both that a substantial proportion of the population is severely handicapped in development of its potential and that among those who achieve the levels of measured intelligence associated with academic success there are marked discrepancies between socio-economic groups in entry to higher education. There appears to be evidence, as in Britain, that a part of this discrepancy is due to environmental factors which cannot easily be modified, though the significance of this evidence is a matter of controversy.[12]

There are three things which appear to be established beyond challenge. Even in those countries with relatively open educational systems there are many people of high measured intelligence who 'drop out' of the educational system: measured intelligence underrates the potential ability of most groups other than the affluent ones; and many students from affluent groups perform tolerably well in the educational system though their measured intelligence is inferior to that of many outside the system.

In a less developed country where only a small proportion of an age group may complete primary school, where there may be great disparities in the regional distribution of school facilities—and, perhaps especially in Africa, facilities are often concentrated in certain areas for chance historical or even climatic reasons—and where the average quality of education is low (simply because of inadequacy of facilities and the numbers of unqualified teachers) the chances are high that many people with considerable natural intelligence will have little opportunity to develop their abilities.

In some countries an attempt is made to be highly selective by a ruthless approach to examinations. This may fail because: (a) the examinations are simply poor examinations. Results may be largely a matter of chance, while some tests may indeed discriminate against the most imaginative—or even the most intelligent—students; (b) the examinations may be a good test of the abilities required at a given stage, but have poor prognostic value; (c) if examinations are national rather than local the relative performance of students may owe more to the differential quality of facilities in different regions or different localities rather than to the innate abilities of the students. Since there are very great variations in the quality of schools in many of the less developed countries the prognostic interpretation of test scores, even if the test is *per se* an excellent one, is a hazardous business; (d) if students are obliged to face important examinations at an early age the influence of home environment is particularly important—which means that there is implicit discrimination against low-income families; further, to the extent that schools are of poor quality the 'home background' becomes more important; (e) students who pass may not be able to continue for economic reasons, while more affluent students who fail may be able to try again—and in so far as a very high failure rate makes it likely that even some good students will occasionally fail it may *reinforce* the bias against clever students from low-income homes.[13] For all these reasons it would seem wise to postpone selection as long as possible, though shortage of resources may severely restrict the options.

Unfortunately, simple solutions like offering scholarships may have only limited value. Experience in Britain, for example, appears to have been that scholarships or free education have been beneficial to middle-income rather than lower-income groups. The percentage of students from various social classes attending secondary school has changed little in the last thirty years.[14]

So far nothing has been said about pre-primary facilities. There is a considerable amount of evidence that the years up to 5 are the most critical determinants of measured intelligence and the period when the greatest changes can be affected.[15] Formal programmes are particularly important for children from low-income homes because their 'natural environment' is unlikely to stimulate whatever potential capacities they may possess. Since little has been done to develop such programmes in the most affluent countries it might seem Utopian to suggest that the less developed countries should do anything about it. But if the findings of Bloom and others were to be replicated in the less developed countries expenditure in this area might have a substantial pay-off.[16]

II *The Teachers*

The simplest and most easily available data about teacher-student ratios are those which compare the total number of teachers in a given stage with the total number of students. When there are a substantial number of teachers with very weak qualifications, this sort of ratio may be seriously misleading and some commentators have suggested that teacher-student ratios should be exclusive of teachers who have not themselves completed at least one stage beyond that for which the students are being prepared.[17]

In some countries data are available for the numbers of teachers with various levels of qualifications. Where there have been significant changes in the provision of teacher-training there may be a complex pattern of distinctions which do not always have much functional significance. On the other hand, other aspects of the quality of the teaching force tend to be ignored. When one is dealing with university graduates, for example, it is important to have some idea of the class of degree that has been obtained, since it makes a considerable amount of difference whether the graduates were among the more successful men and women of their year or whether they scraped through at the bottom of their class and were not considered suitable candidates for other jobs: a school system staffed by outstanding graduates of the secondary system may be a lot better off than one staffed by the lame ducks of a higher level of education. Differences in the average level of experience may be of great significance, and the magnitude of the problem in some countries, or in parts of countries, is disguised by the fact that the data do not show the large proportion of short-term teachers.

Aggregative data for the country may be useful in providing an indication of the general 'health' of the educational system: if, for example, the proportion of university graduates among secondary teachers is significantly lower than in countries at a similar stage of development it should be treated as a warning signal and planners should carefully assess their priorities. But disaggregated data which show comparative teacher-student ratios and measures of teacher quality among the regions, districts, or where practicable, particular schools within a country are very much more useful.

There is a widespread belief, reflected in policy decisions in both developed and less developed countries, that high priority should be attached to reducing teacher-student ratios. The proposition that students will make greater progress when they have more claim on the personal attention of the teacher accords with common sense, but it appears to have been difficult to obtain objective evidence that, within fairly broad limits, class size has a significant effect on student performance. Attempts have been made in the United States to test the proposition by comparing the performance of students in different size classes and in these tests, class size appears to have had a minor effect.[18]

Since the circumstances in which these tests were carried out were quite different from those prevailing in most of the less

71

developed countries it would be rash to use the results as a basis for policy. The very large classes, overcrowding and inadequate facilities that characterise many schools in the less developed countries clearly provide very unfavourable circumstances for the development of student potential, but it is disturbing that virtually no evidence is available which would enable one to make a sound decision as to what constitutes a 'satisfactory' student-teacher ratio. The analysis of comparative data from within a country would provide a lead-in to an adequate treatment of this problem.

Some of the protagonists of small class size argue that its value only appears in the long run, and that while examination results may not be any better, the real quality of learning is improved and this is reflected in subsequent creativity and adaptability. This would appear to be a testable hypothesis, but since it has not been pursued in countries relatively well endowed with research facilities it might be unrealistic to suggest that much could be done in the less developed countries. The broader problem, to which reference has already been made, of the validity of examinations will demand attention and it may eventually be possible to deal with this particular aspect with more confidence.

It is equally important to know a great deal more about the level or levels of qualification and experience, if any, above which the effectiveness of the average teacher increases significantly. This may require a very high degree of disaggregation, because differences in teacher quality are frequently accompanied by major differences in other important inputs.

In many countries the term 'qualified teachers' is used to differentiate those who have received some recognised form of teacher training from those who, regardless of how many years of education they have had, are not graduates of a teacher-training programme. In countries which have a stable teaching force and where most graduates of teaching colleges become teachers the emphasis on specific vocational qualifications may not need to be justified, but in many of the less developed countries many graduates of teacher-training programmes either do not become teachers at all or spend only a relatively short time as teachers. In these circumstances the value of lengthy specialised teacher training requires closer examination.

It may be useful to provide some teacher training for most higher-level students so that any of them would be able to perform with some minimal level of adequacy as teachers in the short run while more extensive teacher training should be provided only for those whose commitment is indicated by several years' work as a teacher; in addition, appropriate incentives should be provided to persuade temporary teachers to become permanent ones. The present position, in which specialised training is provided *before* career choices are effectively made, has two major disadvantages: first, students who spend a substantial proportion of time on specialised teacher training but subsequently spend little time as teachers are less adequately prepared for the careers that they will undertake than would be the case if their education had been less vocationally oriented, and, second, students whose principal interests lie elsewhere but who might be attracted by a short-term or part-time tour as teachers may have little or no training and experience to enable them to fit in easily to that type of work.

III *Plant and Equipment*

When educational facilities are highly sophisticated it is very difficult to disentangle the effects of specific features: to estimate the trade-off, for example, between a larger assembly hall and a larger student lounge. Moreover, wealthy communities can afford to provide amenities which no one expects will have an observable pay-off in the near future: buildings which are aesthetically pleasing, music facilities and paintings, may, apart from the immediate satisfaction they give, be deemed to stimulate a wide range of desirable qualities, but their beneficial properties are likely to remain a matter of faith rather than knowledge for a long time to come.

Unfortunately, the task in the less developed countries is usually much simpler. One wants to know how much difference it makes whether a primary school has one, two or three rooms—or whether it is possible to conduct effective teaching when there are no rooms at all.[19] The question is often not whether desks and chairs should be of a more or less expensive design, but whether there will be *any* desks or chairs at all, rather than a few bricks piled on top of each other. Evaluation of the effect of libraries and teaching aids turns on the availability of basic readers, maps and even blackboards and chalk, and the extent to which these things affect the capacity of an average—or even a good—student to complete a cycle of work in a reasonable time.

Judged by the criteria used in the more developed countries, most schools in the less developed countries would be regarded as inadequate, but even on the most favourable reckoning of the resources likely to be available for education in the foreseeable future 'minimal standards'—according to American or British criteria—could not be achieved in more than a small proportion of schools without a drastic reduction of the school population. What one needs to know is whether significant improvements in performance could be achieved with the resources available: whether an extra room or glass windows or adequate roofing or a small investment in teaching aids would have a discernible pay-off. Putting it in another way, is there any minimal amount of teaching aids that provides a threshold below which the provision of schooling has little effective value? It is possible that a few shillings worth of supplies in each school may make a great difference to the effectiveness of an educational programme.[20]

It is probable that many primary schools in the less developed countries have so few resources at their disposal that they are unable to provide an education that has any lasting value.[21] It does not follow from this that 'more' should be provided for primary education—in many cases budgets are already stretched to the limit—but more attention should be paid to the potential effectiveness of expenditures, and if resources were concentrated in a smaller number of schools the total number of graduates might increase significantly.

While primary facilities are often grossly inadequate, provision at the secondary—and even more at the higher—level sometimes appears to be lavish. The discrepancy between costs per student in the primary and those in the secondary school is due in part to the boarding facilities offered at the secondary level, and the minimal requirements of facilities and qualified teachers are no doubt more onerous at the secondary level, but it is possible that it owes something to the circumstance that secondary school entrance is often the point at which the potential member of the professional and bureaucratic élite is first clearly distinguished from the artisan.

However, despite a fair amount of polemical writing both for and against 'fine buildings', there is very little hard evidence about the relationship between differences in the quality of buildings which might involve substantial resources, on the one hand, and the differences in the quantity and quality of student output on the other.

IV *Cost Data*

Getting information about physical productivity is a necessary first step in understanding the nature of the options facing the policy-maker. One must, however, go beyond this and examine the prices of inputs and, if possible, outputs before one can determine which of the options offers the best economic return.

Various methods for estimating the most appropriate outputs were described in the previous chapter and discussion here will be confined to inputs. Information on prices, whether they be market prices or shadow prices estimated by the planners, is vital for three reasons. First, it may be the only convenient way of measuring plant and input once one gets past very simple structures: the permutation of rooms, floor space, quality of materials and other factors may give a range of possible input mix that is too wide to be accommodated by any practicable scheme of classification on the basis of physical characteristics. Second, the relative costs of inputs are as significant as their productivity: if qualified teachers were twice as productive as unqualified ones but cost three times as much (and assuming there are no other differences between them and no limits to the possibilities of substitution between qualified and unqualified teachers) it would be most efficient to employ unqualified teachers. Third, one must be able to relate efficiency criteria to the over-all financial constraints within which the programme is obliged to operate: increasing the number of teachers or the range and quality of materials might substantially increase output but would involve costs that could not be met by the amount allotted to education in the budget.

Interpretation of cost-data, however, is sometimes a rather complex matter. There are both conceptual and practical problems involved. Financial cost may not reflect the real cost to the community: for example, something which might appear to be 'free'—that is, for which no cost has been assigned—may involve a diversion of resources from some other task. In that case, there is an economic cost involved—opportunity cost— whether or not there is any accounting cost, and the cost is the value of the work which would have been done had the factors of production been used for some other purpose.

Sometimes the labour for building a school is provided 'free' by the local community—that is, the workers are not paid wages of any kind. If, however, workers are obliged to spend less time farming or fishing or trading, for example, than would be the case if they were not helping to build the school then the cost of construction is the value of the output that is lost as a result. It is sometimes observed that participation in self-help schemes is regarded as an alternative to paying taxes and that when a community builds a school 'free' it may default on part of its taxes. On the other hand, enthusiasm for providing educational facilities in the locality might induce people to give up their leisure: the work done building the school is an addition to the amount of effort and labour-time devoted to productive effort, and in this case the building would be provided free.

Similar problems of estimation arise in the treatment of some types of aid, whether it be from governments or other agencies such as missionary bodies: if a certain amount of resources can only be provided for, say, teachers' salaries but would not be forthcoming for anything else, then as far as the receiving country is concerned the services it will buy can be treated as a free good; on the other hand, even though in a particular aid appropriation, resources may be assigned a specific use, it may be the case that the donor would be able and willing to assign them to alternative uses, so that doctors or engineers, for example, could be provided instead of teachers.

The extent to which prices reflect real costs is often a complex matter, and practical decisions depend to a considerable extent on judgments about the nature of the opportunity costs involved. Planners should at least be aware of the problems posed for the interpretation of conventional accounting data.

In many countries, cost data are rather sketchy and are classified, if they are available at all, according to the source of payment rather than educational function. Costs are frequently divided among the central government, local government, and sometimes other agencies such as local communities or private bodies. Cost data may cover only the contribution of the central government and this may be misleading both with respect to estimates of efficiency and of resources being committed to education; capital costs are often covered by a different agency from the one which is responsible for current costs, and decisions about capital and current expenditures may be based on different criteria and expectations, though neither can be adequately assessed without information about both types of expenditure.

The treatment of capital costs is more difficult than recurrent costs. The latter are properly estimated on the basis of the amount spent in a given year, but the cost of buildings, for example, should be considered in terms of the life of the building not of the year in which the money was actually spent. Various methods of depreciation could be used, but as yet there are few countries where data on capital expenditures are presented in this way.

When costs are related to source rather than function, executive decisions are made not on the basis of the real total cost of a project but on the basis of the cost to the agency that is making the decision, and costs incurred by other agencies, no matter how significant they are to the community, are not infrequently treated as free goods from the standpoint of the agency.

In many of the less developed countries there are administrative and sometimes political obstacles to the consolidation of cost data in a way which would facilitate effective economic appraisal of alternative policies. The costs of education, however, absorb a substantial proportion of the budgets of the less developed countries, involve substantial levels of direct or indirect taxation and take up resources which could be used to meet other highly desirable objectives. A high priority should be given to the organisation of data in the most useful manner so that one may ensure that the resources devoted to education are being used effectively.

SUMMARY AND CONCLUSION

Efficiency is a relationship between inputs and outputs. The most efficient system is one that achieves a given output at the lowest cost or gets the greatest output from given inputs.

Conceptually, 'outputs' could include every change that occurs as a result of the process one is examining. In practice, one is usually limited to those outputs which are achieved during or immediately after the process and which can easily be measured. This limitation is probably more significant with respect to education than is usually the case with 'physical products' and much of the dissatisfaction with attempts to estimate the efficiency of different educational methods is due to the feeling that the usual measures of output are a poor guide to the 'real effects' of education.

The inputs are also more difficult to handle for education since different 'qualities' of student cannot be discerned as easily as different qualities of material, and the quality of student-input may be the most significant single determinant of the quantity and quality of outputs. Even for simple student-teacher ratios and their relationship to output the type of information available in many of the less developed countries is seriously inadequate and may be misleading: aggregate data may conceal critical variations among regions or districts; if repeaters are not distinguished from students entering a class it is impossible to estimate the rate of flow through the system, and both the costs and effectiveness of different types of teachers are subject to a wide range of variation.

Reliable information about the relationship between numbers and quality of teachers on the one hand and student progress on the other provides a useful and necessary first approach to the range of options available to educational planners but should be supplemented by data on the plant and equipment with which the teachers are operating. Before policy decisions can be made the physical relationships must be expressed in terms of financial cost and related to the educational budget.

The 'educational budget' and the claims against it may, however, give a misleading impression of the costs to the community involved in an educational programme. The major problem is that significant aspects of the expenditure necessary to carry out a programme may be incurred by different agencies, each of which make their decisions without regard to the complementary expenditures necessary to achieve the objectives of the programme. In many cases, published data on educational costs cover only part of the total expenditures and important elements are 'buried' in other accounts which cannot be related to specific activities. It is also possible that there may be a substantial divergence between accounting costs and economic costs.

If one had adequate data on the 'physical relationships' and their cost implications one would be in a position to begin an effective evaluation of alternative programmes. The 'economic' or 'efficiency' implications of the data should not however be treated as the sole determinants of the appropriate choice: available data, even under very favourable circumstances, may provide an inadequate reflection of 'real' levels of achievement and, in any case, the *objectives* of the educational system, as of society at large, may quite properly be influenced by ideas about personal, social or religious fulfilment which run counter to measurable indices of economic achievement.

Estimates of efficiency are, nonetheless, prerequisites of sound decisions about policy alternatives. There are two principal reasons for this: first, they provide evidence about matters involving substantial resources which would otherwise be, and usually are, the subject of guesswork and, second, they make it possible to estimate the costs of achieving objectives different from those that would be indicated by the efficiency criteria. In short, they provide a context in which 'judgment' might be distinguished from prejudice.

NOTES AND REFERENCES

1 Efficiency is a relationship between cost and return. The most efficient method is the one that gives the greatest return for a given cost. Alternative returns must, however, be measured in some common unity: if, for example, the quantity of output was to increase but the quality diminish, one would need some method of weighting the different qualities, ideally achieved by the price system, before one would be able to say whether the return had increased or decreased.

2 We 'do not yet have quantitative data on intellectual insight and curiosity, social maturity, personal, or cultural awareness or many other desirable by-products of education' (Woodhall, M. and Blaug, M., 'Productivity Trends in British University Education 1938-62' in *Minerva*, vol. iii, no. 4, Summer 1965). The inculcation of a sense of religious or civic duty has been in the past, and in some places is presently, considered more important than academic performance. But even if one disregards all these other objectives of the educational system, examination results may be inadequate simply because some examinations are deficient as a measure of academic achievement.

3 Woodhall, M., and Blaug, M., op. cit., p. 23; Blaug, M., 'The Productivity of Universities' in *Universities and Productivity*, papers prepared for the Universities Conference, Spring 1968, convened by the Joint Consultative Committee of the Vice-Chancellors' Committee and the Association of University Teachers. Reprinted in Blaug, M. (ed.), *Economics of Education 2* (Penguin Modern Economics Readings). See also Danniere, A., *Higher Education in the American Economy* (Random House, paperback, 1964), esp. p. 138.

4 Danniere, A., op. cit., provides a systematic treatment of the problems of by-products and what he calls bi-jointners. See also Carter, C. F., in *Universities and Productivity*.

5 It does not follow from this that research done in universities in the less developed countries will be either useful or sound: the staff may be of insufficiently high quality, they may be primarily concerned with obtaining jobs elsewhere, in which case their research may be of the sort which could better be undertaken in the place to which they want to go, or as part of a rejection of 'foreign values', objectivity in research may be regarded as a sinister and potentially subversive foreign influence.

6 A comprehensive treatment of this problem is to be found in Davis, R. C., *Planning Human Resource Development* (Rand McNally and Co., 1966). See also Williams, T. D., 'Wastage Rates and Teacher Quality in Guatemalan Primary Schools' in *Comparative Education Review*, February 1965; Michel Debeauvais, 'The Balance between the Different Levels of Education' in Robinson, E. A. G., and Vaizey, J. E. (eds.), *The Economics of Education* (MacMillan/St Martin's Press, 1966), and Budart, N., 'Problems of Measuring Educational Yield in order to Assess Educational Productivity' in Hallak, J. (ed.), *Educational Costs and Productivity* (International Institute for Educational Planning).

7 These data may not be publicly available in many of the less developed countries, but their provision appears to be relatively common in Latin American countries. Guatemala, for example, provides data on the number of students who pass the annual examinations and on the number of repeaters in each class (see Williams, T. D., 'Educational Development in Ghana and Guatemala: Some Problems in Estimating Levels of Educational Growth' in *Comparative Education Review*, October 1966).

8 Experience in the Ivory Coast has been analysed by Clignet, R., and Foster, P., *The Fortunate Few* (North Western University Press); there are pertinent comments on South-east Asian experience in 'Education in the Development of South-east Asia', T. H. Silcock's contribution to Piper, D. C., and Cole, T. (eds.), *Post Primary Education and Political and Economic Development* (Duke University Press, 1964), and the situation in Guatemala is discussed in Williams, T. D., 'Discrepancy between Goal and Function in Educational Planning' in *Comparative Education Review*, June 1969.

9 See for example the *Report of the Committee on Higher Education*, Command 2154-1 (*The Robbins Report*), especially Appendix One, part 11: Factors Influencing Entry to Higher Education, and Douglas, J. W. B., *The Home and the School* (MacGibbon and Kee Ltd., 1964).

10 ibid.

11 Jackson, B. and Marsden, D., *Education and the Working Class* (Penguin Books, 1966), give a number of examples. One of the most striking ones, though perhaps trivial in some ways, was the insistence of headmasters that students play the Rugby Union (amateur and middle-class—in most parts of Britain) rather than Rugby League game (professional and working-class) which was the popular sport in the area.

12 Coleman, J. S., et al., *The Coleman Report. Equality of Educational Oppor-*

tunity (US Government Printing Office, Washington, 1966), emphasised the importance of the home environment. Some of its conclusions have been challenged on the grounds that the data may be validly interpreted in a quite different way (see Bowles, S., 'Towards Equality of Educational Opportunity' in *Harvard Education Review*, Winter 1968, issue on Equal Educational Opportunity. Subsequent issues of the Review have contained a running debate begun by Jensen, A. R., 'How Much Can We Boost I.Q. and Scholastic Achievement?', Winter 1968; Discussion in Spring 1969 and 'A Reply' in September 1969). The differential qualities of schooling offered in one city have been described in some detail for Chicago in the *Havighurst Report* and in hearings before the House of Representatives Committee on Health, Education and Welfare. A vivid and sympathetic account of the difficulties faced by Negro students in a Boston slum school is to be found in Kozol, J., *Death at an Early Age* (Penguin Books, 1968).

13 See Williams, T. D., 'Discrepancy between Goal and Function in Educational Planning', loc. cit.

14 Table 15 of Appendix One, Part 11, of *The Robbins Report* gives the percentage of boys aged 18 attending university between 1928 and 1947 on the one hand and in 1960 on the other as being distributed:

	1928-47	*1960*
A Non Manual	8·9	16·8
B Manual	1·4	2·6
C All	3·7	5·8
A divided by B	6·4	6·5

15 Bloom, B. S., *Stability and Change in Human Characteristics* (John Wiley and Sons Inc., 1964).

16 The question of the appropriate age at which schooling should begin in the less developed countries is a complex one. Even if Bloom's findings were to be replicated, there would be two considerations favouring a later start. First, some people feel that, whatever may be the long-run effect on intellectual development of an early start, older children will have acquired the discipline to 'pay attention' for longer periods of time and are more likely to understand the material advantages which follow from success in school; that they will consequently learn more quickly and that it is better to use scarce teaching resources where the immediate educational pay-off is greatest. Second, older children will move relatively quickly into the labour force where their education will pay off in terms of additional income; since the discount rate is high, it is important to narrow the gap between outlay on education and return in the form of output or income. On the latter point, see Le Thank Khoi, 'Rendement et Productivité de l'Enseignement' in *Educational Cost and Productivity* (IIEP).

17 cf. 'Teachers below a minimal level should not enter the "ratios at all" '

(Davis, R. C., op. cit., p. 183). See also Williams, T. D., 'Wastage Rates and Teacher Quality in Guatemalan Primary Schools', loc. cit.

18 Harris, S., *Higher Education: Resources and Finance* (McGraw-Hill, 1962), p. 530 ff.

19 In a debate in the Ghana Parliament, J. H. Allassani, a former Minister of Education, referred to '. . . grass sheds and huts. . . . Classes in these structures are most inconvenient because the structures do not keep off the rain, and they are ideal nests for snakes, scorpions, lizards and rats.' In replying to the debate the Minister, Duwuona-Hammond, did not minimise the problem and was mainly concerned that people should not have the impression that the Government was discriminating against the Northern Region. Children in Accra were also being taught under the trees; '. . . the impression that sub-standard buildings are only provided in the North, but not in the South, should not be accepted' (*Parliamentary Debates 1962*, First Series, vol. 29). Complaints that there were schools with 'no buildings where classes are held under the trees' were still being made in 1965 (see the speech by Mr Tampurie on 19 January, *Parliamentary Debates 1965*, vol. 38).

20 'In many situations (the costs of expendable supplies) do not run above $0.50 per pupil per year. Yet failure to provide even these minimal supplies may markedly reduce learning in the developing countries' (Davis, op. cit., p. 217).

21 'So-called "side benefits" are cited as a justification for dead-end schools. These side benefits are largely political rather than economic or social, i.e. some local chieftain is hailed for providing a school, even when it does not produce. Something is better than nothing. But the advantage of singling out the non-productive is that it makes clear that the provision is not without cost. Even such pitiable outlays as are made could produce more somewhere else' (Davis, op. cit., pp. 131-2).

CHAPTER 4

ECONOMIC PRIORITIES AND EDUCATION IN DEVELOPING AFRICA

JAMES PICKETT*

The purpose of this paper is to examine some implications of African economic conditions for educational policy: and to consider some of the problems which arise in the attempt to relate economic circumstances to education. It is argued that, economically, low levels of development characterise most African countries. That this has particular implications for education and manpower policy is, of course, not a new idea. Harbison and Myers, for example, have adumbrated policy suggestions for countries in which traditional agriculture is the main present activity and in which prospects for early development of manufacturing industry are poor; and they explicitly count many African countries in the wider group of countries for which their prescriptions are intended.[1] The present paper attempts, however, to provide a reasonably detailed and systematic specification of the African economies; seeks to relate this specification to the identification of policy objectives; and differs sharply from Harbison, Myers and other commentators in its educational policy conclusions.

The paper is organised in three parts. The first considers the characteristics and policy problems of the African economies; the second seeks to establish that education is—from an economic point of view—of particular significance in African conditions; and the third examines some of the more important

* I am grateful to Messrs R. K. A. Gardiner, D. J. C. Forsyth, D. Katz and Dr T. D. Williams for stimulating discussion of the topics considered in this paper; to the Department of Adult Education in the University of Manchester for allowing me to try out some early ideas and to the participants in the Edinburgh seminar for helpful comments. Mr Andrew Flatt was efficient and helpful in providing data and performing related calculations. Responsibility for errors and omissions remains, of course, with me.

questions which arise once the economic significance of education is accepted.

I. CHARACTERISTICS AND POLICY PROBLEMS IN THE AFRICAN ECONOMY

Developing Africa—by extension of the currently fashionable synonym for poor countries—may be defined as the African continent and its associated islands minus the Republic of South Africa. The exclusion of the Republic could be justified on many grounds, but, for present purposes, it may simply be noted that South Africa differs markedly from other African countries in its level of economic development and in its economic structure. Even with the exclusion of South Africa, there is considerable political, social and economic variety in African countries, and it is, therefore, necessary explicitly to justify an attempt at collective examination of these countries. Such justification clearly cannot take the form of arguing that the diversity is manifest within the framework of a coherent economic entity, since intra-African economic links are at present notoriously weak. It must rather be sought in the presence of important common characteristics and problems in the different African economies; and it is thus appropriate to attempt to identify a range of common characteristics—with common policy implications[2]—which would embrace at least a majority of countries in Developing Africa.[3]

In this connection it may be asserted, then hopefully demonstrated, that the main, and related, characteristics of the African economies are low levels of development and slow historical and contemporary growth; and that African economies have enough in common to permit the specification of a representative set of characteristics and policy objectives. It may be accepted that, fully specified, levels of development should be construed in terms of more than narrowly economic criteria; and it may be agreed that there are substantial difficulties in giving wholly meaningful interpretation to data on conventional national income statistics. Nevertheless, weak attitudes

85

and institutions, for example, are almost certain to be reflected in attained levels of output which national income accounting does measure systematically if approximately. In the circumstances, levels of development in Africa may initially be judged by comparing African GDP per head with that of other selected countries.

For this purpose, it is possible to compare product levels of 43 African countries in 1966, first with those of selected developed countries, and second with a number of developing countries outside Africa. Thus, in 1966 product per head in the USA, the UK and the USSR was US$3,839, US$1,908 and US$989 respectively; and, by contrast, all the African economies—with the special exception of Libya (US$990)—recorded GDP per caput of less than US$500. Indeed, apart from Gabon, Liberia, Zambia, the Ivory Coast, Mauritius, Rhodesia, Senegal, Algeria, Ghana and Tunisia, all the African economies had a product per head of less than US$200; and in 18 countries the relevant figure was US$100 or less. The African levels were thus clearly very much lower than those of the most advanced developed market and centrally planned economies, the USA and the USSR; and also very much lower than that of a middle-range developed market economy, the UK.[4] Moreover, African levels were generally below those prevailing in Latin America, where product per head was less than US$200 in only one country and greater than US$300 in 10 countries. Asian levels, on the other hand, were more like those of Africa, although the proportion of Asian countries at very low levels (say US$100 or less) was probably smaller than in Africa. The Asian countries in the very low income category included, however, the most populous—India, Indonesia and China.[5]

If, as measured by reasonably current levels of product per head, the economic distance between African and developed countries is very great, the difference in product per caput provides some measure of the magnitude of the task African countries set themselves when they seek deliberately to create modern economies characterised by a substantial and sophisticated capital stock, a marked and developed propensity to apply

86

science, and a skilled and well-trained labour force. It is well known that the developed countries now have such economies; and that they acquired them in the course of the last 200 years or so. What is less well-known, but what is probably more important, is that the level from which the developed countries started their modern development was almost certainly much higher than present African levels; and one way in which this can be quickly demonstrated is to take us$200 as a generous indicator of contemporary African conditions and compare it with estimates of product per head in the initial stages of modern economic growth in the developed countries. Professor Kuznets has done suggestive work on the initial levels of the modern economies, and a rough up-dating of his earlier calculation suggests that, generally speaking, the immediately preindustrialisation levels of product per head in the now developed countries was about us$300 in 1966 prices.[6] The gulf established by this comparison between Developing Africa and, as it were, Developing Europe could be used to underline the contemporary differences between Africa and Latin America, since a majority of Latin American countries are either now at, above, or even well above the us$300 level. Moreover, in a fuller consideration of contrasts among the present developing regions, it would be necessary to point out that although most developing countries in Asia are still below the historical levels of the now developed countries, the more populous of the Asian countries have levels of population which are more comparable with that of Developing Africa as a whole than with those of individual African states; and that these Asian countries should, in their attempts to develop, consequently enjoy whatever advantages attach to large, or at least larger, market size.

African countries are, then, predominantly among those which in contemporary terms have the furthest to go economically. They are also, not surprisingly and for reasons which will be touched upon below, very much among the least equipped to go at all. That this should be so creates a strong presumption that historical growth over the last century, say, must have been slow[7]; it also heightens interest in recent African performance.

It is, therefore, convenient to examine recent years before re-deeming the earlier promise to specify a representative set of characteristics and policy objectives.

In this connection, it should be said at once that, even when all allowances are made for special circumstances—associated with the aftermath of independence, the inexperience of young governments etc.—African performance in recent years has been generally disappointing. This is not to say that there has been no economic progress, nor even that no very impressive achievements can be identified. It is, however, to say that, judged by the fundamentally realistic standards implied in the target set for the first UN Development Decade of securing a real rate of growth of 5 per cent per annum in total GDP by 1969, the African performance leaves much to be desired. Thus, between 1960 and 1966 estimates of the Economic Commission for Africa suggest that there were 13 African countries (comprising 22 per cent of the total population of Developing Africa in 1966) in which product per head actually declined in real terms. In a further 6 countries (with more than 17 per cent of the 1966 population) real rates of growth of product per caput were positive but less than 1 per cent per annum; and in another nine countries (with 33 per cent of the 1966 population) real rates of growth were more than 1 but less than 2 per cent per annum. In sum, therefore, there were at least 28 African countries (comprising some 72 per cent of the total population of Developing Africa) in which product per head grew annually and in real terms, by less than 2 per cent between 1960 and 1966; and in which, therefore, given that population was generally increasing at an annual rate of 2·5 per cent, the prospects for achieving the target of the first Development Decade were extremely small.

To some extent the attempt at economic development in Africa in the 1960's may be seen as a co-operative effort involving the African countries themselves and the developed countries, notably, of course, the former metropolitan powers. It would, therefore, be interesting, indeed fascinating, to attempt to explain, judiciously and objectively, the disappointing performance in terms of African and developed-country policy. Short of such an attempt, it may here be suggested that much that was wrong in both policies is capable of being traced to a failure properly to appreciate the weight and importance of the African economic legacy from the colonial period; and it is important to stress that this point does not depend on particular views on the question of imperialism. At root, the imperialist charge is that African countries were positively exploited by the former metropolitan powers. All that is required in the present context is acceptance of the fact that, whatever the metropolitan powers may or may not have done to or for the African countries, they had not by 1960, say, endowed them with economies that were sell-suited to the pursuit of modern economic growth, and that policies designed to secure such growth in African conditions must begin with realistic recognition of the kinds of economies African countries now possess, as well as the kind of international economy in which they have to operate.

Modern economic growth may be construed in terms of self-reinforcing and continuing increases in output per head; and the process of modern growth has resulted, in a limited number of countries, in high and increasing income levels and large and expanding markets. The attainment of modern economies has been consistent with varied experience and political systems, but has universally been associated with a number of common features, including an increasingly widespread dissemination of rational attitudes and methods and structural transformation, resulting notably in an increased weight of secondary and a decreased weight of primary activities. To identify factors associated with modern growth is not, of course, to explain it. It is, however, possible to follow Chenery[8] and to suggest that growth is likely to be speeded up by the adoption of policies which allocate resources in a way consistent with the historical patterns of the developed countries and held back by contrary policies, although to be useful this thought has to be substantially qualified. In the meantime, it may be suggested that some comparison of relevant characteristics is now developing and now developed countries can at once provide further measure of the economic distance between them and provide the basis for the formulation, at least in broad terms, of policy objectives. Such a comparison could be organised in various ways. For present purposes, however, present African circumstances are judged in terms of the income level and market size of Canada in 1870; and in terms of contemporary African structure, which, it can be quickly established, differs significantly from that of historical Canada and of the present developed economies.

The purpose of this comparison and the related examination of African economic structure is, it may be recalled, to identify a group of African countries with common characteristics and problems in the context of their economic distance from the now developed countries; and the comparison and examination can usefully take the form of judging the African economies in terms of three related but not perfectly correlated criteria: lowness of income level; smallness of market size; and unfavourable economic structure. Given this, it seems reasonable to begin by comprising the set of developing African countries with average product levels in 1966 of less than us$200, and subsequently reducing this set by countries which fail to meet the second or third criterion or both. In this way, it should prove possible to approximate a set of countries in which something like maximum difficulty might be expected in the course of economic development and in which the general outlines of economic strategy should be similar.

In 1966 there were at least 29 African countries with average product levels of less than us$200.[9] That these were in fact 'poor' countries may be graphically seen by comparison with the 1870 average product level in Canada which may be estimated at us$467 in 1966 prices.[10] None of the African countries in 1966 matched the Canadian level of 1870; the ratio of African 1966 to Canadian 1870 levels ranged from 41 to 10 per cent; and in somewhat more than half of the African countries the average product level in 1966 was less than 20 per cent of what it had been in Canada in 1870.

In 1870 the Canadian population was relatively small at about 3·5 million. As a consequence, there were a number of African countries in which total GDP in 1966 was a higher fraction of the Canadian GDP of 1870 than produce per head was of Canadian average product; and total product in the UAR and Nigeria was substantially greater than the earlier Canadian output. It is not, however, permissible to conclude from this that there are a number of developing African countries in which market size as measured by total output is such as to suggest that they are well placed to pursue economic growth. It is probably true that of all the present developed market economies Canada experienced a growth pattern with greatest relevance to the transformation of the now developing countries. In using the historical market size of Canada as a criterion for judging the viability of contemporary African economies, however, a number of qualifications are necessary. Thus, in the first place it has to be remembered that Canada enjoyed some very important advantages that are not now available to developing Africa. These included an ability quickly to establish growth-oriented institutions; a relative ease in attracting foreign capital and labour on a large scale; and, particularly between 1896 and 1914, unusually favourable external trading conditions. In the second place, the fact that Canada had substantially higher income per head in 1870 than the present African economies conferred further advantage; for example, compared to present African circumstances, the Canadian demand pattern was different, more conducive to growth, and with a higher savings rate. Finally, it must also be remembered that the scale and competitiveness of modern industry is much greater now than it was in 1870.

These considerations suggest that for present purposes the measure of market size which could be designated as the minimum required to ensure, other things also being favourable, fairly rapid transformation should be set significantly above the Canadian level of 1870. How much above is a somewhat intractable question. It may, however, be accepted that the smaller the present African income per head, the larger the multiple African market should be of the historical Canadian market; and this thought may be used to determine, in an admittedly arbitrary way, which of the African countries are now handicapped by small market size. Thus, the convenient but arbitrary criterion requires that all countries in which the relative discrepancy in average product is not at least offset by the corresponding but opposite discrepancy in total product should be classified as being of small market size; and on this criterion only the UAR is excluded from the designation.[11] It is, moreover, worth recording that 21 of the 28 remaining countries had total products in 1966 which were less than 50 per cent of Canada's 1870 output; and that there were 16 countries in which the relevant ratio was less than 25 per cent.

It has already been noted that modern economic growth has generally been associated with a marked shift in the relative importance of primary and secondary activities. It may now be recognised that low income levels and small market size reflect low levels of productivity and might be expected to be associated with a production structure in which primary activity, agriculture and mining, accounts for a high proportion of total output and employment. The question as to what specifically constitutes a 'high proportion' is one which must again be answered with a certain arbitrariness. It could readily be established that the weight of primary in total output in the 28 African countries under consideration is much higher than that now prevailing in developed economies; and that in the considerable majority of the African countries the relevant ratio is higher than it was in Canada in 1870. In a number of countries, however, the 1966 ratio is lower than the earlier Canadian figure; and the question arises as to whether these countries should be excluded from the set of African economies now characterised by particularly unfavourable conditions. Generally speaking, the answer is probably no. Without overlooking the economic importance of commerce and other services, including administration, it may reasonably be suggested that development depends critically on agriculture, mining and industry. If, therefore, the weight of primary in total output is below a specified level, it is important to know whether this is due to the size of the manufacturing sector or to the size of the service sector. Taking this into account and using the earlier importance of manufacturing in Canada, it is appropriate to establish twin criteria, and to suggest that, in the conditions of 1966, any low-income African country of small market size in which primary output accounted for more than 30 per cent and manufacturing output less than 15 per cent of GDP, should be regarded as one with an extremely unfavourable economic structure from the point of view of modern growth.

On these criteria, only Congo (Kinshasa) need be excluded from the set of countries confronting extremely difficult conditions.[12] The remaining 27 countries may be characterised by their low income levels, their small market size and their economic structure which in terms of output, and certainly much more in terms of the distribution of the labour force, suggests a strong dependence on primary activity, much of which is organised on a traditional—i.e. non-modern—basis. In 1966 these 27 countries accounted for about two thirds of the total population of Developing Africa and for well over 40 per cent of the total product.

It is tempting to try and classify the 27 countries further, and in particular, to attempt to divide them according to the importance of minerals in production and exports. Such a division would recognise that, generally speaking, external demand conditions are more favourable for mineral than for agricultural products. Since, however, the linkage effects between mining and other sectors are known to be weak in Africa, and since most of the labour force is still engaged in agriculture even in the mineral-rich economies, the distinction between mineral-rich and other economies would bear more heavily on the prospects for financing developments than on the basic process of economic transformation. In many contexts the prospects for development finance would be of extreme importance. Since, however, the present concern is with basic economic characteristics and related policy questions it does not seem necessary to subdivide the 27 countries according, in effect, to their export prospects.

This decision may be reinforced by the thought that the 27, and indeed other, African countries have at least one other fundamental characteristic in common: they are poorly endowed with the kinds of skills appropriate to a modern economy. More will be made of this subsequently. For the moment, it may be noted that this is perhaps the most serious deficiency of all; and, in anticipation of later argument, it may be suggested that the resolution of the skills problem will be a necessary, if not sufficient condition, for the establishment of economically and politically viable African states.

The African economies are part of the world economy; and African peoples are increasingly aware of the economic standards which prevail in the wider world. There is surely some 'international demonstration effect' now at work; to take the matter no further, those who would argue that this effect reaches only an African élite should be called upon to explain the rapid rate of urbanisation, now observable in African countries, in terms other than a desire of literate and illiterate alike to improve their material conditions as a consequence of becoming aware of 'developed' standards as these are reflected in their own national capitals and large cities. Short of such an explanation, it must be accepted that the pressures on even the least equipped of the African countries are not merely that they should grow, but that they should grow rapidly and in a modern way.

This observation may be used as the basis for comment on the controversy which has taken place on the pace and method of economic advance in Developing Africa. In large measure this controversy can be seen as a confrontation between those who would settle for whatever growth may emerge more or less spontaneously and those who believe that State responsibility and effort are required in order to secure an accelerating rate of growth. The essential feature of this confrontation has been to some extent obscured in the past by a tendency for the supporters of spontaneous growth to be identified with the view

94

that traditional pursuits should be encouraged and the supporters of the State to be identified with a belief that heavy immediate emphasis should be placed on non-traditional economic activities. It is now apparent, however, that a wish to emphasise the importance of traditional activities is consistent with either broadly laisser-faire or broadly *dirigiste* views; and that, therefore, the matter should be settled at the basic level.

Put this way, it may be suggested that the difficulty with the spontaneous view is that it fails to show, as it should be required to do, that largely or modified laisser-faire growth will be adequate in contemporary circumstances; and it is no answer to this charge to contend that the present developed countries took rather a long time to acquire their modern economies nor to suggest that there has been in this century substantial economic growth in some developing countries, say in West Africa, which was clearly not State-contrived. It is no answer because the presence of the modern economies makes a difference to the problems and prospects of the traditional economies; because, on examination, the spontaneous growth looks slow in comparison with historical growth in the developed countries; and because it has not in any case generally brought African countries to the point at which they are endowed with modern economies.

It is true, of course, that no amount of aspiration will *per se* produce a rapid rate of growth, and it cannot be pretended that the African economies can be very substantially transformed in any short period of time. It is also true, however, that any government which wishes peacefully to remain long in power must seek to secure a rate of growth of total output which, if it does not offer any quick, and potentially frustrating, promise of catching up' with the developed countries, does at least demonstrate that substantial steps are being taken toward the establishment of a modern economy. It is most doubtful in this circumstance if any African government could afford to rely on spontaneous growth, and the general decision to adopt comprehensive development planning is, therefore, both understandable and commendable.

95

This is not to say, of course, that African governments can seek growth at any price. In so far as the 'international demonstration effect' increases material appetites, it does so in a way that sharpens the expectation of early satisfaction. Awareness of higher living standards can, as J. S. Mill and later writers have insisted, provide incentives which may result in greater effort being put forth to achieve such standards, yet Nurkse was certainly right to worry about the effect of such awareness on savings and thus implicitly to deny the possibility of a Stalinist type solution to the development problem. African governments must thus confront the problem of achieving an acceleration in the growth rate in a manner consistent with the continuing and undelayed distribution of the fruits of growth. This means, *inter alia*, that average consumption levels should probably rise, and rise significantly through time, and that the rate of growth of employment should be no less than that of the employable labour force.

The specification that African countries should grow rapidly subject to the constraints that average consumption levels should rise perceptibly and substantial unemployment should be avoided represents the minimum requirements for peaceful economic transition. There is, of course, much political and social tension now to be found in Africa; and this fact increases the difficulty of attaining the minimum requirements. Much depends on governments and on their ability to avoid vicious, and to promote virtuous, circles. What is reasonably certain is that the failure of governments to define clearly and to achieve certain basic objectives will increase political and social unrest; that increased political and social upheaval will lessen the chance of growth; and that this in turn will further increase political and social tension.

The scope for manoeuvre is thus small; and although it is for sovereign African states themselves to determine the policy objectives they wish to pursue, as well as the manner of their pursuit, it may be strongly contended that, at least for the economies that have been described here, success will depend greatly on a willingness to give high priority to the resolution of the skills problem, and on a willingness to accept that the path to a modern economy lies paradoxically through an early emphasis on the improvement of traditional agriculture. Among the reasons for endorsing this view about the importance of agriculture is the fact that such improvement offers scope for early rapid growth and the creation of a base for substantial subsequent expansion. Since traditional agriculture is now characterised by fairly primitive methods, high returns should be available from simple technical improvements and little capital investment. These returns are, however, only likely to be obtained if sufficient effort is made in a number of complementary directions. In particular much will depend on extension services and on the receptivity of farmers. It is therefore appropriate, for this and other reasons, to turn more directly to questions of education.

2. EDUCATION AND LEVELS OF ECONOMIC DEVELOPMENT

Economics is essentially abstract. It legitimately proceeds by simplification. In recent years, however, the suspicion has grown that development economics has proceeded by over-simplification and that economists have been too prone to offer mono-causal explanations of the growth process, focusing, for example, on the need for entrepreneurial talent or the importance of capital formation. As a healthy reaction, there has been increasingly explicit recognition of the complexity of growth and development. This recognition has included the narrowly economic aspects of the problem. It has also, however, led to the strong suggestion of the need to go beyond, indeed in some formulations possibly to ignore, the traditional concerns of the economist. This widening view of the development problems has been accompanied by lively controversy, which still continues.[13] To become embroiled in this continuing controversy is not part of the present purpose, which is to establish that education in a broad sense has particular economic significance in present African conditions. Two comments on the subject matter of the controversy provide, however, a useful introduction to the main present concern.

Recognition of the fact that economics abstracts not from reality but merely from economic aspects of reality, and of the fact that this may inhibit the full relevance of economics to social problems is not new.[14] That there has long been difficulty in making social, including economic, analysis wholly relevant to social problems is not, however, an evident argument in favour of either disbanding or ignoring economics. Indeed it may be argued, on the contrary, that economics, because of its strong emphasis on rational choice, has particular relevance to developing countries; and it may in all modesty be suggested that economics is not a bad discipline for the socially conscious intellectual who wishes to range widely in his policy concerns. Thus, even the elementary habit of viewing output as resulting from the conjoint activities of land, labour and capital provides a substantial framework for ordering extra-economic thought. Moreover, even if economics were not capable of providing this kind of organising framework, it would still be important to recognise the significance of economic questions and to accept, in a word, that a development plan may come to grief as much because of wrong-headed monetary policy as because of wrong-headed social attitudes.

The second preliminary point to be made is that to accept complexity is not to accept that all factors at work are of equal importance. The main message of complex causation runs rather in terms of inter-connections, and the main caution requires that the consequences of operating on particularly significant variables should be worked out as fully as possible. To see the matter in this light is to guard against the danger of moving from the inadmissible view that capital formation is all important to the equally inadmissible view that capital formation is not at all important.

This said, it is now convenient to turn to the question of the economic importance of education in Africa and to begin by considering briefly some possible implications of a development model adumbrated recently by Chenery and Strout.[15] The basic purpose of the Chenery-Strout model is to examine ways in which, and the extent to which, foreign assistance can accelerate the process of economic transformation in developing countries. To this end two sets of assumptions are deployed in the model-building. The first accepts the view that developing countries are subject to persistent resource bottlenecks and limited structural flexibility; the second follows the neo-classical belief that domestic resources can substitute, if with decreasing efficiency, for imports essential to development. From what has been said earlier of African economies there must be some presumption that they are characterised by structural rigidity rather than flexibility. Attention is focused, therefore, on some aspects of the Chenery-Strout model flowing from the first set of assumptions.

Chenery and Strout distinguish three types of resources: supply of skills and organisational ability; supply of domestic savings; and the supply of imported commodities. They then identify corresponding constraints on the growth process and suggest that the hypothesis of an economy with limited flexibility is appropriately dealt with by means of a programming model which determines the highest rate of growth consistent with the operation of the most powerful constraint. Within this framework three phases of the transition to self-sustaining, and increasingly self-supporting, growth are analysed. In the first phase the crucial constraint is a skill limit, applying to managers, administrators and skilled labourers, reflecting the widespread belief that 'absorptive capacity for additional investment in any period is limited by the supply of complementary inputs, which can only be increased as a result of the development process'.[16] In the second phase the main limit is domestic savings and the economy is absorbing as much foreign assistance as it can obtain, given the general limits on the supply of such assistance and its own borrowing capacity. In the third phase an inability to make structural shifts in domestic production to meet the changing pattern of external and internal demand means that 'shortage of imported goods will provide a limit to further growth quite apart from the investment limitations'.[17] Chenery and Strout are cautious as to the ordering of the three phases. If the parameters of an economy are stable, as they might be presumed to be in a low-income, slow-growing economy, their expectation is that the economy will move from phase one to either phase two or phase three. They further judge that the import constraint is most likely to operate in rapidly growing economies.

The present interest in all this lies in the possibility that the African economies are skill-constrained and the related suggestion that this constraint can only be removed by the development process itself. Understandably for their purpose Chenery and Strout are not at all explicit as to how the process of development should remove the skills constraint. If, however, it were established that this was the effective African constraint it would clearly be necessary to specify a mechanism for overcoming it; and such specification would, equally clearly, have implications for education. Is Africa, then, skill-constrained? It might be thought, given what has been said about African economies and what could be said about African educational systems, that there must be a fair presumption that it is. The notion that the skill constraint is generally the most powerful in developing countries has, however, been recently challenged.[18] It is, therefore, worth attempting to strengthen the African presumption. To do this rigorously within the framework of the Chenery-Strout model would be extremely difficult. This is basically because the model is *ex ante*, while whatever relevant African data there are, are *ex post*. It can, however, be argued that much can be inferred from changes in the international currency reserves of the African countries. In particular, it can be suggested that, under certain circumstances, the accumulation of reserves constitutes *prima facie* evidence of a skill constraint; and it is, therefore, useful to consider the reserve position in African countries in recent years.

Information on reserve changes between 1960 and 1967 is available for 15 of the 27 countries discussed in the previous section[19]; and of the 15, no fewer than eight recorded an increase in reserves over the period. In Mauritania, the increase was due to the marked rise in exports of iron ore and the resultant fact that export earnings were well beyond the capacity of the country to import. In the other countries the increase was associated with a continued deficit on current account, which suggests that the inflow of foreign long-term capital and transfers was greater than the trade gap, and, therefore, greater than the contribution of foreign funds to domestic capital formation. It is true, as has been pointed out in the UN document from which information on reserves was taken, that an increase in reserves may reflect economic prudence, and that changes in reserves should be related to some desirable level. The UN document itself suggests that reserves should be 25 per cent of the annual import bill and only admits rising reserves as evidence of inadequate absorptive capacity if the reserve to import ratio is 25 per cent or above. It thus places four of the eight countries now being considered in the group of countries it describes as being subject to a resource gap.

What is thus in issue is the likely reserve policy of low-income countries. It might be thought that poor countries would be strongly tempted productively to employ, if they could, as much in the way of foreign funds as they could lay their hands on, even if this meant that their reserves fell to what, according to other canons, might be a dangerously low level; and some support for this suspicion may be had from the fact that the reserve to import ratio in most African countries is below, and in some countries well below, 25 per cent. Moreover, it can be argued that the reserve criteria are not symmetrical; although an increase in reserves in the circumstances described may be taken as *prima facie* evidence of inadequate absorptive capacity, it is not so clear that falling reserves establish that absorptive capacity is adequate. This is because, to be meaningful, absorptive capacity must be subjected to some criterion of economic efficiency. It is, however, known that the motives governing the giving and receiving of foreign assistance are varied, and the frequent complaints about wasteful, if impressive, edifices at least suggest that the ability to lay claim to foreign resources is not necessarily co-extensive with the ability to deploy such resources in a manner calculated to increase the growth capacity of the economy.

The notion that African countries are skill-constrained is, therefore, still an appealing one, and it can be bolstered by some thoughts of Professor Galbraith and by some consideration of present educational conditions in Africa. Thus, in a series of lectures in 1965, Galbraith contends that 'The African countries . . . are strongly interested in education. And gradually a design for development is emerging which places primary emphasis on this.'[20] In elucidation he explains that at Harvard attempts were being made to classify developing countries according 'to the obstacle or combination of obstacles which, in the given case, is the effective barrier to economic advance'.[21] The attempt was admittedly impressionistic, but it did produce a fourfold classification, Model I of which was designated 'The Sub-Saharan Model'. The model is most relevant to the present discussion and characterised by the fact that the principal obstacle to development is the smallness of the cultural base and the related difficulty in securing its extension. It is properly and commendably explained that the smallness of the base is due not to lack of aptitude but of opportunity; and it is made clear that the lack is of trained and educated people capable of performing the tasks of government and running an increasingly complex economy. The suggestion is then made that in developing countries, to which the model applies, the first task is to enlarge the cultural base.

All this is certainly plausible, but, it may be objected, is so much assertion. Such an objection could be countered to some extent by a few figures on the number of African graduates given by Galbraith himself. More powerfully, it can be countered by the juxtaposition of the characteristics and problems of African economies adduced earlier with some general account of existing educational conditions in Africa.

The earlier account sought to establish that a contrast between the African economies—with their low incomes, small markets and unfavourable structure associated with low productivity—and the developed countries at once made rapid growth imperative and extremely difficult to achieve. It was further suggested that much of the difficulty would fall on the government. It was not, however, thereby meant to suggest that development was a matter for government alone. Indeed one of the difficulties in a situation in which the relevant skills are scarce and the government charged with heavy development responsibility is that the government will pre-empt so much of the available skills that little will be available for the corresponding development of the non-government sector. Developing this, it may be admitted that the specification of skills has thus far been rather vague, and it may be suggested that an attempt at somewhat greater precision may help to throw further light on the character and magnitude of the skill constraint in African conditions.

This attempt may conveniently be organised within the framework of development planning. Development planning requires, in its preparation, an over-all framework and, within this, integrated sector and project programmes. This in turn requires the skills to discern and fashion into a coherent whole a large number of viable economic and social projects. It might be thought that this is no exacting requirement, since the skills in question are those of, say, a relatively small number of economists, agronomists and engineers. Development plans should, however, be made to be implemented; and implementation greatly increases the skill requirements. At one level, it is not sufficient that the government should obtain, frequently on a temporary basis, the skills of a few experts; and, at another level, the skill requirements ramify throughout the entire economy and affect all grades of labour. At the level of government a viable plan with some prospect of implementation will only emerge if all the operating ministries and agencies of government are continuously involved; and this requires that each ministry and agency should have its own adequately staffed planning committees and planning units. At the project level it is not enough that a particular line of production should be shown to be feasible in terms of general economic analysis. The establishment of a plant as a going concern requires a competent manager, skilled supervisors and labourers, and unskilled workers with a minimum understanding and acceptance of factory discipline. A good development plan is much more than a collection of projects. A careful examination and aggregation of the skill requirements of individual projects is, however, as good a way as any of determining quickly the absorptive capacity of an economy. Moreover, if government effort is to have maximum impact, there should be widely dispersed entrepreneurial and other talent to take full advantage of government initiative.

It may be suspected that the identification of plausible projects at the level of general analysis and the subsequent detailed elaboration of the skill requirements would, in low-income African countries, establish the realities of the skills constraint. Short of such an exercise, certain reasons may still be advanced for believing that, if African countries should grow rapidly, they are substantially inhibited in their attempt to do so by lack of skills. It is well-known, for example, that, however inexact the available data, illiteracy rates are generally very high in Africa. This means three things: that the stock of persons with any kind of education is extremely low; that, since literacy is a prime requirement for an industrial labour force and a helpful feature in an agricultural one, there must be some strong presumption of difficulty in organising economic advance; and that the stock of moderately- to well-educated persons must be very small indeed. In these circumstances, it is difficult not to believe that education and the acquisition of skills is the crucial bottleneck in many African countries. Nor does this difficulty become less in face of the following general account of the African educational system at the beginning of the first UN Development Decade:

Perhaps the most graphic single indicator of the inadequacy of the system is to be found in enrolment ratios. Thus, as far as primary education is concerned, there were 24 countries in 1960 in which enrolment comprised less than 25 per cent of the relevant age group; 20 countries in which enrolment comprised between 25 and 50 per cent of the age group; and only nine countries in which more than 50 per cent of the relevant age group was in primary schools.

At the second level of education, there were five countries in which 20 per cent or more of the relevant age group was at secondary school in 1960; there were 48 countries in which enrolment ratios were lower than this; and in 26 of the 48 countries the ratio was less than 5 per cent. Because of the possibilities for variation in the time pattern of university and other higher education, enrolment ratios at the third level of education are particularly difficult to define and to measure. It is nevertheless certain that the numbers of students receiving higher education in Africa in 1960 constituted less than 1 per cent of any plausible measure of the appropriate age group.

In addition to the brute evidence of the enrolment ratios, it has to be remembered that drop-out rates were high in most countries; and that, therefore, only a small fraction of beginning students at each level actually completed their studies at that level. There was, moreover, a shortage of teachers—even for the limited tasks in hand; and a high proportion of the teaching staff comprised insufficiently trained or completely unqualified teachers. In many countries there was a shortage of classroom and other facilities; and many of the existing installations were of poor quality. There was a pressing need for more textbooks and for improvement in the quality of such textbooks. The curriculum followed was still often that which had been established in the colonial era; and, since it bore little relation to the environment of the pupils, it was not calculated to inspire either enthusiasm or persistence.

In assessing the characteristics of the educational systems at the beginning of the first Development Decade, it has to be remembered that there is a long gestation period in the production of middle and high level skills; and that, therefore, it would be necessary to add the time required for professional persons to pass through the system to the time taken to improve the system to the point at which it could begin to meet the needs of a modern economy. It has also to be remembered that, for a number of reasons, education in Africa is relatively more costly than it is elsewhere.[22]

With more time, space and data, it would be possible to establish much more strongly the thesis that education is of crucial significance to African economic development. In the meantime, it may be hoped that a *prima facie* case has been established, and that it is now appropriate, on that premise, to turn to some questions which arise in a consideration of the relationship between economics and education in low-income countries.

3. ECONOMIC AND EDUCATIONAL PRIORITIES

Argument thus far has suggested that education is of strong

importance in the economic circumstances of many African countries. This importance heightens rather than diminishes the need for careful ordering of priorities. The consequent purpose of this section is to examine some of the more important questions of choice which arise in the determination of economic and educational policies in low income countries. In particular, attention is focused on education as an economic priority, on priorities within the educational system itself, and on the kinds of education which should be offered.

(a) Education and Economic Priorities

In a sense, the crucial question concerns the degree of priority which should be given to education in relation to other methods of increasing the development capacity of the economy. This is a complex question, even when it is somewhat narrowly viewed as a technical problem in resource allocation, and it is, therefore, useful as a preliminary to attempt to dispel the confusion which is often associated with the comparison of the aims of the economist, frequently portrayed as being unworthily materialistic, and those of the educator, which are frequently taken to show a more praiseworthy attachment to spiritual values. In general form, strong expression has been given to comparisons thus unfavourable to economists by Thomas Carlyle, who said, 'of all the quacks that ever quacked, political economists are the loudest. Instead of telling us what is meant by one's country, by what causes men are happy, moral, religious or the contrary, they tell us how flannel jackets are exchanged for pork hams, and speak much of the land last taken into cultivation.'[23]

This implied separation of the material and the more-worthy-than-the-material is, or ought to be, unacceptable. The suggestion that economists have particularly narrow vision is neither particularly accurate nor particularly helpful. Apart from the fact that it is not clear that anyone is in a position fully to specify 'by what causes men are happy', at least two things can be said in defence of economics. The first is simply that, since resources are limited and aspirations infinite, eco-

106

nomics is necessary; economists make a most useful social contribution in insisting on the relevance of opportunity cost. The second is that, far from detracting from the finer things of life, the purpose of economics is to promote them or at least make them possible. Thus, the basic aim of economic planning, for example, is to enlarge the total supply of goods and services; and the effect of such enlargement is certainly to widen the range of human choice and, hopefully, to increase the sum of human happiness.

Even when the need for allocating scarce resources according to rationally determined criteria is accepted, the determination of the amount of resources to be allocated to education remains difficult. One set of difficulties arises from the fact that, in Myrdal's terminology, education has an 'independent' as well as an 'instrumental' value, and this fact underlines what would in any case be evident—that the allocation of resources to education cannot be divorced from the content of education. This set of difficulties can be considerably and reasonably reduced by adopting Myrdal's thought that 'from a development point of view the purpose of education must be to rationalise attitudes as well as to impart knowledge and skills', and by endorsing his value judgment that 'no independent value attached to education is considered to be valid if it conflicts with the value of education as an instrument of development'.[24] It should be recognised, however, that this way of proceeding somewhat reduces the distinction between the 'independent' and the 'instrumental' value of education, and that it amounts, for example, to the suggestion that university students can follow whatever courses they most value, provided they elect to study engineering or economics or whatever subjects are judged to be economically viable. Such conditioned choice can, of course, still be of independent value to individuals, and some neglect of range of choice that might be required by conscious concern with the independent value is presumably justified in poor countries, if such neglect can be shown to lead to more rapid general development.

The acceptance of all that has been said thus far still leaves unanswered the basic question of how to determine the developmental importance of education relative to other possible uses of development resources. It might be thought that, given the stress that has been placed on the need to choose rationally and in a developmental context, recourse can and should be had to cost-benefit analysis or the related rate-of-return approach to determine where, and indeed how, governments in Developing Africa should expand their educational expenditures, and that they should invest in education for as long as the ratio of benefits to costs are greater than they are for alternative uses of resources. It is true that cost-benefit analysis has much to recommend it; in particular, it does recognise that it is 'important to take a long view (in the sense of looking at repercussions in the further, as well as the nearer, future) and a wide view (in the sense of allowing for side-effects of many kinds ...)'[25] and it does result in a broader and more systematic consideration of all relevant factors in the investment decision than economists have given, until recently, to this question. The very attempt, however, to increase the complexity of the decision-taking process in this way makes this particular process inapplicable in present African circumstances. This is fundamentally because cost-benefit analysis is not a technique for taking decisions in ignorance. The specification of costs and benefits, their measurement and their discounting, in relation to education and all the other things against which education should be ranked, are beyond the accuracy and availability of African data.

It has, in fact, to be accepted that resource allocation in African conditions has to be undertaken on the basis of very partial knowledge both of the initial situation and of the consequences of present decisions. It may, therefore, be argued that rough judgments can be supported by rough measurement, and that expression may be given to the general argument that education should be accorded developmental priority in Africa in terms of simple and aggregate indicators, such as the proportion of GDP spent on education and the enrolment ratios at the various levels of education. To go much beyond this would lead quickly to the realms of the spurious. A resolve to increase the ratio of educational expenditures to GDP by a specified amount over a specified period of time, together with an understanding that educational expansion has to bear some relation to employment opportunities and that educational framework has to bear some relation to the requirements of the economy, is probably as specific as most African governments need to be at present in their general educational planning. General plans have, of course, to be given content. It is, therefore, now convenient to turn to a consideration of the priorities which should be established within the educational system itself.

(b) *Priorities within the Educational System*

The notion of an 'educational system' implies the existence of inter-related components, and thus makes it clear that priorities cannot be absolute, if only because a decision to expand, say, the primary sector of the system would have fairly immediate implications for the secondary sector also. In recognition of this, and to give focus to the subsequent discussion, it is useful at this point to introduce a somewhat idealised educational framework which might be taken as broadly relevant to African conditions. This framework may be used, among other things, to organise a brief characterisation of present systems in Africa. Such characterisation may be followed by an account of frequently recommended policy priorities and may be used to support a critique of such recommendations.

The educational framework is presented in Chart 1. Implicitly or explicitly this presentation draws attention to a number of desirable characteristics which may usefully be cited. In the first place, the diagram simultaneously recognises the need for variety in order to tailor the full range of human talent to the economic requirements of society, and the fact that education is a sequential process with a range of patterns and terminal points. In the second place, therefore, the diagram requires that many sectors should, at one and the same time, be sufficiently self-contained to give those who complete the work of

CHART 1

An Educational Framework

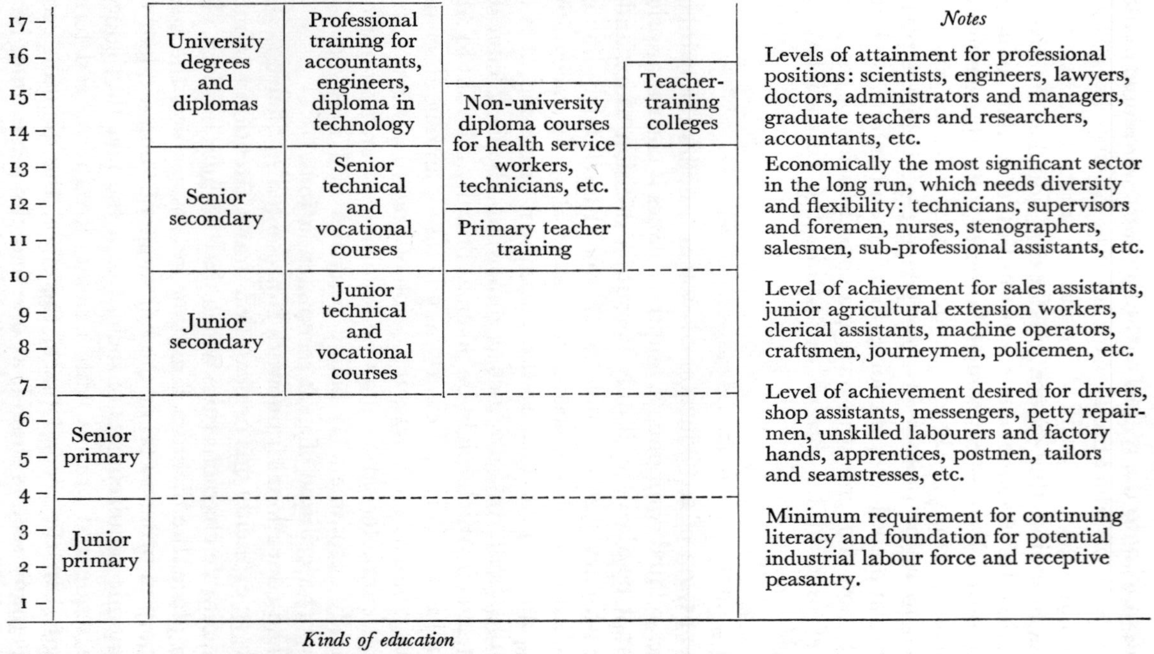

Kinds of education

Years of education				Notes
17 – 16 – 15 – 14 –	University degrees and diplomas	Professional training for accountants, engineers, diploma in technology	Teacher-training colleges	Levels of attainment for professional positions: scientists, engineers, lawyers, doctors, administrators and managers, graduate teachers and researchers, accountants, etc.
13 – 12 – 11 –	Senior secondary	Senior technical and vocational courses	Non-university diploma courses for health service workers, technicians, etc.	Economically the most significant sector in the long run, which needs diversity and flexibility: technicians, supervisors and foremen, nurses, stenographers, salesmen, sub-professional assistants, etc.
10 – 9 – 8 – 7 –	Junior secondary	Junior technical and vocational courses	Primary teacher training	Level of achievement for sales assistants, junior agricultural extension workers, clerical assistants, machine operators, craftsmen, journeymen, policemen, etc.
6 – 5 – 4 –	Senior primary			Level of achievement desired for drivers, shop assistants, messengers, petty repair-men, unskilled labourers and factory hands, apprentices, postmen, tailors and seamstresses, etc.
3 – 2 – 1 –	Junior primary			Minimum requirement for continuing literacy and foundation for potential industrial labour force and receptive peasantry.

Source: Adapted from UNECA document E/CN 14/428

these sectors a sense of satisfaction and achievement as well as socially useful skills and provide the foundation for advance through the system. Thus primary education must lay the foundations for an industrial and agricultural labour force in which the most common skill is that of functional literacy and also provide a sufficiently rigorous preparation for more advanced levels of education. In the third place, the diagram recognises strongly that those who would teach should first be fairly extensively taught themselves.

If the educational framework set out in Chart 1 is ideal in relation to African conditions, this is less because of pattern than because of qualitative and quantitative deficiencies in African education. The boxes in the diagram have some counterpart in African reality. The interesting question concerns the adequacy of the counterpart for developmental purposes. In attempting to answer this question it has to be accepted that information is far from complete and that many indications are impressionistic rather than systematic. It is, nevertheless, useful to establish what is known or reasonably suspected. To begin, as it were, at the beginning, it is certainly the case that primary enrolment ratios are strikingly low; and it has been estimated that in 37 out of 42 African countries in 1964 less than 50 per cent of the 5-14 age group was in primary school, that in 27 of these countries the relevant ratio was less than 33 per cent and in 10 of the countries the proportion was less than one in six.[26] Moreover, the 27 countries in which the primary enrolment ratio is less than one third are largely coextensive with the 27 countries identified earlier as being particularly handicapped in their pursuit of modern economic growth. In principle, low primary enrolment ratios could result from limited entry, high drop-out rates or some combination of both. Unfortunately, the limited information available does not permit detailed calculations on this point. When, however, enrolment ratios are as low as 25 per cent, say, there must be some presumption that both factors are at work. It is certainly the case that in most countries drop-out rates are extremely high, particularly perhaps in the first one or two years, and that only a small proportion of beginning pupils complete what is described in the diagram as junior primary education. Again it would be useful to identify in precise terms the causes of this failure to complete the course. Such identification is hardly possible. Drop-outs, however, are certainly associated with an inadequate number of properly qualified teachers, with inadequate physical facilities and with curricula which are almost certainly irrelevant in the eyes of the pupils.

Given that primary enrolment ratios are low, it is not surprising that secondary and tertiary ratios are also low. Nor, given the general scarcity of resources, is it surprising that teaching and physical facilities should often be judged inadequate at the secondary level also. The difficulties at the secondary level are compounded by the fact that students at this level have already suffered from inadequate primary education and consequently find it difficult to follow a secondary course offered by extremely well-qualified teachers in excellent physical surroundings. At the tertiary level staff recruitment and standards have been organised in international terms and physical facilities are frequently if anything too splendid; in one sense, however, the excellence of African universities has served mainly to emphasise the deficiencies of primary and secondary education in many countries. The conflict between university entrance and subsequent performance standards and inadequate preparation at earlier levels has been a frequent source of discontent.

The notion that vocational as distinct from academic training has particular relevance to the problems of the developing countries has not been without effect in Africa, and many countries have attempted to establish agricultural, commercial and technical schools and colleges at a number of levels. Without prejudice to judgment on the validity of the basic motion, it may be remarked here that, again not surprisingly, these attempts have suffered from the same constraints as have affected the more traditional primary and secondary schools, and indeed that the quality of vocational training is such that it would often be difficult to predicate any argument on the desirability or otherwise of vocational education on the actual experience of many African countries.

This discussion of African educational systems has been necessarily general and necessarily summary. It suffices, however, to make clear that there is ample scope for reform, improvement and expansion, and it could serve to introduce a wide-ranging consideration of topics related to such reform, improvement and expansion. Such wide-ranging consideration would, in turn, embrace questions relating to curricula, relative emphases within the formal educational system and the importance of training facilities outwith the formal system. Questions of curricula are considered in the following section. Much of the present discussion is concerned with emphasis within the formal system. It is, therefore, worth making explicit that this does not imply any underestimating of the importance of informal facilities. The present emphasis is, however, justified, partly because the formal system now predominates and is likely to continue to do so and partly because to be effective informal training requires some formal educational exposure.

The question of emphasis within the formal system has received considerable attention. At the official level the most notable, collective example of such attention is provided by the 1961 Addis Ababa Conference, which was seen as providing 'a forum for African States to decide on their priority educational needs to promote economic and social development in Africa'.[27] Confronted with general inadequacy the Conference commendably resisted the temptation to seek undifferentiated advance in all directions and specified three particular priorities, the expansion of secondary education, curricula reform, and teacher training. It justified the emphasis on secondary education with the view that 'the past decade has witnessed a marked growth in primary school places, but the increase in secondary school places has been insufficient to absorb a fair proportion of eligible school leavers. Current demands for manpower possessing at least a secondary school education cannot be met.'[28]

This emphasis on the expansion of the secondary sector has

been widely endorsed by private commentators. Thus, for example, Sir Arthur Lewis has recently stated that·

The chief need in Africa now is for a lot more secondary schools. The number of jobs requiring a university graduate . . . is very small. Most . . . jobs can be done nearly as well by a secondary-school graduate as by a Bachelor of Arts, at a fraction of the cost. Also the secondary school is the gateway to other jobs for which there is special training—secretaries, nurses, elementary school teachers, agricultural assistants, medical technicians and so on. These are the people on whom the efficiency of operations mostly depends, just as in the army the quality of the non-commissioned officers is decisive.[29]

Harbison and Myers have suggested that:

The typical underdeveloped country should give absolute priority to second-level education over all the other 'highly urgent' educational needs. Almost without exception, those who are to replace foreigners will need to be secondary-school graduates, and many will need higher education to which secondary is the avenue of access. The economic and political leaders for subsequent decades will be the secondary school leavers of the next ten years, and they will constitute the human resource base for subsequent growth. And finally, it will be impossible to develop a good primary education system without substantial numbers of teachers who have a second-level education.[30]

The question now to be considered is whether, in light of Chart 1, the impressionistic attempt to characterise African educational systems and earlier argument, this impressive consensus on the relative importance of secondary education is justified. It may be said at once that there are strong grounds for thinking that it is not. Chart 1 brings out very clearly that primary education is the foundation on which all else has to rest, and the impressionistic comment makes it reasonably clear that some years after the Addis Ababa Conference primary enrolment ratios in many African countries were still low and that the quality of primary education left a great deal to be desired. It would seem to follow that attempts to expand secondary education would be based on wobbly foundations and that, for this and other reasons, relative priority should now be given to the improvement and expansion of the primary schools.

At this point it is useful to recall some of the features of the

African countries earlier identified as being in particularly difficult circumstances from the point of view of modern economic growth. Such countries require to grow rapidly and at a pace that calls for effective development planning; to grow rapidly they should place heavy emphasis on agriculture for some time to come, be especially concerned to transform the traditional sector of the economy into a market-orientated activity, and expect that their growth prospects will be greater the greater the degree of political and social cohesion. In seeking to grow by transforming traditional agriculture and in seeking to preserve or create political and social cohesion, these countries have to reckon with a number of obstacles, not least of which is that the considerable majority of their populations are illiterate. In a sense therefore they lack both the skills to execute and implement development plans and the skills required to understand them even in outline. This double lack is serious and in its implications for educational policy it supports the view that the primary sector is now of crucial importance, even if some of the implications of accepting this view are somewhat unpalatable.

In light of the experience of the 1960's and the first years of political independence, it is evident that the African economies are not going to be transformed quickly or easily. It may still, nevertheless, be suggested that the target of African governments should be the establishment of modern and effectively African economies as quickly as possible. If this suggestion is accepted, it may further be suggested that the speed of such transformation will depend crucially on the care with which the foundations for the future, modern economies are now laid. Emphasis on primary education is consequently now capable of justification both in terms of certain present requirements and in terms of future needs for effective Africanisation. The really basic requirement for effective transformation of the African economies is the continuing literacy of a substantial part of the population. In the short run, it is true, this need could be met by adult education, and, given the importance of agriculture and the need for a capacity to understand government policy, together, of course, with a government capacity to formulate policy and explain it effectively, there is much to be said for coupling proposals to invest heavily in adult education with those for expanding and improving primary education. To expand adult education alone, however, would be an unnecessary neglect of future requirements which, in so far as present expansion of adult education was associated with economic growth, would sooner or later be self-defeating.

If enrolment ratios in African primary schools were substantially raised and the teaching and physical facilities in such schools substantially improved much else would follow. It must be expected that African economies and societies will become increasingly complex and require increasingly large absolute numbers of persons of high intelligence and considerable educational exposure to manage them. Given a normal distribution of intelligence, the securing of such persons in adequate numbers does not require universal primary education. It certainly does, however, require primary enrolment ratios considerably in excess of those which now characterise most African countries. Moreover, since access to education and authority in Africa in present circumstances probably owes even more to accident of birth than it does in the more meritocratic developed countries, and since in any case the bulk of the population is still located in the countryside, the provision of a sufficiently broad base on which to develop high-level talent requires considerable expansion and qualitative improvement in the rural primary schools. It cannot be pretended that such expansion and improvement would, *per se*, do anything to diminish the attractions of the towns. It would, however, result in a more equitable and, it is being suggested, in the longer run a more efficient allocation of educational resources; and it could thus have an important impact on social and political stability. This may be particularly true in countries in which specific educational taxes are levied and where the present dispensation tends to specify the costs to individual communities without producing commensurately identifiable benefits.

It should be emphasised that the present argument is essen-

116

tially concerned with timing and is compounded of the present unsatisfactory state of African primary education and the fairly trite, but important, insight that education is a sequential process that, as every good teacher and student knows, requires careful preparation from the foundations upwards. It differs therefore from the views of those who would now give priority to secondary education in Africa, not so much because it dissents for the reasons advanced from the importance of secondary education as because of the belief that sound secondary education requires equally sound primary preparation. Thus, Harbison and Myers are quite right to insist that secondary graduates are required for the politically important purpose of Africanisation and for expanding the supply of primary teachers. It is doubtful, however, if Africanisation can effectively proceed or the supply of primary teachers effectively be increased by taking very inadequately prepared primary pupils and submitting them to either mediocre or even very good secondary training. Sometimes, as the French have it, *il faut reculer pour sauter mieux*.

The fact that primary education is part of a more general system bears repeated emphasis. It should be recognised, moreover, that the present priority for the primary sector requires, to put it at its least, some contingent planning for the near and distant future. The expansion and increased effectiveness of primary education will, for example, certainly heighten both the demand for and capacity to receive secondary education. It will also increase the number of persons who are often thought to be particularly liable to migrate from rural to urban areas and there become unemployed. This thought relates to a complex problem, of which the most important thing to say is that it cries out for considerably more attention and research than it has hitherto received. In the meantime a number of observations may be made. The first is simply that the implied line of causation from education to migration and subsequent unemployment may be misguided. It is at least possible that people seek primary education in the rural areas because they wish to go to the towns, rather than vice versa. It is equally possible that the illiterate and completely uneducated loom as large among the urban unemployed as the recipients of primary education. This is not, of course, to say that urban, or indeed rural, unemployment is a negligible problem. If, however, the demand for primary education is strong, if people will tend to migrate with or without education, and if the expansion of primary education is in the general interest, then it would seem better to expand education and accord priority to the provision of jobs among other policy objectives, than to restrict education in the weak hope that such restriction will lower urban unemployment levels.

African countries are for the most part newly independent and among the economically least developed of the world. They are thus faced with a cruel dilemma. Understandably, they wish to run their own affairs. They are, however, in a situation which would challenge a much higher concentration of talent than was available to them on their emergence from colonial rule. African governments must confront this dilemma how they will. If, however, they seek rapid growth along the lines that have been suggested here, including the emphasis on primary education, then they will almost certainly be forced to rely on considerable expatriate assistance for many years to come. In this circumstance, it is worth at least suggesting that a serious review of the availability, functions and current use of foreign personnel in planning, education and commerce should be undertaken. In particular, it should be recognised that expatriates should be sufficiently numerous and qualified to perform training as well as substantive functions, that, to be effective, they should perhaps have executive rather than advisory roles, and that the length of time for which they will be required could more efficiently sustain something like career appointments rather than the relatively inefficient present system of short-term contracts. It should be added that if such thoughts present a challenge to African political skills, they equally present a challenge to the generosity of the developed countries—it should be as easy for the rich to be generous as it is for the poor to be skilful.

(c) *The Content of Education*

There is a large, and somewhat heated, literature on the kinds of education which are most appropriate for developing countries. It is not part of the present purpose to add to or detract from this literature.[31] It does, however, seem appropriate to offer a few, brief comments that follow directly from the main concerns of this paper. As a start, it may be repeated that a survey of actual educational conditions in many African countries would suggest that little serious argument could be based on contemporary African experience. It is difficult to resist the feeling that a well-organised academic system and a well-organised vocational system would both be much better than the present system. More generally, the sharp contrast which is sometimes posed between the academic and the vocational should probably be avoided, and the view implicit in Chart 1, that they are complementary and both necessary, should be accepted.

If academic and vocational education are both required, the policy problem becomes one of determining their mix. In the present context, an important question which then arises is whether primary education should be mainly academic or mainly vocational. Not surprisingly, this is a thorny issue which has generated a number of different views. From a developmental standpoint, however, it is important to remember that primary education is the foundation for subsequent education and training, academic and vocational, and, for some people, preparation for modern economic effort. Its main purpose should therefore be, in Myrdal's words 'to introduce methods of modern scientific thought'.[32]

To do this, it should induce the ability to read and comprehend, fluency in verbal expression and a basic numeracy; and if these things are construed as being academic, then primary education should be unashamedly academic. It should not, however, be remote from the interests and backgrounds of the pupils or it will be ineffective and provide a foundation for nothing but rapid escape from schooling. In rural areas this constraint places extra, but not impossible, demands on the

119

teacher, and it underlines the importance of having well-equipped and enthusiastic teachers.

In absolute terms this paper has covered much ground. In relation, however, to the vast theme of economics and education it is far from being exhaustive. Its author is only too conscious that to attain even its present limited breadth, the paper has necessarily and very evidently been short in depth. Essentially, however, it represents an attempt to challenge the prevalent view that an expansion of the secondary schools should be the priority objective in present African conditions. This challenge has been mounted on mainly economic grounds and from the standpoint of an economist. If the challenge is accepted it would be wholly in keeping with a major economic principle—that output expands with the division of labour—if others were to supply the depth and the detail that the present paper so lamentably lacks.

NOTES AND REFERENCES

1 Harbison, F., and Myers, C. A., *Education, Manpower and Economic Growth* (McGraw Hill, 1964).
2 One common characteristic is smallness of market size; one policy conclusion, frequently associated with this characteristic but not discussed here, concerns the need for economic co-operation.
3 Unless otherwise stated, data in this section are from UNECA, *Economic Conditions in Africa in Recent Years* (E/CN 14/438).
4 It should be noted that differences in accounting techniques understate Soviet product relative to that of the US and UK.
5 Asian figures are from various issues of the UN *Yearbook of National Accounts*.
6 A representative figure of US $200 in 1952-4 prices was adopted from Kuznets, *Economic Growth and Structure* (New Haven, 1964).
7 See, UNECA, op. cit., ch. II.
8 Chenery, 'Patterns of Industrial Growth' in *American Economic Review*, September 1960.
9 In a total of 42 for which estimates were available.
10 The estimate required extrapolation of some data from Kuznets and a rough but conservative adjustment for price changes.
11 In fact the discrepancy in market size between the UAR and Canada was considerably greater than the inverse discrepancy between products per head.

12 On these criteria, the Congo was something of a borderline case. But the potential of the Congo for diversification and growth is sufficient to justify the exclusion.

13 See, for example, Knapp and Martin (eds.), *Teaching of Development Economics* (Allen and Unwin, 1964).

14 See Durbin, E. F. M., 'Problems of Research in the Social Sciences' in *Economic Journal*, September 1938.

15 Chenery and Strout, 'Foreign Assistance and Economic Development' in *American Economic Review*, September 1966.

16 ibid.

17 ibid.

18 Maizels, *Exports and Economic Growth in Developing Countries* (Cambridge, 1968).

19 UNECA, op. cit., ch. VII.

20 Galbraith, K., *The Underdeveloped Country* (CBC, 1965).

21 ibid.

22 UNECA, op. cit., ch. IV.

23 Quoted by Viner in 'The Economist in History' in *American Economic Review*, December 1962.

24 Myrdal, G., *Asian Drama* (Allen Lane, 1968), vol. iii, chapters 29 and 31.

25 Prest and Turvey, 'Cost-Benefit Analysis: A Survey' in *Surveys of Economic Theory*, vol. iii, 1966.

26 UNECA, *African Economic Indicators* (1968), ch. II.

27 UNECA and UNESCO, *Final Report, Conference of African States on Development of Education in Africa* (Addis Ababa, 1961).

28 ibid.

29 Lewis, *Two Decades of Growth* (The Aggrey, Fraser-Guggisberg Memorial Lectures, 1968).

30 Harbison and Myers, op. cit.

31 See, for example, Blaug, M. (ed.), *Economics of Education 1* (Penguin Books, 1968), Part 5.

32 Myrdal, op. cit.

CHAPTER 5

EDUCATION IN SOCIAL DEVELOPMENT

G. E. HURD

i

There are few terms in common usage in the social sciences which carry so many meanings as the term development. Progress, growth, change, industrialisation: these are some of its more frequent meanings. There is often an explicit or implied evaluation of the process. Thus, many administrators or practising politicians speak of development only when referring to the achievement of their goals. Among social scientists, too, such evaluation is often present, especially but not exclusively in relation to political development which is often taken to refer only to the emergence of a 'democratic' political system. To give a single example, Joseph LaPalombara, in his essay 'Bureaucracy and Political Development',[1] excludes the activity of the military in politics from his purview on the grounds that military coups are undemocratic. The argument would seem to be: 'it's a "Bad Thing", therefore it's not development'.

In this paper the usage is very different and implies no such evaluation. The term development is used to refer to a process in which institutions become differentiated from one another. In the simplest societies there are no specialised religious, economic, political or educational institutions. Their emergence constitutes social development, as does subsequent differentiation within these spheres. This meaning of the term development is close to that of those economists who distinguish between economic development and economic growth, reserving the former for structural changes in the economy and using the latter for the more easily quantifiable changes in per capita income, gross national product, and the like.

It is upon structural questions that I wish to focus. A sociological perspective draws attention to the social structure and the way in which it is changing (or in other words, to the relationships between the institutions of a society) and suggests that no part of society can be understood in isolation from the society as a whole. It is this insistence upon relating an institution to the rest of society that is peculiarly sociological. In the analysis of education this insight is often lost, paradoxically because of another sociological contribution to the study of education—the discovery of the social nature of man. This is best summed up in the term 'socialisation', and both the study and practice of education owe much to Emile Durkheim's analysis of what he called 'the systematic socialisation of the younger generation'.[2] Socialisation is the one function of education that is invariably understood by educationalists and that has been incorporated into general educational theory, possibly because it coincides with the objectives of educators. It is also the aspect of education emphasised by anthropologists, since in simple societies there are no specialised educational institutions as such. The process of education, i.e. socialisation, is carried out by the whole community: typically, boys learn the skills of hunting or farming from their fathers or other adult males; girls learn how to cook, sew, and perhaps farm from the women of the community. As the adult roles of the society become more complex, however, specialised educational institutions *develop* and a large part of the socialisation process is carried out within them. In short, the emergence of *formal* education *is part of* the process of social development.

Certainly, no sociologist would deny the importance of the socialisation process wherever it may take place. The learning of values, customs and beliefs is equally significant whether it occurs in school or in the context of family life. Indeed, even where formal systems of education exist, some of the most significant aspects of socialisation continue to be performed elsewhere. Thus, P. and S. Ottenberg describe how the Ibo of the early 1960's had successfully adjusted to a money economy and negotiations involving contract law. Yet these changes occurred not within the formal educational system but mainly in the context of trade.[3] Such findings are of crucial importance to those who are interested in the relationship of educational *institutions* to the wider society and they are obscured to some extent by referring to all such socialisation as 'education'.

Conceptualising formal education in institutional terms as part of the development process enables us to focus on the relationship between educational changes and other changes. Rather than simply asking how education affects economic growth or political change we can more easily pose problems of the *inter*-relationship between the developing educational system and other aspects of the development process. But this institutional view of education has other, perhaps more important, implications. Schools and colleges are consciously established as institutions specialising in the socialisation of young people. But the establishment of specialised educational institutions and the appointment of special persons to perform the socialisation process has many other consequences, some of them unintended, some of them unwanted, and some of them not even recognised. For example, the role of education in the independence movements of Africa is frequently remarked upon but less frequently analysed; educational systems are related to systems of social stratification and often act as channels of social mobility; and, perhaps most importantly, educational systems act as selection agencies, allocating members of the population to different occupational positions according to certain criteria. Apart from the intrinsic interest of these structural problems, independence, economic growth, social equality employment and educational provision are invariably important parts of government policy. An understanding of the way in which these objectives interact is therefore of considerable practical importance. Without such an understanding educational policy may be, and in the past has been, both in industrial and 'developing' societies, directed to goals which cannot be achieved through the educational system.

ii

In the attempts to reach an understanding of the structure and functioning of 'developing' societies, researchers have, with few exceptions, fallen under the influence of one or two dominant traditions. Some emphasise disproportionately the importance of the traditional social structure and, at worst, attempt the analysis of contemporary societies as if nothing had changed in the last one hundred years. This approach is less common than it was. At the other extreme many sociologists, as well as economists, political scientists and others who draw on the sociological tradition,[4] transfer concepts and theories forged in the analysis of industrial societies to the analysis of a very different situation. Each tradition, of course, is useful in so far as it draws attention to one aspect of reality. The structures of traditional societies are relevant for the understanding of contemporary societies, forming, as they do, a base line for more recent developments. The structures of industrial societies are also relevant, but only partly because they constitute a model for the planned development of the less developed societies, a model which is often consciously adopted, particularly in its economic aspects. More importantly, industrial societies constitute a world context within which all development must now take place. The countries of contemporary Africa and Asia are usually treated as if they were undergoing a process identical to that experienced by industrial societies. It is far too frequently assumed that any development which occurs in 'developing' societies will necessarily follow the pattern of the industrialisation of Europe, America or Soviet Russia. The exception that is invariably allowed is that 'short cuts' can be taken by the late-comers to the development process; that certain stages of, say, technological development can be missed out. What is less often recognised is the effect upon the internal development of the societies of Africa and Asia and, to a lesser extent, Latin America of the existence in the world of countries which are already industrialised. The establishment of relationships *between* societies at different stages of development may result in a line of development of a very different kind. The only *systematic* recognition of this is by marxists, whose theoretical assumptions highlight the international relationship of 'exploitation'.[5] For the rest, although there has recently been considerable lip service to the importance of the relationship between industrial and 'developing' societies, this crucial relationship is usually left out of analyses of specific institutions.

Nowhere is this international relationship of more significance than in education, for the very existence of educational systems derives from it. Education in 'developing' societies cannot be properly understood as an extension of a process which was present in the traditional society. It must be understood as a newly differentiated institution which socialises, but also has many other functions. On the other hand, it is quite unrealistic to suppose that in a situation of 'institutional transfer' educational institutions will function in quite the same way as in the metropolitan country.[6] When industrial and traditional societies come into contact the result is neither 'traditional' nor 'modern'. The common distinction between traditional, modern, and syncretistic institutions, while usefully drawing attention to the degree of change involved, is misleading in so far as all institutions in 'developing' countries may properly be viewed as syncretistic.

iii

With this in mind let us turn to what is probably *the* crucial latent function of education in 'developing' societies, namely, selection and allocation. This may be viewed as a service performed for the economy, supplying it with suitably trained personnel. It is often argued that a 'modern' society, by which is usually meant a society with a high per capita income, must necessarily allocate members of the population to the various social positions impersonally on rational grounds and that this necessitates all social positions being open to all members of the society. In brief, the argument is that modern societies are necessarily characterised by universalism and achievement.[7] The allocation of social position according to birth or according to particularistic considerations of kinship or friendship is said to constitute a blockage to economic growth. The argument is based upon an analysis of the industrialisation of the western world, although whether modern industrial societies *are* characterised by universalism and achievement is open to serious doubt.[8]

Even more dubious, however, is the assumption that the institutionalisation of universalism and achievement will result in economic development and economic growth in 'developing' countries. Universalistic recruitment to occupational positions requires the development of some mechanism to select the 'best' man for the job. This may consist of some sort of on-the-job evaluation of performance or it may involve the educational system in the process of pre-occupational selection, probably by examination. In the West, it is argued, such recruitment patterns were crucial to the process of economic development and growth, although, as we have already implied, particularism has survived through family firms, the 'old school tie' network and the like, and ascription has combined with achievement in the partial dominance of the upper and middle classes over the educational system. But the implications of bureaucratic universalism are very different in 'developing' societies.

One of the major characteristics of most 'developing' societies is their heterogeneity. Nowhere is this clearer than in the countries of tropical Africa where colonialism superimposed regional and urban/rural differentiation upon the existing ethnic differentiation. The regions of these societies were differentially exposed to European contact and so to formal education which was, at first, part of that contact. Thus, in the coastal countries of West Africa, educational systems are more highly developed in the coastal areas than in the interior with a consequent inequality in access to education. In such a situation the attempt to mediate universalistic recruitment through the educational system results in very considerable regional inequalities. In ethnically diverse societies it leads similarly to tribal or racial inequalities. In stratified societies it leads to 'class' inequalities. None of this, in itself, refutes the argument that universalism promotes economic growth; it has yet to be demonstrated that such inequalities are inimical

to economic growth. There may, however, be political consequences of such inequalities and they may be instrumental in
bringing about extreme political instability. This, of course,
has economic consequences. To stress the importance of this
one has only to point to the tragic case of Nigeria. The insistence upon appointments to the Northern Civil Service on a
universalistic/bureaucratic basis resulted in large numbers of
Ibos entering the service and so achieving positions of power
and/or influence in the North.[9] The consequent tension was
one of the important factors underlying the Eastern secession
and the Nigerian civil war. Clearly, the transference of universalistic criteria of appointment does not always promote
economic growth.

Most African governments are acutely aware of this problem
and supplement their 'bureaucratic universalism' with special
rules facilitating achievement in the less developed regions.
Northerners in Ghana and Nigeria, for example, are given
preferential treatment in entrance to a few of the secondary
schools. In this way an attempt is made to heighten the inte-
grative function of education and to minimise its divisive
function.

Essentially the same problem emerges with regard to the
disproportionate access of élite groups to the educational system.
It is quite possible for bureaucratic universalism to operate at
the level of occupational recruitment, to be mediated through
the educational system through the requirement of educational
qualifications, and yet for channels of achievement to be largely
blocked. This will be the case if entry into the crucial parts of
the educational system is dominated by the children of the
élite. The question becomes: who is selected for the education
that will qualify them for powerful and remunerative occupations? Historically, in *all* societies, the children of the élite have
been prominent among those selected; there has been a substantial inter-generational maintenance of socio-economic position, even in societies which are largely universalistic in their
criteria of occupational placement. Contemporary 'developing'
countries would seem to be no exception. Here, too, there are

sharp differences in the access of various occupational groups to the schools and consequently in the life chances of the various groups.

In African societies this has not yet become a political problem comparable to that of tribal and regional inequality of access to élite positions. There are a number of reasons why this is so. First, there has so far been a lack of class consciousness among underprivileged Africans. This is perhaps less to do with the continued strength or traditional 'vertical' patterns of identification than with the predominantly rural nature of the societies. In the towns, however, there are some indications of a growing identification with 'horizontal' groupings which may well become significant in the future. Furthermore, such evidence as is available suggests that, in one country at least, of all occupational groups it is the urban manual workers who are the least well represented in secondary schools[10]—the very group among whom resentment might be expected to crystallise into something akin to class consciousness.

There is, however, a second and probably more important reason. In so far as there are pressures for changes in African systems of education the demand is not for a redistribution of access to the schools but for further expansion of the educational system so that more can 'benefit' from it. And 'benefit' in this context means, to those who are making the demand, gaining access to good jobs.[11] There is no widespread recognition of the fact that *all* educational systems are élitist in the sense that they are selective. In other words, the allocative function of education is not recognised. (Incidentally, it would not be difficult to demonstrate a similar lack of awareness in Britain and other industrial societies, even among professional educators.) The common belief, and herein lies the misunderstanding, is that expansion of the educational system can, in some way, alter the occupational structure. But with the single exception of creating a demand for more teachers, educational expansion does not directly affect the provision of jobs at all. What has happened as educational systems have expanded is that higher and higher levels of education are needed as 'qualifications' for the same job. Given levels of education are devalued.[12] Thus, wherever educational systems act as agents of occupational selection, only a minority can be chosen. The difference between educational systems lies in the point at which such selection is made. Where primary education is very rare, the selection point is at entry to primary school; as primary schools become more common, selection is delayed until a later stage. In England until recently, and in some parts still, the major point of selection has been at entry to secondary school; more and more in contemporary England entry into higher education is becoming a crucial point. In North America, where a much larger proportion of the age group goes to college, significant selection through drop-out takes place during the undergraduate course and upon entry to graduate school. In short, manipulation of the numbers entering various levels of the educational system cannot affect the provision of jobs. However the educational system is expanded, only the strongest survive, although the death of the weak may be postponed.

iv

How is all this related to further social development? Contrary to general belief, the nature of allocation to occupational position is not directly related to social, i.e. structural, change, even when such allocation involves some social mobility. Social mobility, whether through the educational system or through some other channel, does not necessarily, nor usually, imply change in the structure of society, but rather, movement in the position of individuals within that structure. On the other hand, a change in the *amount* of social mobility in a society is likely to involve structural change. The educational system, however, cannot of itself produce such a change[13]; its function is confined to the promotion of the mobility of individuals.

In what way, then, is the educational system related to changes in the distribution of wealth, power and prestige and to changes in the relationship between groups that are based on this distribution? There is a widespread belief in the power of formal education to change or maintain class systems, a belief which has been reflected in such varied political programmes as the British Labour Party's post Second World War campaign for comprehensive education, President Nyerere's 'Education for Self Reliance' and Lord Lugard's emphasis on 'traditionally-oriented education' which would reinforce the power and prestige of the traditional rulers in Northern Nigeria.[14] However, here, as elsewhere, the autonomy of the educational system is much less than that usually ascribed to it and it is perhaps more effective in maintaining the status quo than in bringing about change. The social classes of industrial societies, the élites of Africa, the land-owners, peasants, and urban manual workers of Latin America, are all groups rooted firmly in the social structure and especially in the economy. They do not owe their existence primarily to a particular form of socialisation, whether within the educational system or elsewhere, although this may be important for styles of life and status consciousness. They are at least equally, and in most cases more, dependent upon the unequal power relationships, both economic and political, which exist between them, and, in the case of social classes, on feelings of solidarity and actions based upon those feelings. Whilst conceding that educational reform might possibly make some impression upon the status dimension of stratification it is difficult to see how it could significantly affect the distribution of power and wealth. To the extent that education has only a limited efficacy in bringing about economic change[15] its function in changing stratification systems is similarly limited. The growth of a class of intellectuals who are professional educators, and who in many 'developing' countries exercise considerable influence, is the only development that could not have taken place without formal education. For the rest, the determination of change in stratification lies elsewhere than in the educational system. And as long as élite positions exist in a mid-twentieth-century society with universalistic recruitment, the educational system will perform a selective or allocative function irrespective of the nature of the system, and the nature and content of the socialising process within the schools and colleges will be determined largely by the requirements of the occupational role.

The relevant questions for the understanding of social stratification in 'developing' countries, then, concern the nature of stratification in these societies before contact with industrial societies (and here there were enormous differences—such as between India and some of the stateless societies of Africa—whose effect will not be wiped out in a mere generation or so) and the development of the occupational structure, especially in industrial, commercial and political fields. This brings us back to the second theme with which we started—namely the importance of the world context within which development takes place. The functioning of formal education in the social structure of 'developing' countries, especially ex-colonies, is distinctive because it did not develop spontaneously in response to other indigenous developments. It was, moreover, the most easily diffused of all Western institutions. The other relevant factor is that in colonial societies the newly differentiated occupations were largely in the employ of the government. These two factors combine to produce societies far more bureaucratic than were, say, the industrialising societies of nineteenth-century Europe. Educational qualifications are *the* significant criterion of occupational placement and the schools and colleges have an enhanced prestige and importance as a result.

In spite of this, their importance is confined to the level of the individual. With regard to the social position any given individual will occupy in society the level of education he reaches is likely to be crucial. But we are forced to conclude that educational changes have few implications for social changes such as changes in the system of social stratification. This may be a bitter pill to swallow. For just as education was the institution most easily diffused from the West, so, of all the institutions of contemporary societies, it is the one most amenable to manipulation. It is far easier to change the educational system than to change the economy or the class structure. Such manipulation is unlikely to produce the desired social change.

NOTES AND REFERENCES

1 LaPalombara, J., *Bureaucracy and Political Development* (Princeton University Press, 1963), pp. 3-33.
2 Durkheim, E., *Education and Sociology* (Glencoe, Free Press, 1956).
3 Ottenberg, P. and S., 'Ibo Education and Social Change' in Weiler, H. (ed.), *Education and Politics in Nigeria* (Verlag Rombach, Freiburg im Breisgau, 1964).
4 For example, the sociologist Daniel Lerner, the economist Bert Hoselitz, the political scientist David Apter and the economic historian W. W. Rostow.
5 See, for example, Frank, A. G., *Capitalism and Under-development in Latin America* (New York, Monthly Review Press, 1967).
6 See Foster, P. J., *Education and Social Change in Ghana* (Routledge and Kegan Paul, London, 1965), for a clear analysis of this problem.
7 See, for example, Hoselitz, B. F., *Sociological Aspects of Economic Growth* (Glencoe, Free Press, 1960), chapter 2; and 'Social Stratification and Economic Development' in *International Social Science Journal*, 16, 2, 1964. For a trenchant critique of this approach see Frank, A. G., 'Sociology of Development and Underdevelopment of Sociology' in *Catalyst*, 1967.
8 See ibid.
9 See Kirk-Greene, A. H. M., 'Bureaucratic Cadres in a Traditional Milieu' in Coleman, J. S. (ed.), *Education and Political Development* (Princeton University Press, 1965).
10 See Hurd, G. E., and Johnson, T. J., 'Education and Social Mobility in Ghana' in *Sociology of Education*, 40, Winter 1967.
11 See Foster, P. J., op. cit.
12 For a further development of this argument see Hurd, G. E. and Johnson, T. J., op. cit.
13 ibid.
14 See Nyerere, J. K., *Education for Self Reliance* (Dar Es Salaam, Government Printer, 1967). Peets, H., 'The Role of British Colonial Policy in Nigeria' in Weiler, H. (ed.), op. cit.
15 On this point see Banks, O., *Parity and Prestige in English Secondary Education* (Routledge and Kegan Paul, London, 1955); Foster, P. J., op. cit.; Anderson, C. A., and Bowman, M. J., *Education and Economic Development* (London, 1966).

CHAPTER 6

POLITICS AND CITIZENSHIP

JOHN P. MACKINTOSH

There was a case recently of student unrest in one of the developing countries of Africa. The Prime Minister was alarmed since these were the men and women he was going to need to run the country and to replace the remaining Europeans in skilled posts. So he and his ministers went down to the university and spent three hours listening to the students' complaints about their conditions, about the deplorable standards in political life, the way the ministers lived, the failure to combat neo-colonialism and so on. At the end the Prime Minister announced that to meet these discontents he would order an immediate cut in ministerial salaries of 20 per cent and the closure of the university so that the students could go back to their villages for a year and discover once again what life and work was for most Africans.

This episode illustrates many of the problems to be considered in this chapter, the purpose of the chapter being to examine the major difficulties facing politicians, educational administrators, teachers and pupils in developing countries. The examples have been taken mainly from West Africa and from Scotland, partly because these are areas where the author has direct personal experience and partly because it is useful to contrast one of the more advanced developing areas of Africa with a European country which has always been relatively poor by European standards but where there has been a great deal of emphasis on education and where the process of establishing an educational system has been long drawn out and cautious.

First, some of the relevant underlying assumptions and approaches to education both in Western and in developing countries must be noted. It has not been sufficiently stressed that educational systems are products of a given society and reflect its history and values. Many people have found it surprising that the former colonial powers exported their political systems to their dependencies despite the fact that neither European liberals nor African nationalists have found it easy to devise other, more indigenous institutions. Indeed it is a contradiction in terms to imagine that indigenous institutions can be devised; either they are in existence or they are not indigenous. However, it was appreciated that facets of the Westminster model of government—such as an impartial civil service, an independent judiciary and a two-party system were alien plants in Africa or Asia, which would require to be specially fostered or protected in a new and strange environment.

But the same reservations did not apply to educational institutions. The pattern of primary, secondary, adult and higher education of the former colonial power was often accepted as having general validity, the educational institutions of Western Europe and the United States being imported wholesale and then left to settle down in a totally different social setting.

The second peculiar feature of this process sprang directly from this rather uncritical adoption of Western methods and objections. While political institutions were, it was realised, open at times to criticism and reform (even total rejection), the universality of the educational importations was generally accepted. A few of the Africans who undertook their studies abroad were irritated by the overtones in Western education but the vast majority accepted education simply as the acquisition of certain skills, a degree or a qualification which would mean so much in terms of job opportunities at home. There is also the fact that most of these students arrived in Europe at a time when the use of educational institutions as a means of indoctrination was totally out of fashion (with the one exception of Catholic schools); it was out of fashion because of the abuses of the fascist period in Europe and because the national traditions of the European states were sufficiently developed to be allowed to play a subordinate or subconscious part in education. Since there was little overt emphasis on this aspect of education, Africans could import European methods and teachers, accepting what many liberals themselves believed, that this was a neutral force in national terms; it was simply the best method of removing prejudices or limitations on personal development and of acquiring new skills and capacities.

Yet it is wrong to imagine that there has ever been such a neutral type of education and the mere transmission of skills was certainly not the principal role of educational institutions during the long period when the European and North American nations were forming and becoming cohesive units. Indeed education has always been more an inculcation of beliefs and a method of creating a common outlook than a series of vocational training schemes.

As an illustration, the Scottish experience is instructive. Education was started in a systematic fashion in the seventeenth century as a direct product of the religious turmoil which did so much to mould the Scottish character and outlook. The parochial organisation of schools called for by the Statute of 1696 was suited to the existing church and civil organisation. The subjects taught were intended to enable all children to read the Bible and a few to go on and acquire the skills needed for the professions of the day, the Church, law and medicine. The four Scottish universities were really operating at what would now be considered a secondary-school level, the total result being a very cheap educational system fitted to the needs of the country—no more than it could afford—and one which drew strength from and confirmed the leading Scottish characteristics in terms of religious observance, thrift, application, an indifference to many aspects of culture and an emphasis on certain specific types of achievement. As a result, despite the modern standardisation of teaching methods and the fact that Scotland has not had a separate political identity since 1707, the educational system has been a major factor in preserving the quasi-nationalism of the Scots. Boys and girls from the Scottish landed families who have been educated at English public (fee-paying and private) schools and at English universities may at times claim to be Scots but they are not so regarded by those who live, work and above all have been educated in Scotland. This is the great divide, not name or family or place of birth. It is the experience of going through the Scottish educational system that provides the quality, the atmosphere, the outlook which leads those who have spent all their lives in Scotland to recognise someone as a fellow Scotsman.

Similarly in the rest of Western Europe and in the United States, the national traditions have been maintained or created in large part through the schools. Bismarck felt that Germany would not be properly unified unless the 'state within a state' represented by the Catholic schools was combatted and to this end he launched the 'Kulturkampf'. When the submerged nationalities were battling to overthrow the German-Magyar domination of the Hapsburg Empire, the critical question was whether their language could be recognised as the official language of instruction and whether the pre-Hapsburg history of an area and of its language group could be taught in the schools.

Thus particularly in the early stages of education, the language, the history of the community, the link either with religion or with common patterns of social conduct and with common concepts of duties, the songs sung, the recreations encouraged, all these help to produce a certain outlook among children. Though too much emphasis on these aspects may seem out of place to both European and African intellectuals and academics who want to register scientific achievements and achieve scholastic recognition by world standards, no country has ever been created out of small or amorphous units without an emphasis of this kind.

As part of the slow process by which Western schools fulfilled this purpose, the pattern of education was moulded to fit the needs of the society to attune with what could be afforded and the kinds of training that were required. At times the system would lag behind contemporary needs and there would be a public outcry. In the case of Scotland, pressures of this kind led to the first major intervention by the State, the 1872 Education Act. The authors of the Act had to accept that the parochial system already referred to had only worked in a partial manner and was totally inadequate in the new, expanding industrial areas of Scotland. Again similar pressures in the 1960's have produced the first batch of new universities founded in Scotland since the sixteenth century. But such adaptations are easier in an indigenous and slowly developing system of education.

Returning to the situation in developing countries the consequences in the cases where there has been a failure to appreciate the importance of these two factors—the socialising effect of education and the need for a proper adaptation to community requirements and resources—must be recognised.

To take the second, more practical type of error or misjudgment first, the most obvious mistakes have arisen where the educational system imported lacks the appropriate distribution of effort for the new society. For instance, in certain developing countries, as part of a political programme and out of pride in the new opportunities offered by independence, some political parties promised to introduce universal free primary education. This was done in both Eastern and Western Nigeria producing two unfortunate results. The first was that a disproportionate amount of the annual budget was absorbed by education, the cost in Western Nigeria at one stage rising to 41 per cent of the revenue raised and in Eastern Nigeria to 46 per cent. This was an error simply because too little money was left for other forms of development on which the vigour of the whole community and its capacity to maintain an educational system depended.

Also, once free primary education was introduced, the output of primary-school children exceeded the jobs off the land which by tradition had been the preserve of adolescent school-leavers who had been taught to read and write, a situation which caused considerable discontent.

A second example was the tendency to regard a university as a prestige symbol so that if one region of a country had one, the others expected the same. In Nigeria this led to ludicrous duplication with the University of Ife being set up alongside the University of Ibadan simply because the latter was a federally maintained institution and the Yoruba felt that they had to have a university of their own. The great weakness of the Ashby Report on higher education in Nigeria (1960), which proposed five universities, was that no attempt was made to compare cost effectiveness of this expenditure with the gains that would have been made by a different distribution of resources either in education or as between education and other forms of development. Moreover the proposals of the Ashby Report were out of phase with the rest of the educational programme in that there were not enough qualified secondary-school leavers to fill all the university places. Once such errors have been made, distortions and problems succeed each other. For instance, in Nigeria, those responsible for university admissions found that with many poorly qualified applicants clamouring for places, it was hard to take a realistic view and exclude those on whom the expenditure of public money was unlikely to be worthwhile. Yet the political pressures aroused if candidates were rejected and an academic year began with empty beds in student residences and empty places at laboratory benches were tremendous. The alternative, to admit a large number of low-level first-year students so that the 10 or 15 per cent who might rise to a suitable standard could be isolated while the others were eliminated, met with tremendous resistance whenever the process of elimination was attempted. It could be argued that if the failure rate was higher than in other—European—universities, perhaps this was the result not of the admissions policy, but of bad teaching. In any case by then considerable sums of public money had been spent on each student which would be lost if their training came to nothing. Also there was the view that many partially trained people were of more use than a few highly qualified and a mass with no training at all. (This was the same philosophy on a grand scale that lay behind the thinking of the Indians who used to put B.A.(failed) after their names.)

The danger of this tendency is that if carried far enough, say to the end of the first degree, it means that graduate engineers are turned out whose bridges fall down, the public has to endure doctors who cannot diagnose and civil servants man important posts when they are not really up to the job.

Not only ought the educational system to be geared to the appropriate inputs of children and outputs of trained scholars at each stage and to the cost the community can afford but there are problems of recruiting and holding the appropriate numbers and quality of teachers.

At the one end of the scale university teachers with international qualifications must be retained. It is a great loss, if pay drops so low, as has happened in India and Pakistan, that some of the best scholars prefer to move to African, British or American universities. Similarly the salaries of doctors, civil servants and applied scientists have to be fixed at levels which will also attract any expatriates needed in an interim period. On the other hand, so many school teachers will be needed that they cannot all be put on anything like the same scale. But a wide gap between teachers' salaries and those of other graduates creates difficulties in that it will tempt school teachers to neglect their duties while they work for university entrance. If entrance carries a grant and graduation trebles a man's salary, perhaps also providing a car loan and a cheap house, the tendency to concentrate on this is understandable. The result will be a steady drain of talent out of school teaching thus making the task of producing a satisfactory stream of educated secondary-school children particularly hard.

Having considered these problems which face the politicians and educational administrators, it is appropriate to return to the content of the imported Western system of education to appreciate that while there must be a conscious adaptation in order to produce an emphasis on citizenship and on a common nationality, to achieve this is difficult and often involves a number of very tough political decisions.

In most developing countries where there are a number of tribes or communities, one of the most tendentious problems is that of language. To choose any one language as the medium of instruction is to give the group speaking that language an obvious advantage. To select a common non-indigenous language such as English or French clearly creates problems in that language is a carrier of culture, it offers access to a literature, it favours certain thought patterns and makes the task of nation-building harder. But there is little point in trying to maintain a dying language by ordering schoolchildren to learn it (as is done in Eire) or to try and invent or resurrect a former historic language. Usually the answer is to select one common or nation-wide medium for teaching and administration and to encourage the study of the local native tongue as a second language. This is the position of Celtic or Gaelic, for instance, in the Gaelic-speaking parts of Scotland. But there is no clear-cut or general answer to this problem—each situation has to be considered as a separate case.

The content of education also presents some problems. Clearly it is ridiculous for children in the Caribbean to be learning the history of the Tudor period in England or to be using the duodecimal system in their money calculations if their countries have adopted a decimal coinage. Scientific education is more international in that its disciplines are less dependent on local conditions, though experiments, problems and examples are all more relevant if they involve materials or case studies which are known to the pupils.

In arts subjects it is important to move as rapidly as possible to studies of geography, history, literature and civics based upon the past and current experience in the country. The difficulty is that there may be no written form to the local language and no literature. The history of the area may not have been compiled, its archaeological past may be largely undiscovered.

This is where the universities have a major role to play. It is tempting for African scholars to work on subjects well known outside Africa in order to be read and recognised elsewhere but they also have a duty to bring their disciplines to bear on the material available in their own countries. This is where the special institutes of African and Asian studies have done valuable work and it is important to stress that there is nothing inherently superior or more 'central' in conducting detailed research into, for instance, medieval European history than in achieving an understanding of the Fulani *jihad* or the nature of the Yoruba kingdoms. From this kind of work it should be possible to prepare histories of the new countries stretching back before the colonial period. Similarly the stories and fables can be written down to provide a background. Recently a modern literature in English but by African writers about African situations and characters has been developing while as each year passes, there is more recent history, law and politics to describe.

The object of education is partly to provide certain skills, to train minds in particular disciplines, partly to convey a greater range of experience and to give confidence by providing a framework of reference to the pupil, so that much must be taught which is deliberately aimed at taking the pupil outside the narrow confines of his current situation. But this can only be done if the starting point is familiar, if the broader standards are related to something which is already known and understood.

Here it is worth considering the problem from the point of view of the pupil adapting to an imported or largely strange system of education. The great problem for teachers in all countries and in all periods has been to awaken the minds of the pupils, the substitute being rote learning of a series of responses. The inspectors allocating charitable funds to Scottish parochial schools of the eighteenth century used to complain of 'reading without understanding'. Each school child would rise in turn and read three words, ignoring full stops or commas, and was aghast when the inspector asked what the words meant.

For African and Asian children, being placed in a school system often conducted in a foreign language, requiring certain batches of facts to be learnt, however meaningless in terms of the pupil's experience, the break-through to 'reading with understanding' is much harder. Studies of pupil reactions have shown that for many the whole process is a mystifying procedure and the children either imagine that pure repetition of learnt facts will produce a pass at the examinations or become puzzled as to what is wanted, regarding the process of evaluation as entirely arbitrary. The result is strain and all sorts of attempts to corner the system while only a handful realise the purpose of the exercise and really develop. The numbers so doing would be enormously increased if the syllabus was rooted in matters meaningful in terms of the pupil's own experience so that the teacher could build on this understanding in explaining the pupils' role in their new state and its place in the world.

It is important to remember that the tasks of the formal institutions of education are much greater when there is little in the way of a penumbra of films, television shows, newspapers, foreign travel and accumulated personal experiences to fill out the background on which teachers can build. The isolation of many developing countries even from their African and Asian neighbours is something which many Europeans do not appreciate.

Finally, if an appropriate system of education is introduced and if it teaches children in a way which combines reasonable pride in their own country, a knowledge of its traditions and an appreciation of the broader world context, if all this can be done, there still remains the more precise and intricate problem of the role of the teacher in politics.

Two extreme positions are possible. One exists in Britain where teachers are not supposed to press their political views on their pupils nor are they, themselves, allowed to run for local government elected posts. This would be a very serious matter in many developing countries where the élite capable of running for local office is so limited that to exclude teachers would be to keep out a major and possibly indispensable source of talent. Moreover the particular reason for doing so, that local authorities employ the teachers, may not be applicable in many developing countries. The second extreme view is held by teachers and politicians who have taken part in a struggle for independence. They may have been forbidden to preach nationalism or even to indicate their sympathies by the colonial power and the reaction is often an insistence that all education is political and that teachers have a duty to indoctrinate their

143

pupils. Marxists take the same view that freedom is an understanding of the processes of history and an identification with the winning side.

While there is obviously a broad truth in the proposition that all education implicitly conveys values and therefore political values, once the period of the independence struggle is over, the matter becomes more difficult. Then it should be accepted that education helps, in the manner described above, in nation-building but politics can mean something more specific, party politics. Once it has been accepted that there are several views as to who should run a new nation and how it should be done, it would be most dangerous for the members of a state-subsidised general system of education to become involved in pressing the case of one party or another.

A series of conventions has to be built up which allows all teachers reasonable freedom of action as citizens, which accepts that normal patriotism can be inculcated in the schools but which prevents individual school masters using this privileged platform as a method of influencing election results. The problem of school teachers under military rule when political parties are suppressed is not very different. The duty to hold the new country together on a basis of equal treatment for all groups remains and so does the importance of indicating that one can be patriotic and yet differ on issues of political policy and priority. What is required under civilian rule is a series of conventions which sets out the degree of private political activity to be left open to the teacher, the bias of the schools in favour of reasonable national sentiments and the refusal to allow schools to be used as a method of building up partisan support for one party or another.

These then are the main problems for those organising, conducting and enduring education. There can be no doubt of the vital role education plays in creating and strengthening national feeling nor the damage that can be done if the doctrine goes further and claims special privileges and priorities for one nation above all others. Yet this must not obscure the real value of education in the context of nation-building and there is much evidence that now it is being administered and taught in a manner which is helping to stabilise the new nations of Africa and Asia. Education, it is being appreciated, is an essential factor in a continuing and broader programme of personal as well as national liberation.

CHAPTER 7

THE ROLE OF ADULT EDUCATION

J. LOWE

i

The main theme of this paper is that nation-building depends upon winning popular support for rapid change. That support will be won only if adults perceive the relevance of the aims of development to their own particular condition, and labour both hard and ingeniously to fulfil them. The first task of adult education is to ensure that this indispensable recognition takes place. The second is to instruct people how to work to some purpose. The third is to help people cope with the sometimes surprising and always taxing social consequences of national development.

A well-endowed, nationwide adult education service is a vital prerequisite of national development. Economic progress can be achieved only through the creation of an agricultural surplus and some measure of industrialisation, and this entails applying scientific and technological skills to the methods of agricultural and industrial production at all levels. Since most of the problems facing developing countries must be solved before the next generation grows up, such skills have to be taught to the existing adult population. The human factor is of unique importance and requires to be stressed precisely because too much weight is often attached to an investment in mere physical resources. In concentrating upon the utilisation of material resources economists are prone to overlook the fact that in the last resort it is the investment in human skills—the production of trained manpower—that counts. Sometimes, indeed, they write as though education had little or nothing to do with economic growth; yet the one commodity, by and large, that developing countries command in abundance is human labour, and that labour can only be exploited in economic terms if, through education, it is made more productive and hence more efficient. Without adult education the best a developing country can hope for is to provide unskilled labour for enterprises owned and run by expatriates.

An adult education service is also vital as a means of encouraging people to welcome innovation and to adjust to disruptive social change. In order that development may take place at an acceptable rate it is necessary not merely that people should take part in programmes planned from above but that they should play their part in formulating and implementing plans on their own initiative. They cannot carry out this role unless they are sufficiently well informed to be able to choose selectively from among the options open to them. Not that the task of engaging people in the development process is easy to define since unsophisticated people have difficulty in grasping concepts about the nature of change. A field adult education officer in the rural areas of Kenya, say, must realise that he cannot translate government directives into action unless the local population first accepts them and understands what must be done to implement them. He must also be aware that the local people are sometimes extremely bewildered by what is happening around them. They can hardly be expected to foresee the likely effects on their customary habits of the advent of a new road or a new school, or the placing nearby of a training centre or small industrial plant, or the movement into the neighbourhood of a battalion of the national army. In many towns the social consequences of rural immigration have been appalling with drunkenness and violence becoming everyday evils. How can people be helped to spend their leisure time in less destructive ways? In other words, the primary task of adult educators is not to make formal academic education more widely available but to assist people to interpret what social and economic change implies for them in the context of their own environments and to see how they may contribute personally to the general good.

For all this, money is necessary. One argument persistently advanced to reject large expenditure upon adult education is that adults represent a poor investment since they are resistant to new ideas and often have only a short productive life left to them. There is a germ of truth in both those reservations but no more. Adults in even the most traditional societies can be induced to change their attitudes if they are sufficiently strongly motivated. Moreover, it is self-evident that in societies where the great majority of the population has had little or no formal education there is a large pool of under-utilised intelligence only waiting to be activated by the appropriate stimuli. The suggestion that adults represent only a short-run educational investment falls to the ground mainly because it fails to take account of the fact that an adult, in his role as parent, trade-union leader, politician or manager, can immediately apply what he learns, whereas much of what the young are taught cannot be applied or is obsolescent by the time they are of an age to apply it. Thus, if reforms designed to make the school curricula socially more relevant are introduced in 1970, not until 1980 or so will they affect the performance as adults of the new intake of children and by that time a host of unforeseen changes may well have rendered the reforms irrelevant. In any case, if it is true that adults resist new ideas, then we should despair of progress in the rural areas. For while young people can be educated to accept change, experience shows that when they run up against the conservatism of their parents they tend not to stay and fight but to throng into the towns. In short, it is arguable that in developing countries money spent upon adult education offers not only quicker but more certain dividends than does expenditure on primary and secondary education for children.

Needless to say, it would be politically naive to expect governments to shift their emphasis from children's education to the education of adults. It would also be educationally undesirable. What is required is general acceptance of the concept of lifelong-integrated learning now being propagated by UNESCO, which treats education as a continuing process and not as something confined to formal schooling. Since the social and physical environment is now in a permanent state of flux, as are the methods used in industry and commerce, people must be helped to respond flexibly and imaginatively. This entails the creation of a four-tier system of education, of which adult education is the fourth tier. The adoption of such an encompassing framework presupposes that no sector of education will benefit at the expense of others; the available resources will be equitably distributed in fulfilment of a rational development plan. Such a framework also presupposes that the main aim of education is to enable people to adapt to their environments by becoming functionally more effective.

ii

Each developing country has its own special problems, as well as its own special goals and special approaches in trying to reach them. Nevertheless, there are certain problems common to all developing countries which adult educators have to identify and help resolve.

There is, first of all, their sheer magnitude. The task of adult education specialists in India, for example, is so intimidating that a Westerner might scarcely see any point in undertaking it. Then, nearly all the developing countries either came directly under colonial rule or fell within a colonial sphere of influence and therefore had to embark upon the herculean task of creating a new nation. Nearly all have to deal with ethnic pluralism, and to overcome the kind of linguistic divisions that are discussed in a paper below.* There are tribal conflicts, of which the Nigerian civil war was a virulent manifestation. There is a more divisive separation between the urban and rural environments than is commonly supposed and a perilous cleavage between the new professional and business class and the masses, the haves and the have-nots. Some countries are scattered over such a vast area that communications alone make the problem of providing an adequate educational service almost insuperable; thus the main reason why the Caribbean Federation did not work had probably less to do with the

* pp. 179-209.

rivalry between Trinidad and Jamaica than with the geographical dispersion of the islands. Communications pose a specially fearsome problem for the scattered territories of the South Pacific. There are also many countries which on the face of it look economically viable, but when closely examined are seen to be extremely vulnerable; in an ideal world there would no doubt be a pan-African economic common market, but in practice the tendency is for African countries to disintegrate rather than to federate in larger units. These are some of the harsh impediments which adult education in developing countries has to help overcome.

A further difficulty is the fact that adult education is frequently interpreted in rigorously narrow terms so as to mean essentially academic studies—the completion or continuation of a formal education programme. The greater part of the adult education provision that is socially constructive in a practical way commonly goes under the heading of community development. At the very least, community development and adult education are aspects of the same social objectives, and at best, they are institutionally complementary. But in many countries there is an open organisational conflict between adult education on the one hand and community or social development on the other, as though education were one thing and social development were something else. Western countries have historically made the mistake of equating education with the formal curricula of schools and universities. Is it necessary for developing countries to commit the same error?

A shortage of trained staff is a world-wide problem. It is particularly acute in developing countries because of the lack of trained graduates. When even people with a poor degree may hope to become foreign service officers, for instance, there is little incentive to look upon the field of adult education as offering a worthwhile career. Consequently, posts are usually filled by non-graduates, and those adult educators who are graduates are sometimes of inferior quality. Until high-level personnel can be attracted to the senior posts it will remain difficult to establish a strong profession.

Almost everywhere there is little suitable accommodation, and a lack of relevant books, teaching aids and supporting equipment. One of the shortcomings of foreign aid is that so much of the donated equipment is completely unrelated to the capabilities of the people for whom it is intended. Thus, recently an American agency presented an adult education centre in East Africa with an electric typewriter, which worked splendidly for a time. When it went wrong, however, it was found that there was nobody who could repair it nearer than in Nairobi, seven hundred miles away. By the time it had been conveyed to and from Nairobi, the cost of repair amounted to £40. That is a small example of misplaced aid. There are places where teaching machines are rusting away because nobody knows how to use or maintain them or because the programme content is not germane to the experience of the people who might want to master it.

Until very recently there has been widespread neglect of rural development and undue concentration upon the needs of urban populations. The reasons for this are well-known, one being that those who plan and administer educational programmes like to live in or near towns. The result is that in some countries adult education methods have not been used, or have been used ineffectively, to help arrest rural depopulation and decay, despite the fact that the incidence of rural depopulation is significantly lower in those countries where the central administration has had the wisdom to allocate resources to rural development; in several French-speaking countries, for example, extension workers are recruited from village communities and sent back after training to work in their own neighbourhoods, apparently to good effect. It is the young people who tend to flee from the rural areas because they see no future in staying at home and wrongly assume that excitement and plenty beckon from the towns. They might be persuaded to stay if they were trained to do something useful and profitable.

Even when developing countries decide to give precedence to agricultural output, they feel compelled to embark upon some measure of industrialisation. Yet they do so lacking a reservoir of entrepreneurs and managers and desperately short of skilled manual workers. The problem is how to produce the irreducible minimum of trained workers at great speed. Some firms are prepared to spend heavily upon in-service training, especially when they have seen the wisdom of relying upon local rather than expatriate skills. But private enterprise cannot be left to tackle the problem on its own account. It is the responsibility of governments, through the adult education service, to introduce industrial training schemes.

iii

An effective system of adult education requires careful planning; it cannot consist of a collection of 'ad hoc' arrangements. Nor is it sufficient to write into national development plans a statement or two about the crucial contribution of adult education.

Planning for adult education must be related to development planning in general. In anticipating manpower needs, for example, it is not enough to rely upon full-time educational institutions to produce the required quotas of professional and skilled manual workers but a matter of estimating how much time and money could be saved through the appropriate training or retraining of sections of the adult population.

Planning is in vain, however, unless it is carried out at the highest government level. Indeed, experience suggests that it is desirable to assign responsibility for the promotion of adult education to a junior minister and to ensure that within the civil service the senior official in charge of adult education should enjoy the same rank as the officials in charge of other sectors of education.

To draw upon the views and experience of practising educators is an essential stage in the planning process, a point which may seem obvious enough until one pauses to consider educational planning in, for instance, Britain. When school teachers, educational administrators, adult educators and community developers, are consulted about the goals of planning, there is every hope that they will become the foremost protagonists of the national programme. It is equally important to harness the idealism and active support of the educated élite, difficult though it may be in many a developing country to persuade people who have had the good fortune to acquire education that they might perhaps feel a sense of responsibility for educating others less privileged than themselves. Up to a point this aim has been achieved in Tanzania.

To have to plan is to learn that it is necessary to make harsh choices. This is a salutary exercise, distinguishing, as nothing else can, between pipe-dream and reality. When resources are severely limited, everyone cannot be given educational opportunities; neither is it sensible to give people the kind of education that will arouse expectations that cannot be fulfilled, leaving a country flooded with bitter and frustrated people who vent their spleen in destructive behaviour. Thus, it may well be realistic, though regrettable, to focus upon particular groups and particular areas. And it will almost always be necessary to provide a practical education which will appeal to the human desire for personal gain or a conscious wish to serve the community.

Centralised control is usually essential. It is all very well to preach the sanctity of local autonomy and voluntary initiative, but in the absence of a national scheme, buttressed by a powerful administrative infra-structure, the general impact is always feeble. The risk of the stifling hand of bureaucracy taking over has to be run—and guarded against.

Co-ordination at all levels is no less important than firm national control. Probably no country, however small, can afford to do without a national association to serve as a forum for the exchange of ideas and as a clearing house for the dissemination of information. Co-operation between ministries—Health, Social Services, Education, Community Development, Agriculture, Information—and between all government agencies has been found to be necessary. The harmonisation of services and activities in the field is especially important so as to forestall the characteristic anarchy that ensues when agricultural extension officers, health visitors, community development officers, and adult educators, enter into competition and duplicate one another's work. Regional and local consultative committees have to be formed. At the same time, it is neither sensible nor just to snuff out voluntary bodies; there are not many of them, especially in the rural areas, and they are rarely in a position to oppose or obstruct the national policy. Within any general scheme they should, therefore, be encouraged to complement and, where appropriate, to reinforce the work of the statutory authorities.

While it remains inevitable that formal schooling will always receive the lion's share of the available financial resources, it is essential that adult education should be awarded a fixed percentage of the total education budget. At a conference on the Development of Education in Africa, held in Addis Ababa in 1967, it was proposed that 5 per cent of national expenditures on education should be allocated to adult education. That percentage was arbitrarily based on guesswork and may have been far too little. Nevertheless, the proposal was uniquely constructive. Alas, the recommendation has not been adopted anywhere, although to their credit a few countries, notably Zambia, are now spending largish sums of money on adult education.

In relation to planning 'evaluation' has recently become a vogue word. Too often, however, its appearance in planning memoranda does not signify much, for it is one thing to say that every programme must be carefully evaluated and another thing to design effective evaluation controls and find personnel with the skills to administer them. Yet to build an evaluation design into every project is always desirable, if not invariably essential, for three reasons. First, the only foolproof way of ensuring that adult educators define clear goals is to force them to work out a model for testing whether these goals have been reached. Secondly, when resources are severely limited it is vital to reinforce success and to recognise failure as quickly as possible, and this pre-supposes making accurate judgments rather than relying upon hit-or-miss, subjective techniques, as most adult educators are content to do. Thirdly, demands for public support are most likely to be acceded to if they are based upon verifiable data. No senior adult educator should lack the skills, though many a one does, to devise methods for assessing the effectiveness of the programmes carried out under his direction.

iv

The successful implementation of national schemes for adult education depends, finally, upon securing the active participation of community leaders, establishing a vigorous adult education profession, making full use of schools, and selecting appropriate methods of communication. These four desiderata will now be considered.

The enlistment of community leaders is a very high priority. Occupying influential posts or playing dominant roles in local communities there are many people whose social contribution would be greatly enhanced if they were better informed about the economic and political situation and instructed in the elementary techniques of communication and business procedures. There also continue to be customary chiefs or elders who exercise a decisive influence on their communities. Unless these men endorse adult education programmes and, preferably, help carry them out, it may be very difficult or quite impossible for adult educators, coming in from outside, to register any impact. The question of how to involve the professional and business élite in the towns is seldom satisfactorily answered. The privileged commonly take their good fortune as no more than their proper due and see no obligation to devote their time to the welfare of those less fortunate than themselves. Adult educators must always try, despite the odds, to inculcate in the business community a sense of social commitment; in this endeavour university departments of adult education bear a special responsibility. In the last resort, however, governments hold the key to activating the élite. For instance, they can, and perhaps should, insist that all university students undertake a period of community service as a condition of obtaining a grant. Again, Tanzania may be cited as a country that has instituted this practice.

Full-time adult educators often give the impression of being weak propagandists in their own cause. As a result, the profession of adult education does not carry much prestige and adult educators rarely form a pressure group to be reckoned with. The obvious solution is for them deliberately to develop and publicise their own distinctive brand of professionalism. This is the only way in which they will become numerous and demonstrably efficient; and only when they give the appearance of being a large and confident body, pledged to success, will they exercise significant political influence. The recent trend towards the creation of national and regional associations of adult education ought therefore to be accelerated.

The most efficient way of providing a comprehensive and socially purposeful education service in a developing country is to regard the school as the focus of community interest. Combining facilities for children, young people and adults in the same building obviously ensures the economical use of scarce physical resources. When a community is very poor, it may be unable to afford any more than a one- or two-room school; in that case, young people and adults will largely frequent it in the evenings. When means permit, however, it is desirable to attach to each school a room or rooms for the exclusive needs of adults, so that they may have suitable chairs and equipment and occupy the school during the day-time. Apart from economic considerations there are other reasons for turning a school into a multi-purpose community centre: teachers can more easily be encouraged to treat the school as a change-agent in the community and to revise their view of their functions accordingly; parents are encouraged to identify themselves with the aims of the school, and at home to reinforce the education received by their children rather than detract from it, as so often happens. The curricula can be designed to reflect to a large extent the characteristics and the needs of the locality or, as in the Philippines, to give parents indirect guidance in improving their farming methods and domestic habits. A school takes care of its own model farm; parents can observe the methods that are employed besides learning from their own children. Above all, the creation of 'a community school' prompts people to realise that the main object of education is to raise the quality of life for themselves and their children.

For various reasons it often happens that the curricula and methods used in adult education programmes are more or less exactly the same as those used in the schools. One reason is that a good deal of adult teaching is done by school teachers who do not choose, or do not know how, or have not the energy, to change their customary style. Another reason is that many adult students simply want to pass examinations and so are quite happy to be fed with what seems to be the relevant information. Now it is commonly accepted that to be of practical value both to the community and to the individual the content of programmes has to be pertinent to the actual experience and particular knowledge or skills required by those taught and conveyed by the largely informal methods that adults find palatable. Above all, the nature of development and the necessity for it in the context of nation-building must be introduced into the curriculum. The kind of programme material that is most appropriate is described in Patrick Van Rensberg's *Education and Development in an Emerging Country*. Recognising the need for the 'lifelong learning' approach Mr Van Rensberg has designed a course on the explicit theme of education and development for the young people attending Swaneng Hill School in Botswana.

There is no shortage of textbooks and pamphlets enumerating and describing the battery of teaching methods available to the adult teacher. The problem is how to ensure that teachers in developing countries know of their existence and use them selectively. And this is a question of training. One of the main tasks of the adult educator is to recruit competent part-time teachers and to arrange short training courses for them.

If awareness of potential teaching methods is fairly wide-

157

spread, it cannot be said that sufficient attention has yet been paid to the rich potential of using a combination of teaching methods. Before investing in programmes of adult education which involve organising groups for classroom teaching, adult educators should begin to ask whether they can more conveniently reach out to a much larger audience by using a combination of two or more media—television, radio, correspondence, study kits and programmed texts. The controlling factor is, as always, finance. Few countries are as fortunate as the Ivory Coast in being able to obtain nation-wide television coverage within the foreseeable future, but most can afford to provide radio coverage. The ideal criterion would be that in terms of its own communications and financial resources each country should not fail to exploit the tools of educational technology in as far as they will save time, reduce costs, and increase the efficiency of the learning process.

v

The danger of concentrating exclusively upon education for material development has frequently been alluded to by educational theorists. Moreover, in almost any speech on adult education by a leading politician it will be found that whereas his introduction lays stress upon the need for a pragmatic, bread-and-butter approach his conclusion enjoins us not to neglect the cultivation of the mind, and, perhaps, the refinement of our spiritual beliefs. Alas, this ritualistic coda is genuinely called for, since there can be no doubt that if the aims of adult education are restricted to achieving only economic targets, serious interpersonal problems will arise and the mental growth of each individual will be stunted; even if we do not wish to fall back upon a high-minded appeal to such cherished educational ideals as forming sound attitudes, whatever they may be, and cultivating the aesthetic faculty, we cannot ignore the need to transmit what is best in traditional cultures or to enable people to make intelligent choices in fashioning their lives. As pointed out above, the scope for economic enrichment will continue to be restricted, no matter how much vocational skills are improved, unless people can come to see development as a social imperative and apply their intelligence to making it possible. Thus in the more economically advanced countries it has been found that in order to bring about a steady increase in industrial output, it is not enough to organise initial and in-service training courses for adults which are strictly utilitarian. Training courses must also contain a mind-broadening element.

SELECT BIBLIOGRAPHY

Coles, E. Townsend, *Adult Education in Developing Countries* (Oxford, 1969).
Liveright, A. A. (ed.), *The Concept of Lifelong Integrated Learning* (International Congress of University Adult Education, Occasional Paper II, February 1968).
Lowe, J. (ed.), *Adult Education and Nation-Building* (Edinburgh, 1970).
Prosser, R. C., *Adult Education for Developing Countries* (Nairobi, 1967).
Schramm, W., *Mass Media and Development: the Role of Information in the Developing Countries* (UNESCO, 1964).
Van Rensberg, P., *Education and Development in an Emerging Country* (Scandinavian Institute of African Studies, Uppsala, 1967).

CHAPTER 8

THE EDUCATION OF WOMEN

EDITH O. MERCER, OBE*

i

From 17 to 25 March 1969, just at the time of the Edinburgh
Seminar on Education and Nation Building, there took place
in Addis Ababa under the auspices of the Human Resources
Development Division of the United Nations a regional meeting on the Role of Women in National Development. It
brought together women in public and voluntary services for
health, nutrition, education, welfare, industry and government,
with a view to the promotion of active participation of women
in civic, political and economic life. I mention this as an indication that the subject of women's contribution to nation-
building in the developing countries is a live one. Indeed, over
the past few years it has become increasingly so. Along with
the struggle to secure the recognition of women as human
beings having equal rights with men (as steadily promoted by
the UN Status of Women Commission, a subsidiary body of the
UN Economic and Social Council, and as patiently fostered by
numerous non-governmental organisations and individuals)
there has arisen the parallel concept of equality of contribution
to public and private life, and now in the newer developing
countries the idea of women's participation in the process of
building up the political concept and the economic and social
structure of a nation.

Education, as we know, was for long dissociated from the
idea of nation-building. In the older countries it was seen as a
cultural process, a contribution to the national ethos perhaps
and a means of imparting classical virtues and religious and

* The views expressed are personal to the writer and should not be regarded
as necessarily representing the policy of the Ministry of Overseas Development,
to which she belonged until recently.

moral values, but mostly a privilege for the few, and not as a contribution to development in the sense that we now understand the term. For women too, therefore, education was first of all seen mainly as an objective of women's rights, the access to knowledge and culture. Even in recent decades when UNESCO has been responsible for one meeting after another in various parts of the world on the elimination of discrimination against women in education, the emphasis has been on education as a right rather than as a national economic asset. The last few years, however, have seen a change of attitude. Among other signs, the Fourth Commonwealth Education Conference in Nigeria in February/March 1968 devoted considerable time to the question of education for economic and social development and specifically included women's education.

With differences, one finds in most societies women fulfilling the basic roles of the early care and custody of children, the maintenance of the home in whatever form it may take, the feeding of the family, and, according to prevailing customs, the preservation of its health. Feeding the family may include not only the preparation and cooking of food but also growing it, so that in many societies women have been the cultivators and agriculturalists while men have been the hunters and fishers. At later stages of development women might continue to grow all the family food while men took over the cash crops. In the field of health primitive midwifery competes for a place as the oldest specialised profession for women. In simple societies women were usually regarded as occupying an inferior position to men and were often in a state of servility or indeed slavery, but there could be little doubt about the extent of their contribution to their societies in terms of work and production by the then existing standards. In matriarchal societies, of course, women often had considerable political influence, such as choosing the successor in the royal line, but this influence was only exercised behind the scenes.

In developing countries the old simple communities still exist, with their ancient ways and customs, but they are by no means any longer the whole way of life of those countries. Complex

161

modern economies have arisen, and along with them, the growth of cities, modern specialisation and professionalism, the universal franchise, and a larger concept of nationhood. With these have gone profound sociological changes, which are, however, still in a state of fluctuation between the older and the newer. The position of women in the society of their communities and their countries represents one of the most significant of those sociological changes.

Partly because of their position as conservators and guardians of the family, partly because they travelled less and came less in contact with new ideas, partly because of social pressures on them to remain doing the work that others found it comfortable and convenient for them to engage in, women had fewer opportunities to adjust to and profit by the new developments. This is nowhere better exemplified than in the educational statistics of a large number of developing countries. These figures show as clearly as anything could how far the education of women and girls has lagged behind that of men. In even simpler form the statistics for literacy present a similar picture.

It would not be fair to conclude that the deficiencies in girls' education are wholly due to lack of provision of girl's schools by the authorities. There has also been a reluctance on the part of parents to permit education for their daughters on the same scale as for their sons, and indeed often a reluctance and misunderstanding on the part of the girls themselves.

Educational differences between the sexes exacerbate the social differences. Men who go to training for the professions and public life find that their uneducated wives are unable to undertake the social duties and occupy the position expected of the wives of such men. Furthermore, the level of living in their homes and the upbringing of their children does not correspond to their own new ideas and their wives are not able to respond to these requirements. Women are not available for the more skilled jobs which in more developed countries are customarily undertaken by women and the political franchise extended to women becomes meaningless if they are not sufficiently enlightened to understand at least simply the issues with

162

which their vote is concerned. It can be said with confidence that a need for advancement and participation, although not perhaps precisely formulated, is evident among women in all developing countries, even when expressed as tersely as in the sentence, 'We want civilisation.'

ii

Women's potential contribution towards their societies may be summarised under three headings: home-making, professional work, and public life.

First, as a home-maker, a woman can by knowledge, skill and energy enhance the level of living in her own home. She can improve the nutritional content of the family meals by a better understanding of dietetics. She can add to the comforts and amenities of her house. She can improve family health by better hygiene and child care. She can make clothes. She can grow better and more varied crops in her garden or plot. As an educated mother she can better understand and contribute to the schooling which her children receive. In all this, of course, she needs the help and co-operation of her husband, who has equal responsibility with her for the maintenance of the household and the well-being of the family.

Secondly, she can learn to fill the jobs badly needed in her country, where skills are in short supply: teaching, medicine, nursing, secretarial work, to name but a few. The population explosion does, of course, raise a problem of employment for the under-educated school-leaver or the child who has not been to school. Boys, and to a certain extent girls, in this group are tending to flood into the growing cities where there is nothing which they are qualified to do, and where industrialisation is of too slow and recent growth to present any likelihood of their absorption at the assembly lines of factories (even if automation were not reducing this type of employment in any case). It is not suggested that girls should attempt to join this hopeless quest any more than they do at present. They are to this extent fortunate in that even if they are inadequately educated there are usually still traditional tasks for them in and around the home, and marriage is early. Furthermore, developing countries are predominantly rural countries, and it is the rural areas and rural pursuits which must of necessity absorb the under-educated, whether men or women, for some time to come.

Thirdly, there is the civic contribution to be made by women. In some developing countries women have made a particularly notable contribution to public life. One has only to think of India and Ceylon (and now Israel), which have had women Prime Ministers, and the scattering of other countries which have women ambassadors, women members of legislatures and some paramount chiefs. It is true that the Prime Ministers of both India and Ceylon have been successors to male relatives in the office, but their emergence is significant of a profound change of attitude towards women's participation in public life. It is, of course, not only at these high levels that women have a part to play, and lower down the line it must be admitted that the prejudices against them are often greater.

Women's emergence from the home is often first of all into some kind of community organisation for women, women's associations for the sharing of mutual interests and social occasions. Such groups may be feminist in intention but quite often they are equally concerned with the sharing of knowledge or effort on topics of common local or domestic interest. It is not always easy (for reasons of custom) for women to participate in village committees where men predominate (although they may have meetings of their own), and women who are clear-spoken and decisive among their own sex may be shy of expressing themselves in mixed company. The local councils and the district and regional councils, however they may be called in different countries, are nevertheless places where the voices and views of women need increasingly to be heard if a balanced consideration of issues is to be attained. The particular concerns of women, apart from their views on general topics, will enable them to press for needful measures which may otherwise be overlooked.

Apart from service on public bodies, women have a particularly important part to play in voluntary organisations for social service. This is especially true of women in towns and cities where the old local ties are broken and many people are strangers to the towns and to each other. Developing countries have a particular problem on their hands in this respect. Resources in finance and personnel are inadequate for anything like full state-provided social services, and much of the burden of what needs to be done falls on voluntary organisations and voluntary workers. As in more developed countries much of such voluntary service is given by women, although of course not exclusively so.

iii

It is clear that one of the chief means whereby women can be enabled to make a fuller contribution to national development is by education, but such education may be in very varied forms. The most obvious is the need for more girls to have access to primary education and for the prejudices to their doing so being overcome. In saying this one must remember that universal compulsory free primary education is a long way off in many countries and that the population explosion is steadily postponing its achievement. It is not a question of girls replacing boys in schools, but of the long-term aim of a basic primary education becoming the common equipment of all. For girls as for boys the question is what form that primary education should take. There is a growing scepticism about the content of the curriculum in primary schools. It is thought to be over-academic and designed to lead children away from their existing way of life rather than to equip them to improve it. Rural schools, which form the majority, may teach little that relates to local flora, fauna, local geography, history and social customs, little that relates to the way of life of the children and their parents. It is true that rural schools may have school gardens, but, as sometimes run, they may be more calculated to create permanent aversion than to foster an interest in cultivation. Many educationists are beginning to question whether

165

formal primary schooling for all may not be a mistaken *primary* objective of the politicians of nations in process of rural development, however much public demand for the 'magic' of education may force it on them. This kind of thinking is at the back of the far-seeing declaration by President Nyerere of Tanzania on 'Education for Self-reliance'.

At present, figures show the proportion of women receiving higher education and professional training in developing countries as being still lower than for those having access to primary education. There are many factors, among the most important being finance (any available family money goes on education for the boys), early marriage, and the view that as the girl will get married anyway, further education would be wasted on her. Yet most developing countries suffer from shortages in various professions and are still having to borrow skills heavily from abroad. I have mentioned the examples of doctors, nurses, secretaries and teachers, to which might be added trained social workers and women agricultural extension workers, all occupations for which women have shown themselves well adapted. There is a strong case for encouraging and enabling more of them to prepare for these professions, and the opening up of jobs for them. The case of teaching is a particularly good one, as a better supply of teachers of all kinds would help to break the vicious circle of lack of educational facilities causing shortage of teachers and shortage of teachers resulting in lack of educational facilities. An additional point is that the teaching profession has been badly hit in most developing countries by the fact that men teachers have left it in great numbers for work in politics and administration. There is more than a chance that women would be less easily tempted away and would form a more permanent reservoir for the profession.

I now come to that form of education which has more importance for the majority of women in developing countries than any other. Whatever happens to primary and higher (second and third level) education for girls in the future, the fact is that here and now many women have received no formal education as children. For them and for nation-building, adult education in all its forms is of the utmost importance, and can have a quicker effect on development than the eight or ten years that are needed for a child to come to maturity through school. As I use the term, adult education falls into four broad overlapping categories: (i) general education, (ii) vocational training, (iii) the extension services covering home economics, agriculture, health etc., and (iv) the informal educational work carried out through women's organisations.

General education for adult women (and with them I include girl school-leavers) is in effect the normal school curriculum carried forward, developed and adapted to more mature pupils. Classes in mathematics, language and literature, history etc., may be taken with a view to reaching a General Certificate of Education or similar educational milestone, or for general cultural purposes and personal enrichment. I will not dwell on this more formal type of education, not because it is unimportant but because its nature is well known.

In vocational training, apart from full training for the professions, I include training for a variety of trades undertaken by women, such as hairdressing, cookery, typing and office work, nursery work and as telephonists. This type of training will be undertaken in towns rather than by rural women, for it is chiefly in the cities that opportunities for paid employment in these kinds of work are likely to arise. It is a contribution to the growth of modern amenities in fast-developing cities.

Of greater immediate national importance in my view are measures for the less formal education of rural women, since, as I have said, it is on rural development that national economies mostly depend, at any rate in the near future. In our concern over raising the gross national product, we do well to remember a simple and direct means towards what is after all its ultimate objective: to raise levels of living. The means I refer to is the education of women to make better and wiser use of the resources at their disposal in and around the home. Years ago F. L. Brayne in *Socrates Persists* vividly illustrated the point when he told the story of the bringing of artificial light to a Punjabi village. The men and boys were taught how to make and light oil lamps and keep them going, but they moved about on their travels and nobody had taught the wives, so the lamps went out!

Education related in a direct and practical manner to the way of life of women and their families is nowadays the task of home economists and extension workers attached to the rural services. The success of services of this kind and the enthusiasm and energy with which they have been received by the women concerned suggest that there is no greater urgency than to train and appoint more home economists, women extension workers, and women community development workers. At present the number of women extension workers is few and, although the need for more male agricultural extension workers is also great, that for women seems both greater and less recognised. The role of rural training centres and of community development services in this type of education is also important since, through training, local women leaders can be helped to stimulate local effort among women, and the idea of collaboration for common ends.

It is undeniable that parallel types of education are needed for townswomen. Home economics training is equally desirable for them, and, since they will now be buying food for cash rather than growing it, consumer education, how to purchase wisely despite advertising 'pulls', assumes particular importance.

The fourth contribution to adult education for women comes through women's clubs and societies. By coming together under their own leaders women learn to discuss and undertake improvements in their homes and immediate environment. Such organisations, enjoyable in themselves, also provide the forum for civic education, education in rights, duties and responsibilities within the community. The growth of women's organisations at all levels in the developing world has been tremendous, and their influence very great indeed. Because their outlook has frequently been restricted to the domestic scene, women, even more than men, need help in widening their horizons and understanding some of the issues facing their local communities and their countries. The whole concept of nationhood may be a very new and imperfectly understood one, and a beginning

is often best made by involving women in community development activities and the formation of village clubs and societies.
These activities have an educational function which can lead
on to better understanding of both local government and
national government and a more mature contribution based on
co-operation and partnership between the sexes.

Before I go further I should like to give three African examples of how adult education for women has worked. For two
of them I am indebted to my colleague, Mr A. R. G. Prosser,
who was directly involved in promoting them. All three are
from a pre-independence stage in the countries concerned, but
are characteristic of what has gone on since (and perhaps illustrate incidentally that the fact of political independence is a
stage in a country's evolution rather than the beginning of it).

iv

As an example of how a programme for women's education
may start from nothing and on the initiative of one individual
I would like to quote the Corn Mill Societies of the Cameroons
and the work there of Miss Elizabeth O'Kelly back in the
1950's. The grinding of corn for daily food is one of the more
time-consuming and arduous tasks of the African village house-
wife, and if it has also to be combined with fetching water from
a distance she may have little leisure. Nor is there an incentive
to cultivate additional fields for cash if there is nothing to spend
money on. What happened in the Cameroons was that, on the
inspiration of Miss O'Kelly, the women set about to provide
themselves with cash for a particular purpose. Village groups
of women worked to collect in one year sufficient money (£20)
to purchase collectively hand-operated grinding mills. This
they did by cultivating untilled land to sell the products in the
market. With the mills in operation, the women found that the
burden of their corn-grinding task was greatly lessened, and
with a release of that energy which is so notable a characteristic
of the African woman, and, having learned the uses of cash,
they continued to farm more land and to learn better tech-

niques, with consequent reduction of hitherto 'lean' periods. Some 27,000 women were involved in this scheme.

This in many ways is a simple story compared with the complex organisation of programmes of women's education which has taken place since and elsewhere but I quote it as an instance of how these things can begin.

Ghana is a country which has long had well-developed towns and villages. It is also one in which women have customarily enjoyed a clear social status, partly arising no doubt from the strength of their economic position as traditional traders, and immediately after the Second World War there arose a demand both for schools for girls and for some form of education for adult women who had had none. Mass education teams touring Ghana as early as 1948, in order to organise courses whereby the educated few might teach others, found from the outset that illiterate women were demanding instruction. Of this surge the missionaries already knew and, to the extent of their limited resources, had attempted to meet by establishing small centres to train the wives of ordinands and by founding Mothers' Unions and their equivalents.

In consequence of this demand the Ghana Government decided to include education for women as a priority in its community development programme. The first pilot scheme centred on a film about child welfare which told a simple story contrasting two sisters who consulted respectively the traditional soothsayers and the children's hospital about the well-being of their children. Some 50 villages sent their leading women on a short course in health education organised with the Ministry of Health, and they returned to their villages to illustrate what they had learned. Another experiment centred on instructing the wise old women who traditionally attend childbirth and who were clearly key people. This was successful up to a point but was not favoured by the then medical authorities.

The next stage was the appointment by the Department of Social Welfare and Community Development of a senior woman officer of the British Red Cross Society to prepare a new policy for work with women. A conference of women community development staff led to the construction of a detailed syllabus of courses for village women, as a basis of staff training policy. It covered child care, nutrition, cooking for the family, sewing and environmental hygiene. The recruitment policy of the Department of Social Welfare and Community Development was altered to ensure that one third of the junior staff would be women. (At this stage the appointment of a senior woman officer was apparently not contemplated.) However the services of a home economist from the USA became available and she organised the training of both staff and voluntary leaders over a period of two years.

In the meantime the Red Cross officer had put into effect in the Transvolta region the programme for women's work devised at the conference. The merit of using visual aids in such work was clearly demonstrated. A locally made travelling exhibition on environmental hygiene was set up in one after another of a group of villages. The villagers were escorted round it and the lessons from each exhibit explained. Hundreds of deep pit latrines were dug by communal effort and water supplies improved. Selected village women were given intensive courses at the rural training centre on the syllabus for women's work. Similar schemes were carried out in other regions of Ghana, and a clear pattern of work emerged in most regions, whereby women's village groups were organised by women assistant officers. Even as early as 1950 there were some 16,000 women under instruction. Exhibitions of handiwork, organised on a regional basis proved much appreciated festive occasions. In Ghana, it is interesting to note, it was not necessary to spend time on the special formation of women's clubs as in every village a women's group already existed by tradition and a senior woman was recognised as leader.

All this was not done without problems, not least of which was that of transport and accommodation for the women assistant officers who had to get around in difficult conditions with rudimentary services and who were, most of them, sacrificing better opportunities in towns to which their qualifications would have entitled them.

Parallel with work in rural areas, there were developments in the long-established large towns of Ghana. A nursery school movement had grown up to care for the children of occupied mothers and was used as a focus for programmes of mothers' education. Neighbourhood centres provided both accommodation for nursery schools and class-rooms for the women, including illiterates, where instruction was based on the women's work programme under the guidance of a senior woman officer of the Department of Community Development and Social Welfare. Vocational training centres were set up in each major town to prepare girls for marriage or for employment in offices or as dress-makers. These centres were essentially voluntary organisations and the pupils paid fees but the centres received government subventions and help over their syllabus and staff training.

These programmes in Ghana were not necessarily ideal, and have been modified as time went on. Different emphases have resulted from experience. Women's work in the rural areas is still easier to promote than in the towns where the social organisation is very complex and more research is still needed into the major urban social problems as they affect women.

v

On the other side of Africa in Uganda parallel developments in women's education have been taking place but on a very different social basis. In Uganda there are no traditional towns and indeed no villages in the West African sense, but instead loose family associations of small holdings, the 'shambas'. There has therefore been much greater isolation and an absence of community organisation among women. Furthermore the traditional status of women was lower in East Africa, whatever the improvements that have since taken place, and there was greater need initially to break down the hostility of husbands to education for their women folk.

In these circumstances the women community development officers of the Department of Community Development which had been set up in 1952, decided that women's clubs (rather on the lines of the women's institutes which had been so successful in rural Britain) were the answer to the isolation resulting from the shamba system, and over the years a most effective club movement was organised and developed in the various districts of Uganda. Without existing women's groups to build upon, this meant an immense amount of tuition in club organisation and in the duties of chairman, secretary and treasurer. Usually the arrangement was for a series of women's clubs to meet at Local Government Hall or at club houses constructed by the members and for the women community development officers and their assistants to attend as many as possible of them, to help with practical demonstrations and programme planning. Courses for club leaders were organised, as were in-service courses for the assistant officers. Women would walk miles along bush tracks to attend meetings. At first they tended to want chiefly classes in needlework but once their interest had been aroused it was possible to proceed to child care, nutrition and better homes. That in four years the number of clubs had grown to a thousand and the membership to twenty thousand is an indication of the need which this educational development filled.

At this point assistance came from the United Nations Children's Fund UNICEF over the provision of transport for field workers, stipends for the training of voluntary leaders and teaching equipment for the rural training centres at which they were trained. At the same time a government policy statement declared that special emphasis should be laid on intensive and sustained work with women who because of the part they played in the homes as wives and mothers were a key human factor in the development of the people generally. It announced the appointment of a Woman Assistant Commissioner.

The syllabus for women's clubs, as in Ghana, covered a number of interlocking courses, so that each community development officer could offer her club a variety of courses, but one course led to another so that eventually each club might work through the entire syllabus. The syllabus covered aims and organisation of women's clubs, better homes, decorating the home, hospitality, entertaining visitors, the garden and small farm animals, better family living, the healthy family, feeding the family, cookery and diet, laundry, needlework, fundamentals of care of small babies and infant feeding, school-children, practical hygiene, nursing and first aid.

Although government initiated the programme of women's clubs in rural Uganda, the movement is based on voluntary effort and voluntary control through club officers, and the authorities have merely provided assistance towards a planned programme, through a woman Community Development Officer and a hierarchy of women staff.

Women's clubs have not been developed in the same way in the towns of Uganda but community centres have been organised on housing estates and some women's groups, mainly concentrating on sewing and child care, have worked in these centres. The YWCA has done a great amount of women's work in the urban areas and their periphery, linking their local clubs with the central organisation of the Uganda YWCA.

These examples of movements for the education of women in developing countries have been cited just because they were early and illustrate how these things start, but they have been succeeded by organised programmes in many parts of the world, by no means least the schemes assisted by UNESCO in association with programmes for functional literacy in many countries, of which those in Iran, Tunisia and Tanzania have been among the most significant.

vi

International contacts are an important aspect of work among women. The two-way traffic in ideas brought about by them not only brings new ideas from outside to women's work in particular developing countries but enables women's international organisations to appreciate the strength and problems of the women's movement in those countries. It would of course, be a mistake to think of this movement only in terms of the rural women of whom I have been speaking. To take Uganda only as an example, it has also sophisticated organisations of educated women such as the Uganda Association of University Women and the Uganda Council of Women, the latter of which has done much to formulate requirements for changes in legislation more favourable to women, for example, in matters of inheritance. It is indeed the custom rather than the exception nowadays for there to be in every country influential organisations of its more educated and leading women, whether in Asia, the Pacific, the Caribbean, or Latin America. A valuable educative process for these leading women has been the opportunity for study tours abroad and regional meetings made available through international organisations, both intergovernmental, like UNESCO and the Economic Commissions of the United Nations, and the non-governmental ones, by various trusts and foundations in the USA and Britain, and by the government-financed British Council and comparable organisations elsewhere.

vii

It is time to summarise. The main conclusions of what I have been saying are:

(i) there is a special need to attend to the education of women and girls in developing countries, not only so that they may discover themselves, but because of the increased contribution which education will enable them to make to the economic, social and political development of their countries;

(ii) this means more schools and training facilities for girls;

(iii) it also means more education and training for adult women, particularly of the less formal kind;

(iv) this implies more women qualified to undertake the teaching involved, not only in schools but in rural institutes and the community development and extension services.

To bring about what I have just summarised two things are

175

mainly required. The first is the will to do so. Half the trouble has been public and private reluctance to admit that women's education is really important. Much lip-service is paid to it, not least by politicians, but often when it comes to a particular case in a particular family, the father, the brothers, the husband, and the girl or woman herself are unconvinced. There is need therefore not merely for opportunities for women's education, but for women to press forward to take advantage of those opportunities, and to be encouraged to do so by those about them. A campaign of education of public opinion is therefore one more form of education which is needed. In this inevitably the mass media have an important task. Women themselves, the leading and educated ones, can do much to make the path to education and citizenship easier for their less privileged or more timid sisters.

Secondly, however much of the first ideas and enterprises may be due to the initiatives of individuals and special groups who point the way, a real programme for improved education for women and for opportunities for them to make a full contribution needs, first of all, its serious adoption as a priority in government policy; next, the provision of finance; and thereafter the administrative planning and structure, the supervision and the programming, which will make policy effective. These need not be costly in terms of total government expenditure but they must exist. It is not sufficient to have a theory. Action is the best indicator of sincerity of purpose.

Finally, there is the question of how much the education of women can be promoted from outside. UNESCO and UNICEF, to which I have already referred, have done a great deal, both by conferences and resolutions on the subject and by supplying technical assistance to particular national programmes especially with the aid of the United Nations Development Programme. Donor countries, such as Britain, through the Ministry of Overseas Development, have done much to provide experts in education, in women's organisations and in community development, trainers and trainers of trainers, to help in the establishment of programmes for women, and in financing the training in Britain of women teachers and educators from the developing countries, often on courses specifically designed to meet the needs of those countries. But this outside help can only be given at the wish of the country concerned. This is why, as I have said, the first need is for a broad programme of education for women, with the help of both men and women, to be incorporated in a nation's plans for its own development.

Estimated School Enrolment (female)
by education and by major areas (1959, 1960 and 1965)
(UNESCO *Statistical Yearbook 1967*)

Major Areas	Year	Percentage of girls in total enrolment (both sexes)			
		Total	First level	Second level	Third level
World total	1950	43	43	43	32
	1960	43	44	43	34
	1965	43	44	43	36
Africa	1950	30	30	30	21
	1960	35	37	31	20
	1965	37	38	30	22
America	1950	48	48	50	31
	1960	48	49	50	36
	1965	48	49	49	38
Asia	1950	35	35	35	16
	1960	37	38	35	23
	1965	38	39	36	26
Europe	1950	46	47	44	28
	1960	47	49	45	30
	1965	47	49	46	33
Oceania	1950	46	48	43	29
	1960	46	48	42	28
	1965	45	47	42	26

Illiteracy
Age Group 15-44
1962 (circ.)

Continent or Cultural Region	Percentage illiterates	
	Men	Women
Africa	69	87
America	17	18
Asia and Oceania	41	61
Europe and USSR	2	5
Arab Countries	65	88

From UNESCO Minedlit 5 (CS/0665.14/EDA.8(WS)), 1965.

SELECT BIBLIOGRAPHY

Brayne, F. L., *The Neglected Partner* (The Village Welfare Association, 1949).
—, F. L., *Socrates Persists in India* (OUP, 1932).
—, F. L., *Better Villages* (OUP, 1937), especially chapter **x**.
O'Kelly, Elizabeth, *Rural Life.*
Prosser, A. R. G., UNO Economic Commission for Africa publication.
UNESCO *Statistical Yearbook 1967.*

CHAPTER 9

EDUCATION AND LANGUAGE

NIGEL GRANT

Small comfort though it may be at the present time, it can at least be argued that some of the most pressing problems of education in developing countries—the adequate supply of buildings, textbooks, equipment, teachers, and so on—are soluble in principle. They are, ultimately, a matter of money, and remote though it seems at the moment, it is at least possible to hope for a break-through some time in the future. Other countries have managed it before. But there are other problems where even agreement in principle is lacking, and which no amount of finance can diminish. Of these, the language question is one of the most central and stubborn.

In Britain we are seldom aware of this. Apart from very small linguistic minorities, we all speak (almost) the same language, and therefore take it for granted. It becomes as invisible as the air we breathe. Yet this situation is exceptional in the world as a whole. Many parts of Europe are beset by language problems of varying degrees of intensity, as witness the recurrent trouble between French-speaking and Flemish-speaking Belgians.[1] But it is in the developing countries—ironically, the very places where economic and similar problems are at their most acute—that the problem of the language of instruction looms largest.

As soon as we begin to consider this issue, we immediately run into problems of definition. What is a language? How does one decide whether some particular speech-form is, for educational purposes, to be recognised as a language or dismissed as a dialect? In Europe we tend to see the distinction as clearcut. English is a language, Somerset or Glaswegian is not; French is a language, the Midi *patois* is not; Castilian Spanish is a language, Andalusian is not; and so on. But already doubts begin to creep in; the identification of a 'language' with a nation-state can break down even in the relatively settled conditions of Western Europe. (Can one really regard Catalan as a Spanish dialect, for example?[2]) It is even more likely to break down in most of the developing countries.

Any student of linguistics—or for that matter anyone who uses his ears—will recognise that *any* language varies with region, social class, setting, occasion. Even so-called 'Standard English' covers a range of accepted variants, geographical or occupational; even the same speaker may use different forms of the same language in different circumstances. (To take an extreme case, the latest group of American astronauts were heard to use phrases like 'We are presently involved in high-grade participation' to mean that they were very busy, but one assumes, or hopes, that they do not talk like that at home.) The practice of talking about a language as if it were a thing or organism has its uses, but it can be misleading—it may impose a false unity and equally false divisions at the same time. To speak of different languages is not necessarily to recognise discrete entities, but rather to draw dividing-lines, often vague or arbitrary, for the sake of convenience.

India affords an excellent illustration of this. According to Grierson,[3] anyone travelling across the North of the Indian sub-continent from west to east will find the forms of speech changing gradually from place to place. The Urdu heard at one end and the Assamese heard at the other are quite distinct, even mutually incomprehensible, but one would be hard put to it to say precisely where Rajasthani gives way to Hindi or Bengali to Assamese. Most of the Indo-European languages of the North of India are blurred at the edges like this, and the same is true of the Dravidian languages of the South. The classical literary forms—and the educated colloquial forms, which are rarely the same thing—are distinct enough, but these are not the forms that most people actually speak. In the 1951 Census of India it was not found possible to separate speakers of Hindi, Urdu and Punjabi.[4] The 1961 Census did manage this, but the division was, inevitably, arbitrary in many cases.[5]

The figures, therefore, have to be used with caution; $133\frac{1}{2}$ million people are returned as speaking Hindi, but the range of varieties covered by the term is vast, so much so that Hindi speakers from different areas often have great difficulty in understanding each other. The common official form may also be out of reach of most people. Illiterate Hindi-speaking villagers were not the only people to find the Hindi of All-India Radio hard to follow[6]; so did the late Jawaharlal Nehru.[7]

This may be a temporary phenomenon. The identification of one form of a language with a political unit is likely to strengthen it and iron out the more awkward varieties in time. This happened centuries ago in Western Europe, where the dialects of the Ile de France and Castile emerged as the national languages of France and Spain out of a whole complex of Latin derivatives. Other factors may have the same effect; trade and literature, for the most part, helped to turn Tuscan into Italian, while keeping Ligurian at dialect level.

All of this suggests that there is no *linguistic* difference between a language and a dialect; the dividing lines are drawn according to other criteria. Yet they have to be drawn somewhere. Even in educational systems where the authorities encourage schooling in minority languages, there is a limit to the variety that can be recognised, if only for practical reasons. But where does one draw the line? When faced with a multiplicity of related speech-forms—as in Soviet Central Asia after the Revolution, or as in many parts of India at present—what criteria can be used? Number of speakers? The existence of a literature? Distinctiveness? There is rarely a simple answer, and the issue is usually complicated by other considerations.

Some of these considerations are real enough, some linguistically irrelevant but frequently appealed to nonetheless. It might be as well to clear some of them away at this stage.

(1) *Race.* Language, of course, is a purely cultural acquisition, and has nothing to do with race, whatever that may be. This should not need saying, but some beliefs go deeper than reason. There used to be a great deal of nonsense talked about

this, especially during the heyday of imperial expansion, when it was widely assumed that the biological differences between some human groups extended to the speech organs. If this were true, the implications for educational policy would be profound, but there is not a shred of evidence to support it; people of any 'race' can, and do, learn the languages of others. The confounding of race and language took a hard knock with the discrediting of Hitler's fantasies about an 'Aryan race'; but some of the misapprehensions voiced in current controversies over immigration suggest that the difference between acquired and inherited characteristics is not as widely appreciated as it might be.

(2) *Difficulty*. Beyond question, some languages are notoriously more difficult to learn than others. They may be grammatically complex, like Russian, or phonetically awkward, like Chinese. But these are difficulties in the way of someone who speaks another language already. There is little evidence that this makes much difference to the ease with which young children learn them, and none that considerations of this kind have ever carried any weight whatever with those responsible for decisions on language policy.

(3) *Development*. Talk of 'primitive' or 'advanced' languages can lead on to dangerous ground, but there are some problems here that have to be faced. As a rule, any language at any given point of time is closely related to the conditions of the society in which it is current. Thus, a language spoken by 20,000 people in northern Siberia may be perfectly adequate for the exigencies of nomadic life and Shamanistic religion, but may not be up to the requirements of industrial society. Since the content of formal education is likely to be more closely related to the latter, this can cause difficulties, especially in the matter of vocabulary. This, of course, has nothing to do with complexity; the languages of primitive societies are frequently far more complex than those of societies we are pleased to term 'civilised'. But the means may be lacking for the expression of new concepts, as missionaries of all proselytising creeds have found often enough. There are two chief ways round this prob-

lem—to create new terms from native roots, or to borrow from other languages. The second is probably the commoner, and can be a powerful vehicle for cultural influence. Thus, the languages of Soviet Central Asia have borrowed extensively from Russian; many African languages have borrowed from English or French; Persian and Urdu have borrowed from Arabic, as did Spanish in its own day; English borrowed from French (and a host of others), French from early Germanic, Germanic from Latin, Latin from Greek, and so on until the written record vanishes from sight. On the other hand, building up new terms from native roots has been a preferred method in languages as disparate as Arabic, Chinese, and modern German. By a not dissimilar process, modern Hindi draws on material from its own Sanskrit parent, as a matter of official policy. But since new coinings may be as strange to the average speaker as any foreign borrowing, this method too is not without its problems.

But although it must be conceded that some languages are more fitted than others for use as educational media, and that developing some languages for this purpose can be a formidable task, this does not mean that any need be *inherently* inadequate. Any language has to develop as needs change. Hindi may be less adequate than English at the present time, but so in its day was English as compared with Latin; and it is worth remembering that for a considerable period during the Roman Republic and early Empire, Latin was regarded as inferior to Greek as an educational and cultural medium. Whatever the drawbacks of a language at present, there is no need to assume that these must constitute a permanent disqualification.

(4) *Linguistic Nationalism.* Although it has little to do with the intrinsic merits of any language as an educational medium, linguistic nationalism has proved extremely powerful in the past and shows every sign of remaining so. It is natural enough that the language of any group should become the symbol of its own identity—witness the large number of peoples whose names for themselves mean 'the speakers' or 'the articulate', and for foreigners 'dumb' or 'stutterers'.[8] Majorities are as liable to

feel this way as minorities—the French, for instance, are just as nationalistic about their own language as the Basques or the Bretons are about theirs. In education, linguistic self-assertion by minorities usually takes the form of demanding schooling in their own language, and may extend to a reluctance to learn the majority medium even as a second language; majorities usually assert themselves by requiring the study and use of their own tongues by the minorities, and not infrequently go further in circumscribing or even banning the use of the minority languages in schools. There are plenty of examples of this last pattern, for the enforcement of all-Russian schools on Poland by the tsars to the banning of Breton in the schools of all French governments up to and including the present. In extreme cases, there may be pressure to use a language that few people actually speak. In the Republic of Ireland,[9] for instance, the Irish-speaking proportion of the population is tiny, yet Irish is a compulsory subject in the schools; and although it is not required as the *medium*, it can still take up to 40 per cent of curricular time in the primary schools. But such cases are rare; linguistic nationalism usually combines emotional identification with hard self-interest, and can add to the practical difficulties by making the whole question even more highly charged than it might be.

It does not follow, of course, that requiring minorities to learn the majority language need be put down to linguistic imperialism. In modern conditions, most countries feel the need for a common medium of communication, both for practical purposes and to obviate the disintegration of the national unit. Even systems which positively encourage minority languages require all school children to learn the national language, or try to.[10] When one language is spoken by a majority of the population, its use as the *national* medium is hardly unreasonable; yet, inevitably, this is bound to be of some disadvantage to the minority, whose learning burden is thus increased. As the examples will show, there is no way of pleasing everybody; even striking a balance of offence can be difficult enough.

CASE STUDIES

Out of the great variety of systems with major language problems, the USSR, India and East Africa can serve as illustrations.

(1) *The* USSR

According to the 1959 Census,[11] over 100 different languages are spoken in the USSR; Russian, with 124 million speakers, accounts for nearly 60 per cent of the total. The next two most important languages, Ukrainian and Byelorussian, are closely akin to Russian; with 33 and 7 million speakers respectively, they bring the proportion speaking the major Slavonic languages up to nearly 80 per cent. (For details, see Fig. 1.) For the rest, there are the major Turkic languages (Uzbek with 6 million, Tatar with 4 million, Kazakh with $3\frac{1}{2}$ million, etc.), the official languages of the other Union Republics, with between one and three million speakers each, and smaller groups ranging from over a million German-speakers to tiny populations, mostly in Siberia and the far North—7,000 Nanai, 7,000 Rutul, and even 535 Orochi and 232 Yukagir. Over half the minority languages are spoken by less than 100,000 people each, and about a quarter by fewer than 10,000.

There is also considerable variety in the extent to which the minority languages have developed as literary and cultural media. Georgian and Armenian, spoken by relatively small populations in the Caucasus, have been vehicles for flourishing literatures in their own scripts since the fifth century AD—much longer than Russian, as they are fond of pointing out. But they are exceptional; the Turkic languages of Central Asia (and Tadzhik, which is a form of Persian) did make some use of the Arabic script before the Revolution, but were unable to compete with classical Persian, Turkish or Arabic as literary media. Indeed, these languages are to some extent artificial creations. Modern Turkmen, Kirgiz, Uzbek and Kazakh were developed largely on the basis of the dialects of the chief towns in an area where 2-3 times the number of dialects was current. They were furnished by the Soviet authorities with Latin scripts (later

FIG. 1   USSR: Proportions of population speaking main languages as mother tongues. (*Census*, 1959.)

Figures in percentages; 100% = 208,826,650.

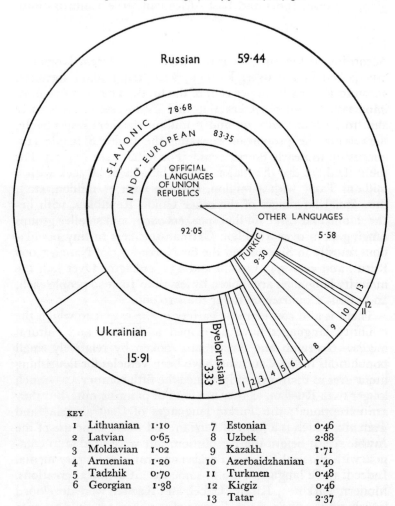

KEY

1	Lithuanian	1·10	7	Estonian	0·46
2	Latvian	0·65	8	Uzbek	2·88
3	Moldavian	1·02	9	Kazakh	1·71
4	Armenian	1·20	10	Azerbaidzhanian	1·40
5	Tadzhik	0·70	11	Turkmen	0·48
6	Georgian	1·38	12	Kirgiz	0·46
			13	Tatar	2·37

Other languages: This category consists mainly of Finno-Ugric, Mongol and far Northern languages, but also includes some Indo-European languages not accounted for in the diagram, such as German, Polish, Ossetian and others.

changed to Cyrillic), used in the schools, given official status and cultivated as literary media, drawing heavily on Russian rather than on Turkish or Arabic for new vocabulary. Other major groups, such as the Buryat-Mongol, a patchwork quilt of languages stretching from central Russia to the Mongolian border, were unwritten before the Revolution; the same is true of the Finno-Ugric languages, with the exception of Estonian. The Baltic languages, written in Latin script, were not Soviet languages until the incorporation of Lithuania and Latvia. Moldavian is practically the same as the Romanian spoken over the frontier, but has been given a Cyrillic instead of Latin alphabet. Finally, the non-Soviet languages, such as German, Yiddish and Polish, spoken by substantial numbers within the USSR, have of course long-established educational and literary use. The remaining languages, however, from Tadzhik, Ossetian and other Iranian languages to the minuscule groups in the far North, were unwritten in pre-Revolutionary times. Many languages, especially of the Turkic, Iranian, Finno-Ugric and Buryat-Mongol types, were provided with alphabets derived from Cyrillic during the Soviet period. It was a lengthy operation, taking over thirty years, and suffered from lack of co-ordination; even so, about forty languages are still unwritten.[12]

Officially, Soviet educational policy is pluralistic. The Constitution (Article 121) states that all have the right to education in the mother tongue.[13] But it must be obvious from the foregoing that this is easier said than done. It is one thing to provide native-language schools for six million Uzbeks or 2¾ million Georgians, quite another to do it for 500 Tofalar or even 2,000 Selkup. In practice, there is a compromise: the full range of schooling is available in Russian, in the official languages of the other Union Republics and, within the Russian Federation, in Tatar and Bashkir. For the rest, provision is more modest. The peoples of the major ASSR's (Autonomous Soviet Socialist Republics, such as Yakutia or Komi, which exist *within* some of the Union Republics) have to make do with schooling in their own languages up to Form VIII—about age 15.

In the minor ASSR's mother tongue instruction usually lasts only for the first four years, secondary education being given in Russian. As for the small groups in the far North, it is sometimes possible to provide schooling in the mother tongue for the first year or two, just long enough for the children to learn enough Russian to continue in that language. The Leningrad Pedagogic Institute (Teacher Training College) has a special Northern Department for teachers from some of the northern nationalities, but the supply of students is always something of a problem; and there seems to be no way at all of making even these provisions for the children of the groups numbered in hundreds rather than thousands, and who lack a written language of any kind. For them, instruction has to be in Russian from the start, which creates initial difficulties and slows down progress for a long time.

The major groups have problems too. There is some evidence that the authorities encourage Russification from time to time, especially in the Baltic states and the Ukraine.[14] Some of the Central Asian areas, notably Kazakhstan, have a high proportion of Russian settlers; for them there is a parallel system of Russian-language schools, where Kazakh is given as an optional subject, and there has been a growing tendency for Kazakh parents to send their children to Russian-language schools rather than their own. This tendency has been noted in many parts of the Union; even in the Ukraine and Byelorussia the major cities are now largely Russian-speaking, while the vernacular schools are found mainly in the smaller towns and the countryside.

The authorities deny that they are pursuing a deliberate policy of assimilation; Russian, however, is undoubtedly gaining ground, and there are powerful forces helping it along, whatever governmental intentions may be. Mobility is one of these, whether from countryside to town or from one part of the Soviet Union to another. Imagine, for example, an Armenian child with ambitious parents and a bent for mathematics. It is quite possible for him to receive all his primary and secondary schooling in Armenian, studying Russian only as a second language. The University of Yerevan has a perfectly adequate Faculty of Mathematics; but if he wants the very best in the country, he will probably aim for Novosibirsk, Moscow or Leningrad, which are outstanding. But these are Russian-medium institutions, and our hypothetical Armenian will therefore have to be competent enough in Russian not only to follow the course, but to vie with native Russian speakers for admission. Competition for entry to the most popular higher institutions is keen enough, quite apart from linguistic complications; and parents, knowing this, may well be tempted to put him in a Russian-language school from the very beginning. If this can happen in Armenia, where the indigenous culture is particularly strong, it is even more likely to happen in places like Central Asia where it is much weaker.

Even if we assume, then, that the larger minorities at least do effectively enjoy their right to mother-tongue instruction, this is clearly not the end of their difficulties. Given that they have to learn Russian as a subsidiary subject, they have a greater burden of learning to cope with than their Russian compatriots; in some republics, the general school course requires an extra year to cope with the additional material.[15] The smaller minorities, for their part, are under much greater pressure to assimilate; small numbers and the undeveloped state of their languages makes them far less resistant to Russian encroachment. It is hard to see how this could be otherwise. Even under a pluralist policy, it would seem that the majority language is likely to spread at the expense of the others. Minority languages which are distinctive, have their own literatures, and are spoken by reasonably large numbers in a geographically concentrated area appear most able to resist the trend.

(2) *India*

Before the arrival of the British, education in India was based on three competing systems—Sanskrit for northern Hindus, Tamil for southern Hindus, Persian and Arabic for Muslims. All were confined to small élites, and were concerned mainly with the learning of the sacred texts, usually by rote. Among the early British administrators, Warren Hastings favoured the encouragement of Sanskrit and Persian-Arabic learning, but his view did not prevail. Thomas Babington Macaulay, who was in any case unsympathetic to the indigenous cultures, recommended in his minute of 1835 a Westernised system of education, restricted to a minority, with English as the medium of instruction. His cultural arrogance seems breathtaking today, but in fairness he was probably more sensitive to Indian needs than most of his British contemporaries. He certainly did not rule out vernacular education for all time, but took the view that the Indian languages would not be viable media until they had undergone considerable transformation. Meanwhile, he settled on English as the language 'most useful to our native subjects'.

> We must at present do our best to form a class who may be interpreters between us and the millions we govern—a class of persons Indian in blood and colour, but English in tastes, in opinions, in morals and in intellect. To that class we may leave it to refine the vernacular dialects of the country, to enrich those dialects with terms of science borrowed from Western nomenclature, and to render them by degrees fit vehicles for conveying knowledge to the great mass of the population.[16]

At the same time, there were moves to develop vernacular schools, but these were largely confined to the primary level. Between these and the English-language system leading to the universities the gulf was wide indeed.

It was only to be expected that the stirrings of political consciousness should bring a reaction against this (at best) paternalistic policy. 'To get rid of the infatuation for English', said Tilak, 'is one of the necessary conditions of *swaraj*.' This viewpoint gained ground among Indian intellectuals and government circles alike, and long before independence—as far back as 1902, in fact—the principle had been accepted that Indian vernaculars were the most suitable media for instruction up to the higher stages of the secondary school. The objection to English-based education, voiced forcefully by Gandhi and Tagore, among others, was twofold. Firstly, it was alien: 'The schools of our country,' Tagore wrote, 'far from being integrated to society, are imposed on it from the outside.'[17] Or again, 'Education and life can never become one in such circumstances and are bound to remain separated by a barrier.'[18] The growth of political nationalism, naturally, gave increased weight to this kind of objection. Secondly, it was ineffective. Gandhi complained that, because of the time taken to learn English, the standard of attainment in everything else was 'pitifully inadequate'.[19] Later findings, on the whole, bore this out. The Punjab University Enquiry Committee of 1932-3 drew attention to the time spent on English and the neglect of the vernaculars, and suggested that 'a large proportion of the pupils are unable to think and write clearly in any language'.[20] Most of the admittedly small amount of experimental evidence available since does seem to indicate that children taught in a foreign medium are at a disadvantage compared with those who learn in their mother tongue.

Although English continued to occupy a pre-eminent place (and became even *more* popular as a subject of study) after Independence, there were many reasons why it could not continue to be the normal medium for secondary and higher education indefinitely. The position of English as the language of the Raj worried nationalists less than might be expected. But English had always been out of reach of all but a tiny élite, cut off thereby from the mass of the Indian people in all fields of public life. A glance at Fig. 2 will show how few Indians could expect to reach the level of schooling where English was taught even well after independence.[21] It might have been possible to rule the country through a small governing class speaking Persian under the Moguls, or an English-speaking civil service under the British Raj, but in a democratic independent India this separation of the educated from the rest of the population would hardly do. The circumstances demanded an *Indian* medium in education and public life.

But which one? Out of hundreds of languages, the Indian Constitution recognises fourteen—Assamese, Bengali, Gujarati, Hindi, Kashmiri, Marathi, Oriya, Punjabi, Sanskrit and Urdu among the Indo-European tongues of the North, and the quite

FIG. 2 INDIA: Enrolments at different levels of the educational system, 1960-1.

Figures show percentages of the appropriate age-groups.

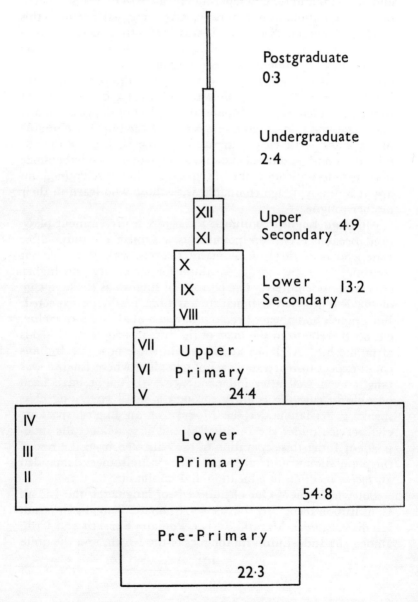

different Dravidian languages Kannada, Malayalam, Tamil and Telugu in the South. These are spoken, in one form or another, by some 87 per cent of the population. (See Fig. 3.[22]) Sanskrit is included for cultural reasons—though, rather oddly, nearly 3,000 claim it as their mother tongue. Of the remainder, Kashmiri and Assamese are spoken by relatively small numbers (small by Indian standards, that is—about 2 million and 7 million respectively), but all the others can claim substantial numbers—Bengali just under 34 million, Marathi over 33 million, Urdu and Gujarati well over 20 million each, and so forth; while in the South, Kannada and Malayalam are spoken by over 17 million each, Tamil by 30½ million, and Telugu by over 37½ million. Many of these languages have considerable literatures—Bengali is the language of Tagore, after all—and some, notably Tamil, can boast a lengthy cultural pedigree.

In this profusion of languages Hindi, with over 133 million speakers is by far the most prominent numerically, but is still spoken by less than a third of the population. Further, its geographical range is limited to part of the North (see Map). All the major languages, with the exception of Urdu,[23] are concentrated in fairly well-defined areas. This makes it relatively easy to find viable *regional* vernaculars (especially with the reorganisation of the states on linguistic lines)[24]; but it also emphasises the cultural cleavage between the Hindi-speaking North-Central area and the Dravidian-speaking South, to say nothing of further, if less fundamental, cleavages to east and west. Hindi is the only possible choice for an all-India medium; yet numbers and geography alike ensure that its choice offends more people than it satisfies.

The Official Language Commission was set up to examine the problem, and it finally presented its report in 1959. As expected, it recommended that Hindi be adopted as the official language of the Indian Union, that English be retained for the time being (the original change-over date was to be 1965), and that the rights of the states to use their own languages in the schools and elsewhere were to be safeguarded. The recom-

FIG. 3 INDIA: Proportions of population speaking main languages as mother tongues. (*Census*, 1961.)

Figures in percentages; 100% = 468,050,000

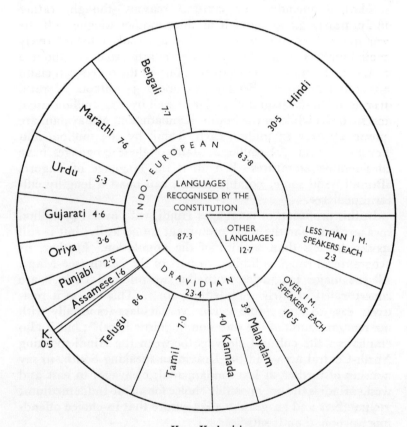

K. = Kashmiri

mendations were accepted in principle by the President's Order of 1960, and were effected in the Official Language Act passed by the Lok Sabha in 1963.

There was never any question, naturally, of making Hindi the normal medium of instruction outside the areas where it was spoken as the mother tongue; nor, on the other hand, has there even been any question of using any other Indian language as the national medium—none of them comes near to qualifying numerically. The adoption of regional languages at *state* level has been generally acceptable; the requirement to teach Hindi nationally as a compulsory subject has come in for strong opposition. This has been most marked in the Dravidian South, and was given point by the self-immolation of a number of Tamil enthusiasts, and later by the successes of the DMK, a Tamil nationalist party, in Madras State in the general election in 1968. To a slightly lesser extent, opposition to 'Hindi imperialism' has been strong in Bengal and Maharashtra as well.

The opponents of Hindi favour either the retention of English as the national 'link language', or no national language at all. The first solution, as a long term policy, is rejected by the Central Government for reasons that have already been touched on—they are unwilling, as one commentator has put it, to keep education in a 'linguistic polythene bag'.[25] The second alternative is also unacceptable because of the danger of linguistic 'Balkanisation'. As Lal Bahadur Shastri said in 1962, 'A change-over [to regional languages only in higher education] without a link in the form of English or Hindi would only make Indians of different States strangers to one another.'[26] The policy of replacing English with Hindi has proved politically costly; but so has hesitancy about pushing it through. The Central Government is under pressure from the other side as well; not only is the Hindi lobby powerful in the Congress Party in the Northern States, it is in danger of being outflanked on the language issue. The electoral successes of the Jana Sangh, a right-wing Hindu party, strongly pro-Hindi, have been achieved largely at the expense of Congress.

Officially, educational policy has been governed by the

'Three-Language Formula' since its adoption by the All-India Council for Secondary Education in 1956—primary education in the mother tongue, followed by the regional language and Hindi at the secondary stage.[27] Under a system that has been cynically described as 'equal handicaps for all',[28] pupils in the Hindi-speaking areas are supposed to study another Indian language. Many make use of the fact that the list includes Sanskrit, and there are many cases where French or Russian is studied instead.[29]

Even when the formula does work as intended, problems remain. Where the home language is the same as the state language, they are certainly lessened, and this is true of the majority; but they do not disappear completely since, as already noted, the form of the language actually spoken in the home may differ markedly from the official written form. Gandhi and Tagore, working in the relatively homogeneous areas of Gujarat and Bengal respectively, could argue for mother-tongue and regional-language schooling as if they were the same thing. In practice, although the drift has been towards standardisation within the states, concessions still have to be made to minorities.[30]

Further, English has proved difficult to replace for many purposes. For one thing, its advantages as an international language are recognised. For another, the development of neither the regional languages nor Hindi has yet reached the point where they are fully viable for all kinds of higher education. Some teaching has been done in these languages in the universities for a number of years, but the results have not been altogether encouraging. According to the Universities Grants Commission in 1965, 'The regional languages have not yet developed to a point where they can replace English as a tool of knowledge and as a medium of communication.'[31] The same is true of Hindi, in the view of the National Integration Conference: 'This link [in higher education] must be Hindi, but since Hindi, like any other regional language, will take some time for its development, English will continue to be such a link.'[32] Since English is to stay for the present as an important

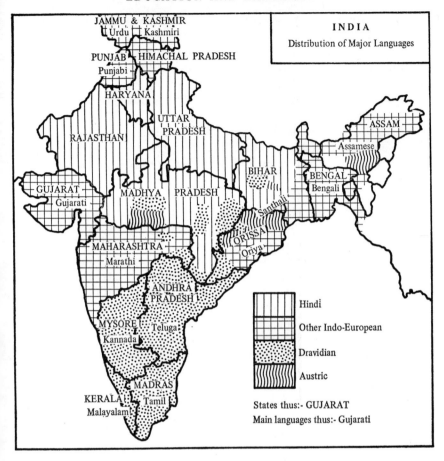

INDIA

Distribution of Major Languages

JAMMU & KASHMIR
Urdu — Kashmiri
PUNJAB — HIMACHAL PRADESH
Punjabi
HARYANA
RAJASTHAN
UTTAR PRADESH
ASSAM
Assamese
GUJARAT
Gujarati
MADHYA PRADESH
BIHAR
BENGAL
Bengali
Santhali
ORISSA
Oriya
MAHARASHTRA
Marathi
ANDHRA PRADESH
MYSORE
Kannada
Telugu
MADRAS
KERALA
Malayalam
Tamil

Hindi
Other Indo-European
Dravidian
Austric

States thus:- GUJARAT
Main languages thus:- Gujarati

medium in higher education, it will also remain as an important subject in the secondary schools for a long time to come.

Again, multiplicity of languages is aggravated by multiplicity of scripts. Assamese uses the same alphabet as Bengali, those of Kannada and Telugu are closely similar, and the Devanagari script of Sanskrit and Hindi can be used for some of the other Indo-European languages; but most official languages have their own, while English requires yet another. A Kerali schoolboy learning Malayalam, Hindi and English will therefore have to master three different styles of writing as well. When the vast majority of Indians are illiterate in any script, and when large numbers lapse into illiteracy due to the brevity of their schooling, this extra burden is no small matter.[33]

There has been some advance. The regional languages are developing apace as media for educational at all levels, and there are some signs that Hindi is beginning to consolidate its position as a national language. But the conflicting social, political and educational requirements are far from being resolved. Undue reliance on the regional languages not only makes mobility more difficult, but increases the danger of the country's falling apart. Keeping English as the sole or even chief medium for advanced education is to create a caste of educated English-speakers in a land already bedevilled by countless centrifugal forces; and even if Hindi should gain acceptance as an effective national language, unity may have been gained at the price of isolation. As Mrs Indira Gandhi said in 1967, 'In the present-day world, we cannot afford to live in isolation. Therefore there should be three languages, regional, national and international.'[34]

This would be a formidable task even for an advanced country. But even primary schooling is not yet universally available in India, while secondary education, to say nothing of higher education, is still obtainable only by the fortunate few. Only 7 per cent of the population was bilingual according to the 1961 Census[35]; the growth of secondary education should increase this figure, but even supposing that this does happen, that the country avoids falling apart, and that it does prove possible to develop the regional and national languages sufficiently to avoid lowering standards with their wider introduction, Indian pupils and students will still be faced with a formidable mass of learning before they can communicate with each other. The author of a recent study has summed up the problem in the form of three questions, all vital:

How far can a new society afford to lose the warmth of local life enjoyed and transmitted through a multiplicity of local languages? How far can the central authority counter-balance the divisive strains of a dozen regions demanding and using their own languages in administration? . . . How far can a technological society support the financial and organisational burden of using three or more languages in the course of its education?[36]

The answers will be awaited with some anxiety.

(3) *East Africa*

Perhaps the greatest problem in most sub-Saharan African countries is that not only the education systems and the media of instruction, but the very states themselves, were the creation of the European colonial powers. The Europeans carved out areas according to their lines of penetration, and the frontiers were essentially the places where the powers finally came face to face. The holdings of Britain and France, Germany and Portugal, were delineated from known coastal or river footholds to straight lines on a map, which may or may not have had anything to do with any observable geographical features; they seldom bore any relation whatever to the ethnic or linguistic composition of the populations. Modern Ghana and Mali are not the old ones, but the names of mediaeval states applied to ex-colonies. In West Africa, the pattern of tribal population was parallel to the coast, whereas the Europeans cut in vertically. Occasionally they took in a whole state (Benin, for example), but were just as likely to slice their way through existing tribal areas. Thus the successor states are regularly faced with fissions and tensions of the kind that has attained such tragic proportions in Nigeria. The languages of Northern Nigeria, such as Hausa or Fulani, are spoken in Niger, Chad and even in Mali, but not in Southern Nigeria; while the Yoruba of south-western Nigeria is spoken in Ghana, Togo and Dahomey, but not in Northern Nigeria. Perhaps the oddest of all is the Gambia, a finger-like excrescence sticking into the middle of Senegal. The national identity of most African *states*, therefore, is largely an inheritance from the colonial powers.

It is not surprising, therefore, that few states can find a viable medium that is both *national* and *African*. Except in Tanzania, where Swahili enjoys national currency, there is no alternative

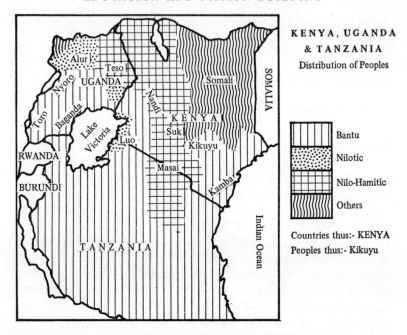

KENYA, UGANDA
& TANZANIA
Distribution of Peoples

Bantu
Nilotic
Nilo-Hamitic
Others

Countries thus:- KENYA
Peoples thus:- Kikuyu

to the former colonial languages, English and French. There have, of course, been moves ever since independence to adapt the imported educational systems to national needs by Africanising the curriculum,[37] but this has not involved dispensing with English or French. Some African vernaculars are employed to varying degrees at the primary stage, but English and French are introduced as subjects early in the course, frequently in the first year, and are employed as the instructional media as soon as possible. In many cases even primary education is conducted in the ex-colonial language throughout, as are secondary and higher education everywhere.[38] So deeply entrenched are they, in fact, that they can in a real sense be regarded as African languages, and in many systems the policy of having secondary pupils study both is catching on, as in the Gambia, where French is taught in secondary schools, or in Senegal, where English is compulsory.[39] This is partly due, undoubtedly, to the international currency of these languages; but the fact that these two particular countries are separated by little else may have a good deal to do with it.

There are several reasons for this continued reliance on European languages in the post-imperial period:

(1) African vernaculars are not, by and large, sufficiently developed to make them viable media for instruction beyond the primary stage. (The Arabic of North Africa is another matter.) Many are not suitable even for elementary schooling, lacking scripts, adequate vocabulary or sufficient numbers of speakers. This is not, as we have seen, an insuperable objection; development of this kind has been common elsewhere in the past, and the major languages at least, such as Fula, Yoruba, Ibo, Luganda, Shona, Sotho, Xhosa and a host of others already have written scripts, and some of them have a vigorous literature as well. In particular, two languages are current far beyond their original areas, Hausa in the west and Swahili in the east; it is true that they are often spoken in forms not immediately suitable for sophisticated use—'trader Hausa' and 'kitchen Swahili' or 'kiSettler'—but this consideration has not prevented the development of lingua francas into great literary languages elsewhere, such as Aramaic, *koine* or Romaic Greek, mediaeval Latin or Urdu.

Swahili, incidentally, is very far from being a 'primitive' language by any standards. It had a lively poetic literature as far back as the seventeenth century, employing the Arabic script and drawing on Arabic for new material. There is no reason why English should not be similarly used for the needs of a technological society.

Some see this as a disadvantage. According to a report in the *Times Educational Supplement* in 1967:

Unfortunately, Swahili, although it has a complicated grammar, and is in no sense a simple language, lacks an up-to-date vocabulary and has rather tended in recent years to absorb English words rather than search for Swahili equivalents. 'Bus stop', for example, is everywhere known as 'bussie stopie' by Swahili speakers.[40]

Why this should be unfortunate is not clear. 'Bussie stopie' may

FIG. 4 KENYA: Distribution of population by tribal groups, 1962.
Figures in percentages; 100% = 8,636,263.

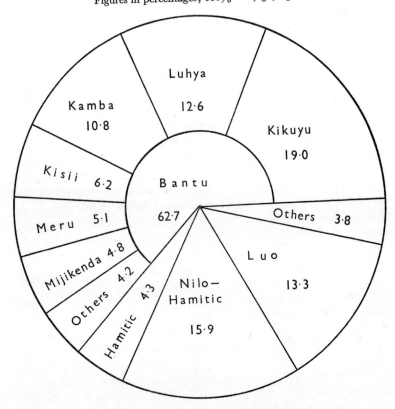

United Nations Demographic Yearbook, 1963.

sound odd to English speakers, but this is hardly the point. *Novel, yacht, algebra* and *tea* may sound odd to a Frenchman, Dutchman, Arab or Chinese, but they are perfectly good English. Enrichment of this kind is a normal process of linguistic development. Bread, for instance, is not native to Africa, and Swahili therefore had no word for it. When the need was felt to fill the gap, the name of an expatriate baker, McCarthy, was pressed into service as *mkate*, by precisely the same process that has given English *damasc, bayonet, volt, pomp* and a host of others. It is hard to see what would have been gained in 'searching for a Swahili equivalent' in one case or an English one in the others. Has German profited much from replacing *Telefon* with *Fernsprecher*, *Geographie* with *Landwissenschaft*, or has Russian by using *mezhdunarodnyi* instead of *internatsionalnyi*?

If President Nyerere found it possible to translate *Julius Caesar* into Swahili, the disadvantages of the language can hardly be inherent; the same is true in principle of the other African languages. But there are more serious objections in the way of ousting English or French in favour of African languages, even if they are as widely current as Swahili.

(2) The very nature of most African states puts them in danger of fragmentation along tribal lines. In hardly any case is any one language acceptable as a national medium. In Kenya,[41] for instance, there are 42 indigenous tribal groups in a population of 8,365,000. The largest single group is the Kikuyu, with little over $1\frac{1}{2}$ million. Among the other Bantu-speaking peoples there are a million Luhya, a million Kamba, and half a million each of Meru, Mijikenda and Kisii. There are smaller groups of Nilo-Hamitic peoples (the Masai, Nandi and others), and the Nilotic peoples are represented by the Luo, with over a million. (See Fig. 4 and Map.) Out of these, there is no obvious—or even feasible—choice for a *Kenyan* language; it is hard to envisage the non-Kikuyu peoples accepting what is, numerically, the best claimant. Swahili has some currency, and is tribally neutral, but it is English that fills the role of official and educational medium in this mixture of minorities.

There are some cases where there seems an obvious choice,

at first glance, for a national language. In Uganda,[42] for instance, formed on the nucleus of the Kingdom of Buganda (but including those of Bunyoro and Toro as well), there is a population of nearly 6½ million. Of these, no less than 51 per cent are said to speak Luganda as their mother tongue, which would seem to give it a strong claim on numerical grounds to be developed as a national language. But it is not as simple as that. The way in which the figures were collected, and the statistics for the various tribal groups (which give the Baganda a much smaller proportion of the population), suggest that the figure of 51 per cent is a considerable over-estimate. Even if it were accurate, such preferential treatment would be unacceptable even to the other Bantu people, let alone the others, to whom Luganda is just as foreign as English. English, then, remains as elsewhere. Vernacular teaching in the primary schools is concentrated on five of the languages—Luganda, Luo, Runyoro, Ateso and Lugbara—but in the towns, where the population is mixed, even primary schooling is generally given in English throughout.[43]

(3) Although pan-Africanism is further off than ever, most African states have resolutely turned their backs on tribalism, and would probably regard the difficult task of developing national vernacular systems, even in Luganda, as hopelessly parochial. Swahili is not a tribal language, and in any case English has continued as an important medium in Tanzania as well. Overwhelmingly, the African countries have chosen to develop educational systems in their original imported media, French and English, which are, after all, internationally current as well as being the most widely understood languages south of the Sahara. (How far Portuguese will fill the same role in Angola and Mozambique when these countries eventually win independence remains to be seen.) The use of the international languages makes the supply of textbooks and teachers much easier; they are the languages of no particular tribe or state, and this helps to outweigh their imperialist associations. It has not passed without notice, too, that it is in the Republic of South Africa that most emphasis is placed on vernacular education—

Zulu, Sotho or Xhosa rather than English, 'Bantu education' in medium as well as content. This can be seen as the educational counterpart of the Bantustan policy, the logical outcome of *apartheid*, whereby Xhosas can have citizenship of a sort in the Transkei and nowhere else. Bantu education fobs the Africans off with a substitute, which is recognised as such, and disliked, by those who have to undergo it. But even if it were admirable in quality, it would still tend to reinforce tribalism and divide Africans from each other. This, of course, is the South African régime's intention, a point which is unlikely to be lost on the independent African states.

But if the arguments for English and French are strong, they do not dispose of the problems. It has already been remarked that children who are taught in a foreign medium progress less well than those taught in their mother tongue, and it has to be recognised that in Africa English is often taught rather badly. In many parts of Africa a large proportion of teachers are completely untrained, especially in the west: according to the Banjo Report in 1962,[44] 26,000 primary school teachers out of 40,000 in Western Nigeria had had no training at all. According to a study published in 1968:

> The importance of the spoken language is not really understood by most teachers. Because their own command of English is often poor, they inevitably lean heavily on the Reader and do not encourage children in the skills of understanding and speaking simple English. Secondly, there is interference from the mother tongue, in grammar, pronunciation, intonation and stress. . . . Thirdly, the classroom environment and teaching techniques are rarely conducive to good language learning. Classrooms are under-equipped, class libraries virtually non-existent, materials for constructing simple visual aids almost entirely lacking. The radio, gramophone and tape recorder are generally out of the question for reasons of finance. As a result the children rely heavily on the teacher and play an entirely passive role—hardly the best way to learn a language.[45]

Such strictures are mainly applicable to primary schools; but since secondary schooling is confined to a small minority as yet, the danger remains that the use of English, as in India, can cut the educated élite off from the rest of the population in Africa as in India. But at least the Africa in questions of policy

205

are clearer; the problem is more amenable to financial and economic solution than in the case of India—though, as was said at the outset, this must offer small consolation at the moment.

CONCLUSION

Complex though the situation is, there does seem to be a fairly consistent trend towards assimilation. This seems to happen whether educational facilities are provided in minority languages, as in the USSR, or not, as in France. The very existence of an official majority language appears to encourage a drift in its favour. Political indentification of a language with a nation, its use in trade, administration and literature, all play their part as well as the educational system. The main effects of using a language in education is to achieve greater standardisation of majority and minority languages alike. A distinctive language like Georgian or Malayalam may be able to resist encroachment while minor variants of the official medium may be largely smoothed away. At the same time, unwritten languages spoken by very small groups are liable to disappear, whether through deliberate encouragement or not. If general schooling is given in another medium, and if such a minor language is left out of the process, only exceptional circumstances, such as identification with a cohesive and self-aware national group, can prevent it from dying out. Conversely, there is little evidence that a policy of linguistic conservation can, by itself, ensure the survival of a language, if other factors are against it. Gaelic, for instance, is mildly encouraged in Scotland, strenuously in Ireland, with little apparent effect. The only example that springs to mind of a policy of this kind succeeding is in Israel; but if there had not been a pressing need for a common medium for the largely immigrant Jewish population, speaking Yiddish, Ladino, German, Rumanian, Arabic and 20 other languages,[46] it is doubtful if the schools could have succeeded in reviving Hebrew as a living tongue.

Much more research is needed on the educational effects of

studying through the medium of an alien language before we can be sure how much more assimilation to expect, and perhaps, accept.[47] It would be a pity if many languages were to die out of effective use; but it would be an even greater pity if the multiplicity that now exists were to continue to deprive millions of educational opportunity. In Britain, where we have the reputation of being the world's worst linguists (not altogether unjustly), we are coming to realise that it is much easier than used to be thought for anyone to learn another language or even several. But it is one thing for a British schoolboy to acquire reasonably competent French and German, then to add tourist's Italian, Spanish or even Serbo-Croat to his list; it is quite another for a child brought up to speak the Adivasi dialect to learn standard Marathi, Hindi and English well enough to study them further. He is, admittedly, an extreme case; but for all the development of education in the mother tongue in various parts of the world, the fact remains that in most of the developing countries a large proportion of children who are to have any chance of receiving education at the higher levels will have to do so in a language other than their own for a long time to come. There is little prospect of baulking this basic difficulty; but it could be made a little easier by improving the efficiency and spreading the availability of schooling in general and language-teaching in particular. This, once again is a question of money. The problem cannot be bought off; but if the world could get its priorities right, it could be made rather less crippling.

NOTES AND REFERENCES

1 e.g. Hauptfuhrer, F., 'Belgium's Culture War' in *New Society*, 28 March 1968, pp. 455-6.
2 Catalan is as close to French as to Spanish. The accidents of mediaeval dynastic politics, rather than anything else, denied Catalan the status of a national language while giving it to Portuguese.
3 Sir John Grierson, *Linguistic Survey of India* (1916).
4 *Census of India 1951* (quoted in Le Page, R. B., *The National Language Question* (OUP, 1964), p. 53.

5 *Census of India* (1961).
6 Dakin, Julian, 'Language and Education in India' in Dakin, Tiffen and Widdowson, *Language in Education* (OUP, 1967), p. 16.
7 Maxwell, Neville, 'India and Language' in *New Society*, 21 December 1967, pp. 892-4.
8 e.g. Shqiptar (Albanian) = 'clear speaker'; Nahuatl (Aztec) = 'pleasant sound'; Euskadi (Basque) = 'articulate'; Slav (and Slovak, Slovene, etc.) are probably derived from *slovo*, 'word' or 'speech'. Nemets (Russian for German) = 'dumb'; Hottentot = 'stutterer' (Dutch); the Greeks called all non-Greek speakers *barbaroi*, people who could only say 'bar-bar' instead of speaking properly.
9 Macnamara, J., *Bilingualism and Primary Education* (Edinburgh UP, 1965).
10 Switzerland is an exception, despite the preponderance of German speakers.
11 *United Nations Demographic Yearbook* (1963).
12 Musaev, K. M., *Alfavity yazykov narodov* SSSR (Moscow, 1965).
13 *Constitution (Fundamental Law) of the Union of Soviet Socialist Republics*, ch. x, art. 121.
14 Kolasky, J., *Education in the Soviet Ukraine* (Ontario, 1968); Belinsky, Y., 'The Soviet Educational Laws of 1958-9 and Soviet Nationality Policy' in *Soviet Studies*, 14, 2, 1962.
15 *Vedomosti Verkhovnogo Sovieta* SSSR, 19 August 1965.
16 Macaulay's Minute of 2 February 1835 in Sharp, H. (ed.), *Selections from Educational Records*, part i (Bureau of Education 1920), p. 109. Macaulay was legal advisor to the Supreme Council of India.
17 Dakin, op. cit., p. 22.
18 ibid.
19 ibid.
20 ibid.
21 Figures for the school year 1960-1. Sargent, Sir John, *Society, Schools and Progress in India* (Pergamon, 1968), appendix A.
22 Figures from *Census of India 1961*.
23 Urdu is the language of Indian Muslims rather than of any particular area.
24 e.g. Maharashtra, Punjab, Andhra Pradesh.
25 LePage, R. B., op. cit.
26 Dakin, op. cit., p. 53.
27 ibid., p. 39.
28 Sargent, op. cit., p. 157.
29 ibid.
30 This is particularly true of the languages of some numerous tribal groups, especially in the North-East Frontier District.
31 Dakin, op. cit., p. 54.
32 ibid, p. 53.
33 A proposal that a modified form of the Devanagari script could be used

for other Indian languages found favour with the Official Language Commission, but not with the Dravidian or Bengali speakers.

34 Quoted by Dakin, op. cit., p. 61.
35 *Census of India 1961.*
36 Dakin, op. cit., p. 61.
37 e.g. Banovitch, Alexandre, 'Tendances actuelles de l'évolution du contenu de l'enseignement dans les pays de l'Afrique Noire' in *General Education in a Changing World* (Proceedings of the Comparative Education Society in Europe, Berlin Conference, 1965: The Hague, 1967).
38 Tiffen, Brian, 'Language and Education in Commonwealth Africa' in Dakin, Tiffen and Widdowson, op. cit., pp. 63-113.
39 Hugo, Ian, 'English for French Africa' in *New Society*, 8 September 1968, p. 373.
40 Fuller, Susan, 'For and against Swahili' in *Times Educational Supplement*, 24 February 1967.
41 *United Nations Demographic Yearbook 1963.*
42 ibid.
43 Burns, Donald G., *African Education*, pp. 28-9 (OUP, 1965).
44 Tiffen, op. cit., p. 82.
45 ibid., p. 83.
46 *United Nations Demographic Yearbook 1963.*
47 The available evidence seems to suggest a disadvantage for the child taught in a foreign medium (e.g. UNESCO, 'The use of Vernacular Languages in Education' in *Monographs on Fundamental Education* 1953). But it is not conclusive; an experiment in Iganga, Uganda, yielded rather different results (Dakin, op. cit., p. 27).

CHAPTER 10

CONTRASTS IN CUBAN AND AFRICAN EDUCATIONAL STRATEGIES

RICHARD JOLLY

This paper considers education and manpower strategy in Cuba after the Revolution, in respect of five main problems common to the experience of many under-developed countries.[1]

In order to emphasise the essence of Cuba's strategy, an attempt is made to contrast Cuban policies with those followed in Africa. This, of course, throws one open to the charge of not comparing like with like, neglecting the complex of social, educational, political and economic differences between the two. Let it be clear at the beginning, therefore, that the argument is not that policies and approaches in any one country should or can be simply transferred to another, even though this has been attempted often enough in, for example, university education. Rather the paper attempts to use features of Cuban education to stimulate questions, possibly rather obvious ones, about educational strategy elsewhere. Since Cuban experience is extreme in its contrasts with current African policies, the differences emerge rather sharply. Since Cuban education has tackled common problems boldly and in many respects successfully, there are important lessons to learn. But—to repeat—this is not to suggest that any particular country in Africa can or should simply copy Cuban policies far from their original context.

Cuba's experience as an under-developed country following an extreme strategy for development gives it great professional interest. Cuba is the first fairly typical developing country to adopt a socialist strategy and centralised planning. The Cuban economy, unlike the economies of China, Russia and Eastern Europe is in size, level of development, structure of trade and geographical location fairly typical of the small, tropical primary-producing, export oriented economies, which comprise the majority of the world's under-developed nations. Cuba has a population of 8 millions, a tropical climate and is heavily dependent on sugar, which alone accounts for about four fifths of exports and a fifth of national product.

This is not to suggest that in all respects Cuba is typical. In terms of national income per head, the Cuban economy before the Revolution was stagnant rather than poor. Cuba's per capita income in 1958 was about $500, ranking third in Latin America and well above average for the third world. But for three decades real per capita income had grown very little and the distribution of income was highly unequal, particularly in its extremes between the rural areas and Havana.[2]

The education profile of the Cuban population before the Revolution reveals many of the same features as the economy. The coverage of education at primary, secondary or university levels was well above the standards of many under-developed countries, even in Latin America, but the proportion of each age group attending school had changed little since the 1920's. Like the economy, education was stagnant rather than poor. This comes out clearly in the largely horizontal contours shown in Diagram 1, the age-education profile of the Cuban population in 1958.

In other respects, Cuban education suffered many of the weaknesses common to under-developed countries. Educational facilities and coverage were far better in the urban than the rural areas and minimal for adults. The content of education was heavily biased in favour of urban rather than rural interests and in favour of high-level professional skills rather than middle-level technical ones. Education was expensive, wasteful and corrupt, absorbing a high proportion of national income and government expenditure, but producing much less than was paid for because of over-staffing, misallocation of resources and bribery.

When the Revolutionary régime came to power at the beginning of 1959, educational expansion and reform became an integrated part of national policy for at least three major

CUBA- EDUCATION PROFILE OF TOTAL POPULATION

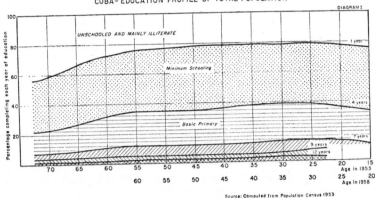

Source: Computed from Population Census 1953

reasons. First, basic education was treated as a constitutional right, to be made universally available both for its own sake and to eliminate the gross inequalities which the previous system embodied. Second, there was a large and obvious need for training skilled manpower at all levels, partly to provide for the new needs of the ambitious development programme, which in the first few years involved a major switch to industrialisation, and partly to make up for the loss of the skilled and professionally qualified persons who left for abroad as refugees. Finally, the ideological reform of education was central to the purposes of the Revolution and the remaking of Cuban society.

In most African countries, educational expansion has also been a dominant part of government policy after Independence, for several major reasons. In Middle Africa,[3] the levels of educational attainment and the proportion of children enrolled in school were among the lowest in the world. This is well illustrated by the age-education profiles of Zambia and Uganda, shown as Diagrams II and III. The need for skilled and educated manpower has been urgent and compelling and has led to large and rapidly launched programmes of secondary and higher expansion. To some degree, Africa has also lost skilled and professional personnel in the form of expatriates and ex-colonial civil servants, though these have often been replaced by new

UGANDA—EDUCATION PROFILE OF AFRICAN POPULATION
(Total Population)

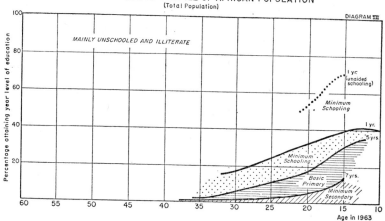

Source: Computed from annual enrollments in aided
schools and population estimates

ZAMBIA—EDUCATION PROFILE OF AFRICAN POPULATION

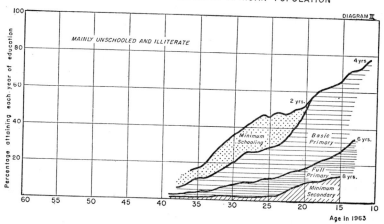

Source: Computed from annual enrollments in aided
schools and population estimates

recruits and other expatriates, provided by an aid donor, often the ex-colonial power. In addition, the right to education has also been emphasised, though in practice it has often implied the right to primary (or even secondary and higher education) for some rather than the rights of all. Common to both Cuba and most African countries have been programmes of rapid expansion of formal education. Data on the expansion of Cuban education are given in Table 1, which shows the growth of enrolments over nine years, beginning with the school year just before the Revolution.

TABLE I

Enrolments in Cuban Education for Selected Years
(thousands)

	1958/9	1962/3	1967/8
Primary	717·4	1,207·3	1,391·1
Secondary			
General	63·5	123·1	177·1
Technical and professional	15·7	42·5	46·7
Teacher training	8·9	18·5	23·3
University	25·6	22·1	35·0
Adult education	—	492·6	425·2
Other	3·7	6·8	14·9

Source: Ministerio de Educación, Cuba, *Estadísticas de la Educación*, 1965/6, p. XLIII
and *Cuba, The Educational Movement*, 1967/8, p. 189

TABLE 2

Average Growth Rates of School Enrolments in Cuba and Middle Africa for Selected Years
(annual average increases in per cent per year)

	Cuba		Middle Africa	
	1958/9-1962/3	1962/3-1967/8	1955-60	1960-65
Primary	14	3	9	6
Secondary	20	6	16	15
General	18	8	—	16
Technical	28	2	—	14
Teacher training	20	5	—	9
University	−4	10	21	20

Source: Cuba: Table 1
Middle Africa: UNESCO-OAU/CESTA/Ref. 1, mimeo (UNESCO, Paris, 16 April 1968)

Table 2 contrasts the growth rates in Cuban education with the growth rates in African education (averages for the 35 Middle African countries) over the decade, 1955-65.

In both cases, the growth rates are extremely high by world standards, higher than is typical of Asia or Latin America and very much higher than in most developed countries. Cuba, particularly during the first four years of the Revolution, and Africa over the last decade are case studies in educational expansion at exceptionally rapid rates.

Rapid quantitative expansion is only one dimension of manpower and educational strategy, and in other respects Cuban and African strategies have differed sharply. Most African countries have to date followed a fairly conventional mix of educational policies along broadly traditional lines. Cuba, in contrast, has made radical changes: radical in institutional, educational and economic terms, as well as in political ones. The rest of this paper takes as given the main outlines of expansion and concentrates on five areas of divergence: manpower strategy, adult education, institutional flexibility, rural education and educational costs. Each is important, though even taken together they are far from comprehensive.

MANPOWER STRATEGY

One of the remarkable features of the Cuban régime has been its conviction that attitudes and commitment are in the last resort more important than education and skills. This is shown most clearly by the willingness of the régime to allow well over a quarter of a million of the population to leave as refugees mainly to Miami. The enormous sacrifice of education and skills which these losses involved is indicated in Tables 3 and 4, which analyse the occupations and education of those who left during the first three and a half years, in relation to the numbers of the active labour force in Cuba during the previous census.[4]

A loss of two fifths of the country's stock of graduate manpower and nearly a fifth of its secondary educated manpower

TABLE 3

Loss of Cuban Employable Manpower from Departures of Refugees to the USA 1959-62 (Sept.) by occupations

Occupation	1952 active population	Registered refugees in US	%
Lawyers and judges	7,858	1,695	21·6
Professional and technical workers	78,051	12,124	15·5
Managerial and office workers	93,662	6,771	7·2
Clerical and sales workers	264,569	17,123	6·5
Domestic service, military and police	160,406	4,801	3·0
Skilled, semi skilled and unskilled	526,168	11,301	2·1
Agricultural and fishing	807,514	1,539	0·2
	1,938,228	55,354	2·9

Source: Fagen, R. R. and Brody, R. A., *Cubans in Exile: A Demographic Analysis of Social Problems* (Spring, 1964), pp. 391-2

is a devastating reduction. Yet the Cuban government apparently was prepared to pay this price in order not to destroy revolutionary morale among those who stayed.

In some respects this priority of attitudes over skills is exactly the reverse of that adopted in most African countries after Independence, when expatriates were retained and recruited, primarily for their skills and often with only marginal concern

TABLE 4

Loss of Cuban Employable Manpower from Departures of Refugees to the USA, 1959-63 (March) by level of education

Educational attainment	Registered refugees in USA (000's)	Estimated percentage of total stock of such manpower in Cuba
Less than 4th grade	2·3	0
4th to 11th grade	35·6	3
12th grade to 3 years' university	14·1	17
4 years of university or more	7·7	38
	59·7	2

Source: as Table 1. N.B. Estimates involve some assumptions which on balance probably tend to understate the percentage loss in the higher educational categories.

for their commitment to the new policies of an independent régime. Of course, many expatriates have been in close sympathy with the new policies and, even when not, the conflicts in attitudes and loyalties have seldom been as sharp or as personal as in the much more political situation in Cuba. But conflicts of interests do exist and the fact that they may not

TABLE 5

Percentage of Expatriates in High-Level Posts in Selected African Countries

Manpower Category†	Botswana 1967	Kenya* 1964	Nigeria 1964	Sudan 1967	Tanzania 1964/5	Zambia* 1965/6
Degree level or equivalent		77	39	12	82	96
Post school certificate, 1-3 years' formal education or training	96	25	5	6	23	92
School certificate	81	54	—	2	31	88
Middle secondary-school level	37	18	—	0	9	41
	31	48	13	3	31	62

* Refers to all non-Africans.
† Some differences exist in the categories used by different countries, but the categories quoted are broadly comparable.
Source: Manpower surveys of countries listed.

always appear acute may in part reflect the dominant influence that expatriates may have on national policy. The proportion of expatriates employed in high-level jobs in selected African countries is shown in Table 5.

In Central and Southern Africa the total proportion of expatriates is much higher than the proportions of educated persons who left Cuba. No doubt the proportion of expatriates who would be totally out of sympathy with the main government policies would be much less, though it might not be so different from the position in Cuba, particularly in the private

P   217

sector and in countries where large numbers of expatriates are still employed.

For the purposes of this paper, the question raised is whether in Africa and elsewhere education and skills have been over-emphasised at the expense of attitudes and commitment. The continuing dependence on expatriates after Independence is, at least in part, responsible for the continuation of expatriate salary scales and staffing patterns, expatriate styles of consumption and aspirations, expatriate standards of housing and so forth. All of these have profound influences both on present society and on the pattern of a country's long-run development. And their long-run cost needs to be weighed against the short-run gains in skills and education.

One example may make clearer the economic issues, quite apart from the political and social ones which may be more obvious. In Zambia, in 1965-6, over 30,000 expatriates were employed in jobs, from sales assistants and engine drivers to senior civil servants and mining executives. At the top, 3,500 of the 3,650 graduate-level jobs, 96 per cent, were held by expatriates. Average non-African earnings were £2,250 per year, average African earnings were £214.[5] Socially, culturally, politically the majority of expatriates lived in a world of their own, far removed from that of most urban Zambians let alone the majority of Zambians in rural areas. It is usually accepted that this is part of the price one must pay for skilled manpower. But do the costs always justify the benefits?

Lest one depreciate too readily the importance of skills and education, it is well to emphasise the costs of the alternative strategy even to Cuba, which had initially a far greater stock of qualified manpower than any African country. (Much of this was under-employed or employed in activities to which the Revolutionary régime gave little priority, such as private legal practice). But even with this favourable starting-point, the losses of skilled manpower have created severe administrative and production problems, to which at least some of Cuba's present economic problems must be attributed. Moreover, even now in many African countries weaknesses in public administration due to inadequate levels of experience or education or training are undoubtedly responsible for considerable economic inefficiency.

Of course, one needs much harder evidence to make a balanced assessment in this complex field. But there is some evidence to suggest that in the private sector in many African countries, skills and education have and are still being over-emphasised at the expense of attitudes and commitment, certainly when judged by national interests and possibly in some cases when judged by the long-run interests of the private sector itself.[6] As regards the public sector, where localisation policies have already sacrificed some of the formal educational and skill standards, a general judgment is more difficult. No doubt there are places in most administrations where skill and educational standards are still unnecessarily high, though there are other places where standards are too low for efficiency. But the real issue is whether the whole strategy is right. In much of Africa for a few more years, the present strategy is probably inescapable, given the extreme shortage of top-level manpower particularly in countries of Eastern and Central Africa. But fairly soon, when the number of local persons with education, skills and experience increases, the strategy will need to be re-assessed in terms of its wider consequences and not only in terms of the apparent needs for skilled and educated personnel.

ADULT EDUCATION

The loss of so much of Cuba's high-level manpower was compounded by the additional manpower requirements of her ambitious development plans. Although Cuba made no systematic projections of long-run manpower requirements, the need for education, formal and informal, for the labour force was accepted from the beginning. So was the need for education at primary levels especially outside Havana—for its own sake, to right the imbalance between the urban and rural areas and also to instil a revolutionary ideology.

Even within the school system it could well be argued that

attitudes were given priority over high-level skills, at least in the sense that primary, secondary and adult education were given priority over university education: university students were widely used as emergency teachers for literacy and primary teaching, often on the promise that they would resume their studies after a year or two. University enrolments during the first five years of the revolution were several thousands below their pre-revolutionary average, though no doubt this also reflected the emigration of some university students and a good number of former university staff.

The priorities of educational expansion are well illustrated by the events of 1961, the 'Year of Education'. In that year, almost all schools were closed down for eight months, and the educational resources of the nation channelled into a single literacy campaign.[7] Many students and most of the teachers formed into an army to wage war against illiteracy. More than 125,000 students and teachers were involved, mostly in the rural areas, with about the same number teaching in the urban areas. Nearly a million adults were enrolled in study, of whom, it was claimed, 707,000 learned to read and to write. Here again, Cuban education was directed towards attitudes at the cost of higher education directed towards skills.

This interpretation must not be over stressed, however, since these priorities for educational expansion were also in part the result of stressing short-run ahead of long-run benefits. This is hardly surprising in view of the losses of skilled persons described earlier, which must have given an unprecedented urgency to short-term training programmes. Again one wonders whether the luke-warm efforts towards accelerated training in Africa, particularly in the private sector, and in spite of endless recommendations by missions and committees, is not primarily the result of a fundamental lack of urgency or conflicts of interest in getting them underway rather than of the technical difficulties or costs in organising such training in Africa.

In Cuba, the programmes for continuing adult education have been vast and impressive. Since the literacy campaign between four and eight hundred thousand adults have enrolled each year in evening classes, mostly in programmes designed to consolidate the initial acquisition of literacy and to raise the educational standards of worker and peasant to the equivalent of sixth grade. These enrolments mean that in each of the last eight years between 10 and 20 per cent of the Cuban adult population have been involved in formal programmes of adult education.

Although the literacy and follow-up programmes have used work-related teaching materials, specialised programmes were started in factories to improve work performance and to give workers a better understanding of how their industrial tasks related to the operation of the factory as a whole. These classes met on the shop floor, led by someone from the factory. At an early stage they enrolled about 72,000. In addition, specific training programmes catered for persons in occupations which the revolution had made redundant, notably domestic servants.

Adult classes have relied heavily upon the formal school system to provide teachers and upon schools, factories, shops, even garages, to provide space for classrooms. Even in the early days such improvisation may not have been always necessary, since ordinary school buildings were generally available in the evenings. But improvisation may have provided effective propaganda: education clearly became the concern of all, integrated into the daily life of the community in a very wide variety of places.

The contrast with African programmes of adult education is enormous both in scale and approach. Formal adult education in Africa is still on a minute scale in comparison with school education. Literacy campaigns in a few countries have involved large numbers for short periods, but with nothing like the proportion of sustained enrolments as in Cuba. If one includes the many types of rural extension programmes, particularly for agriculture, the proportion of population covered in some way is much larger, but the service provided is often patchy and irregular.

Yet a glance at the age-education profiles for Uganda and Zambia reveals the large proportion of the adult population who are illiterate or have only minimum levels of schooling. Without adult education this will remain the position for 20 or 30 years after universal primary education is achieved. Adult education is usually cheap. Moreover the impact of adult education on work performance will affect the labour force immediately and not, as with most school education, only after some years when the student has started work. Lower costs and the difference in the timing of benefits give an edge to adult education as an investment which may often be enough to compensate for its several inefficiencies in other respects in comparison with school education, providing the content and organisation is effective.

INSTITUTIONAL FLEXIBILITY

As noted earlier, the speed of educational expansion after 1959 in Cuba was extremely fast, but not, in fact, faster than many African countries have achieved after Independence or just before. What distinguishes Cuba is the flexibility within the system as it expanded, which enabled it to avoid many of the temporary distortions of very rapid expansion.

The best example is the introduction of special acceleration classes within the normal school system to even out the 'bulges' resulting from the enormous expansion of intake and the sudden increases in the promotion rates at crucial points of the system. In most African countries, the expanded intake of students follows a normal progression up the system, often overloading the classes carrying the swollen enrolments but leaving classes further up the system under-enrolled, ahead of the time when sufficient students will be qualified to join them. In Cuba, special 'acceleration' classes were introduced in many schools, which enabled certain students to cover two years' work in one, thus achieving double promotion at the end of the year, though probably at the expense of a drop in standards. This method did, however, go some way to avoiding under-used facilities, thus expanding total enrolments and spreading the load more evenly throughout the system.

At the secondary and higher levels in Anglophone Africa quality has generally been put before expansion of enrolments and has prevented a more flexible approach. Universities have often continued for several years with spare capacity, small classes, and light work loads, while the members with Grade I certificates from upper secondary schools have built up to that required to fill the university places. In some cases the spare capacity in universities has been used for postgraduate teacher training for prospective teachers from developed countries, thereby providing teachers for the secondary schools, but at the cost of not using the facilities for educating local persons. Since most of the overseas teachers only complete one or two years on contract, most of the social benefit of their training will probably accrue to the developed countries where they will spend the bulk of their teaching life.

Again this is not a simple choice, for the question of standards raises wide and difficult issues on which evidence is scarce. And to some extent it is now too late, since in most countries in Africa the period of spare educational capacity has largely passed. But with a further period of sudden educational expansion, the need for flexibility will return.

RURAL EDUCATION

Perhaps the most impressive part of Cuban development strategy has been its success in shifting emphasis from the urban to the rural areas. This has been done with a wide variety of economic measures involving agricultural projects, housing schemes, health programmes, the distribution of the labour force and differential food rationing. That the balance has been shifted is indicated, at least in part, by the very gradual decline since 1962 in the proportion of total population living in the capital, a great contrast to the situation in most developing countries.

In education, the rural emphasis has been pressed with a number of major programmes, some of which are worth listing briefly to indicate the approach. First, there has been a major programme for building new primary schools, most of which are in the rural areas, not the towns. In Oriente, the most remote of Cuba's six provinces and the one with the most scattered population, a 'school city' was set up to provide boarding accommodation for students from the less accessible areas. In addition, several teachers' centres were built, where teachers from the isolated schools in the mountains could go for a weekend of relaxation, discussion and instruction every two weeks. The plan was for the centre to be run in conjunction with a national programme of correspondence courses for teachers, designed so they could continue their own studies, often with the aim of achieving university entrance, as well as to improve their teaching ability. These and other such programmes have been designed to strengthen the interest and incentives of teachers to work in the rural areas and to maintain their enthusiasm and spirit when they are in post.

In addition, the system of primary teacher training was changed, so as to put the emphasis from the beginning on commitment to work in the rural areas. For many students, the first year of primary teacher training takes place in the Minas del Frio mountain school, where the emphasis is on tough rural living near the Sierra Maestra, where Castro first fought the guerrilla battles which brought him to power. Though the second and third years of teacher training are run on more conventional lines, the first year is primarily designed to win dedication to the Revolution and to produce teachers hardened to difficult conditions and willing to accept assignments anywhere in Cuba's many rural schools.

Special training has been provided to put across teaching methods suitable for the one teacher school (children of many grades in a single classroom) which with the rural emphasis still forms an important fraction of all primary schools, particularly in the places of low population density. This training has been provided in the form of upgrading courses for serving teachers during the summer vacations. As a reward for their diligence throughout the year, the part-time summer courses were held at Varadero, a leading tourist resort where the lavish hotel facilities were used to provide accommodation at subsidised rates for teachers and their families.

Among school students rural values have been strengthened in a number of ways. The literacy campaign was important in this respect, since for many urban students it was their first close experience of rural life. All but an eighth of the *brigadista* teaching force came from urban areas and most of them were given rural assignments. Each student taught one illiterate, lived with his family, sleeping in a hammock and working on his farm. By such means the whole campaign acted as a bridge between the rural and urban worlds and made a deep impression on many who took part.

Since the literacy campaign, several innovations have been adopted in the rural areas. One of the latest approaches is the 'school to the countryside' plan, in which a whole school, with its teachers, students, employees and equipment, moves to the countryside where it encamps on a farm. For a month and a half studies continue but in combination with work on the farm.[8]

EDUCATIONAL COSTS

Cuba, like most countries of the world, has increased substantially the proportion of her national income spent on education. Expenditure rose dramatically from $79 million in the year before the Revolution to $276 million in 1962-3, an average increase of 37 per cent per year in current prices.[9] In 1966 total expenditure on education represented 7 per cent of gross domestic product.[10] These increases may be compared with those of average public expenditure on education in the nine middle African countries for which data are available. Educational expenditure in middle Africa rose by 16 per cent per year from 1960 to 1965, an increase of from 3·0 per cent of GDP to 4·2 per cent.[11]

Expenditure is however a misleading indicator of the real economic cost of education. In the first place, the largest item in economic cost is not included in the educational budget, namely the opportunity cost of the students' time, which at higher levels of education often forms more than half the full economic costs. Secondly, because teacher salaries are the dominant financial item, unit costs (education expenditures per pupil) often indicate little more than the size of the pupil/teacher ratio and the level of teachers' salaries. Since, moreover, in under-developed countries the labour market often works very imperfectly, and teachers' salaries are usually fixed by government in accordance with national scales, educational expenditure has even less significance as a measure of education's opportunity cost. Cost must be judged by direct reference to the real resources used.

In this respect, it is extremely significant that Cuba, from a situation of widespread unemployment and under-employment before the Revolution, even during the peak employment periods of the sugar harvest, moved fairly soon afterwards to a situation of full employment and labour scarcity. Full employment, coupled with the depleted supplies of high level manpower, has increased in effect the opportunity costs of the manpower used in education and thus the costs of the whole educational programme. Manpower in this situation becomes an important constraint to educational expansion.

In Africa, shortage of finance is often *treated* as the constraint to further educational expansion particularly at primary level. Yet it is just this level where persons with the education required to be primary teachers are unemployed. When this is so, the financial signals are misleading. Education appears costly, whereas in fact the resources required are available and unused.

In Cuba, the financial constraint does not operate because plans are made in terms of full employment of the major real resources, particularly labour, and government in effect simply provides whatever finance is needed to achieve this.

Two further aspects of the Cuban approach deserve special mention. First, planning in real resources for education has involved a shift of resources from outside to within the educational system. Printing presses, used before the Revolution for monthly magazines, have been used for producing textbooks and teaching materials, often to the same format of the previous glossies. The houses of refugees, which by law are surrendered to the government on their leaving the country, were taken over as boarding accommodation for scholarship students. The local police stations of the previous regime were turned into schools, including the headquarters in Havana which became the Ministry of Education and housed in addition major schools facilities enrolling several thousand students. This very flexible use of real resources was, of course, made possible by the widespread powers of the régime, but they have been exercised in education with a good deal of imagination.

The second aspect concerns the measurement of opportunity costs, which are no less important with the removal of the financial constraint. For manpower, opportunity cost is defined in terms of the alternative work they would do if they were not in education, full or part-time. It is possible to compute, if only roughly, various totals of the time spent by persons on education, often in the evening after work. Yet to measure the opportunity costs of the time and effort involves specifying the alternatives. This is exceptionally difficult when the alternatives are not individual alternatives within some given social system but rather alternative national policies for the *whole* system.

For African education, the questions raised by the Cuban approach are fundamental. Has too much attention been paid to the financial constraints and too little to the real resources required in education? The scope for adopting Cuba's policies towards housing and printing are probably very limited, though there might in time be some possibilities if one was prepared to use some of the larger civil service houses. But the main possibilities lie in the area of manpower. Given inflexible wage structures and limited revenues, finance can act as a real constraint, even though the real resources required are unemployed. The alternative is some revision of the wage, price or revenue structure. This no doubt is difficult but it is failure to deal with this which makes possible the educational equivalent of poverty amidst plenty: the apparent financial impossibility of expanding education any further in spite of the existence of eager students and unemployed teachers (or potential teachers, even if with low qualifications).

CONCLUSION

This paper has been largely descriptive, drawing comparisons and raising questions but not attempting to answer them. In respect of the five contrasts raised, Cuban strategy has in many ways been radical and successful. Why does Cuba seem to be succeeding in educational areas where so many other countries have failed? This is well beyond this paper but three points can be made. First, success needs to be carefully defined; success as judged by the internal norms of an educational system may be a failure by other tests, political, social or economic. Second, economically success must take into account costs as well as benefits—and Cuban education has been very costly, even allowing for the advantages of a rich but stagnant economy which to a large extent could bring into use resources and facilities otherwise under-employed. Third, Cuban educational policy and reforms have been part of major changes. and reforms throughout the whole society, part in fact of a revolution. Some of the educational policies discussed in this paper could without doubt be introduced without a revolution, but could they all? A major conclusion of Cuban experience is that if educational reform is to succeed, it must be made part of more fundamental changes in the whole society.

NOTES AND REFERENCES

1 This paper draws heavily on my earlier study of Cuban education, published as chapters 4 to 8 of Seers, D. (ed.), *Cuba: the economic and social revolution* (University of North Carolina Press, 1964). Unless otherwise noted, further details and sources of data for the points made in this paper will be found in chapters 4 to 8 (for education points) and chapter 1 (for the economy).
2 Seers, op. cit., chapter 1.
3 Middle Africa is a UNESCO concept, comprising 35 countries, broadly Africa less North Africa and South Africa.

4 The census data refers to a period seven years before the start of the emigration data, and the two cannot, therefore, be strictly compared without adjustments. But the order of magnitude of the percentages in Tables 3 and 4 is broadly correct.

5 Data from the Government of Zambia *Manpower Report* (Government Printer, Lusaka, 1966).

6 See for instance the various African manpower reports and particular reports on localisation in the private sector.

7 A report of the literacy campaign has been published by UNESCO. A detailed description is given in chapter 6 of Seers, op. cit.

8 Reported in Ministry of Education, *Cuba; the educational movement, 1967/8* (Havana).

9 General consumer prices rose by perhaps 10 per cent over this period (ignoring quality changes on which information is not available). This would reduce the increase in constant prices to about 34 per cent per annum (Seers, op. cit., pp. 33-4).

10 *The Economist*, 15 March 1969, p. 40.

11 UNESCO-OAU/CESTA/Ref. 1 of 16 April 1968, mimeo (UNESCO, Paris).

CHAPTER II

EDUCATION IN THE USSR: THE RELEVANCE OF THE SOVIET EXPERIENCE

NIGEL GRANT

Like any other, the Soviet educational system is the product of circumstances peculiar to its own society; it is not, therefore, appropriate to treat it as a blueprint for any other. In the Eastern European countries, the large-scale educational reforms carried out by the post-war communist régimes drew heavily on Soviet experience. In some respects this was reasonable enough, but the widespread tendency to adopt some Soviet practices uncritically had some unfortunate results, and it is noteworthy that adaptation to local realities has been on the increase during the last decade throughout the Eastern *bloc*—a process which the reassertion of Soviet control highlighted by the 1968 intervention in Czechoslovakia has, so far, not greatly altered. In the even more widely different conditions of the developing countries, copying Soviet practice would be even less appropriate. Nevertheless, Soviet experience cannot be dismissed as totally irrelevant; like many of the developing countries today, the USSR was faced at its birth with the need to develop in a hurry, in education as in much else, and many of the problems that have arisen in the past half-century have their counterparts in the Third World now. The attempts to deal with these— the failures no less than the successes—may prove of some use to other countries trying to make up lost ground in education, depending on it for economic and social advancement, and having to do it with severely limited resources.

The most obvious general characteristic that Imperial Russia shared with the present-day developing countries was educational backwardness. Russia was left relatively unaffected by the educational upsurge in the West in the late nineteenth and

The Soviet School System

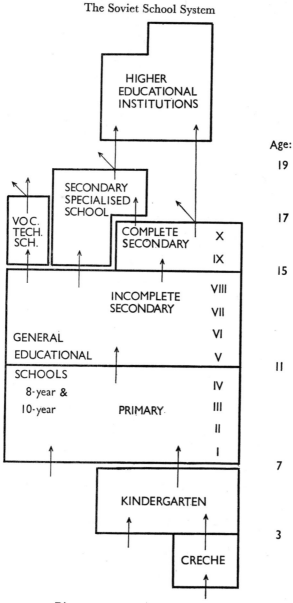

Age:

19

17

15

11

7

3

Direct arrows = into further courses
Oblique arrows = into employment

early twentieth centuries. It is perfectly true, of course, that European Russia was rather better off; at its best, Russian schooling, especially in the major towns, compared tolerably well with that in most of Western Europe.[1] On the whole, this area lagged behind the rest of Europe at that time, but was far ahead of present-day Asia and Africa. But European Russia was not the whole country; it was in the rest—the Caucasus, Siberia, the Far East, Central Asia—that resemblances to the Third World were most marked. The literacy figures give a reasonable indication of the discrepancies throughout the country. In 1914, about 32 per cent of the population were reckoned literate. In European Russia, naturally, the proportion was higher (about 40 per cent), and in the non-European areas it was much lower. In the Caucasus, Georgia, with its long-established literary tradition, came out fairly well, with 20 per cent literate, but in Central Asia, Uzbekistan had only 2 per cent literate, Turkmenia 0·7 per cent, Tadzhikistan 0·5 per cent, while Kirgizia had no written language at all. The peoples of the Far North and Far East were in similar case.

These figures have to be treated with some caution. For one thing, they appear to have been based on the writings of Tsarist Russian authors who sought to justify the annexation of these areas, and who had an obvious interest in keeping the figures as low as possible. When all due allowance is made, however, there is still no question about the low level of literacy in those territories. More seriously, it can be objected that the figures for numbers of schools, pupils and teachers (which present an equally dismal picture) are misleading, since they deal with Russian schools only, taking no account of the traditional Muslim educational establishments.

This is a fair point, but it does raise the question of the quality of the education offered in these schools. In Uzbekistan, for example, an American team has summed up the position thus:

Almost all the schools were in the cities and towns, and were attended mainly by Tajiks. Conducted entirely by the clergy, they served only to prepare boys for professional careers. About 15-20 per cent of the male population in the towns are thought to have attended the primary school, called the *maktab*. They entered when they were about eight, and in their eight years there they learned to read a little by listening to their teacher chant and then chanting in their turn, while looking at often unintelligible religious texts. . . . This rote learning gave them little understanding of what they read, much less the ability to read other writings. The advanced school, the *madrasa*, offered studies in religion, jurisprudence, philosophy . . . and literature. Impressive though this curriculum may sound, the treatment was superficial, and much of legend, local lore and misinformation about the rest of the world found its way in. But a young man who had completed the nine-year programme was considered ready for a career in the clergy, the law, teaching, literature or administration.[2]

It seems fair to conclude that a school system such as this may have mitigated the educational backwardness of the Central Asian territories only marginally; the tribal peoples further north and east, of course, lacked even this kind of provision. Generally, the non-Russian areas of the Empire were fairly typical of educationally under-developed countries.

As is well known, the circumstances under which the USSR came into being made things considerably worse. The October Revolution itself was a relatively bloodless affair, but the civil and interventionist wars which followed were not. The effects of full-scale warfare over most of the country were incalculable in terms of loss of life and destruction of property. Certainly, the political instability, the terror and counter-terror, the large-scale emigration of professional people, and the economic collapse—at one point, postage stamps bore no denomination because of the speed of inflation—hardly provided a favourable atmosphere for long-term activities such as educational planning or investment. Even by 1926, 42 per cent of the population in European Russia were still illiterate, and in the Asian areas the position was almost as bad as before the Revolution—in Azerbaidzhan, for instance, 75 per cent were still illiterate.[3]

Long after the fighting had ended, political upheavals went on—the New Economic Policy, the collectivisation of agriculture, the two Five-Year Plans and the general tightening-up of Stalin's rule—right up to the greater trauma of the Second

Q   233

World War. While not attempting in any way to minimise the social and human cost of industrial development in this period, one must recognise the substantial advances in the educational sphere. Stalin, of course, was no devotee of enlightenment, but he knew as well as anyone else that the economic and industrial modernisation of the country required not only top-level specialists such as scientists, engineers, agronomists, technologists, etc., but a much larger supporting force of technicians and other skilled personnel, whose availability depended in turn on a high level of literacy and general education. To put it more crudely, it is perfectly possible (and historically common) to run an agricultural economy with an illiterate population, but an industrial economy requires a much higher standard of education at all levels. In these terms, the policy was beginning to show results; by 1939, 81 per cent of the entire population were literate, and even in Uzbekistan the figure was over 78 per cent.[4]

But the Second World War set things back once more. The German armies penetrated as far as the outskirts of Leningrad, almost to Moscow, and reached the Volga and the Caucasus before being halted. In the occupied areas, the invaders behaved with the special savagery reserved for operations in Slav countries, exacerbated by partisan warfare behind the lines and a tidal movement of attack and counter-attack over much of the richest land in the Soviet Union. The losses in life and property were hideous; the Byelorussian SSR, for example, suffered the loss of half its population and nearly all of its capital city of Minsk. Estimates of the total number of casualties are still a matter for dispute, but have been put as high as 30 millions, plus the loss of 10 millions in the birth-rate[5]; apart from anything else, this was to have important effects in the 1950's on manpower supply and hence on educational policy.[6] In immediate educational terms, some 82,000 schools were destroyed, a loss of 15 million school places.

Although many of the developing countries have suffered similar upheavals, few have been on anything approaching this scale. They are worth mentioning, however, if only to put educational developments in perspective. The advances made in the USSR are, in many ways, remarkable enough even in fifty-odd years; the civil war and the 'Great Patriotic War', although lasting for only three and four years respectively, inflicted enormous damage on the country, enough to ensure that the *effective* time for educational development was much less than the half-century since the Revolution. (See Table 1.[7])

TABLE I

The Growth of the Educational System: Pupils and Students by Type of Course, in thousands, 1914-69

	1914/15	1940/1	1950/1	1960/1	1966/7	1967/8	1968/9
Elementary, complete and incomplete secondary schools	9,656	34,784	33,314	33,417	43,529	44,451	45,077
Schools for working and rural youth, adult schools, etc.	—	768	1,438	2,770	4,641	4,451	4,118
Total general schools	9,656	35,552	34,752	36,187	48,170	48,902	49,195
Vocational-technical schools	106	717	882	1,113	1,961	2,129	2,263
Secondary specialised schools	54	975	1,298	2,060	3,994	4,167	4,262
Higher education	127	812	1,247	2,396	4,123	4,311	4,470
Further education, etc.	645	9,491	10,591	10,909	15,341	16,516	17,336
Total:	10,588	47,547	48,770	52,665	73,589	76,025	77,526

Of the problems that have arisen in the Soviet context which are relevant to the developing countries, the most important would appear to be the following:

(1) Language problems in education
(2) Literacy
(3) The position of women and girls in education
(4) Education in remote and rural areas
(5) Education for work
(6) The role of science and technology
(7) Socio-political education

(1) LANGUAGE PROBLEMS IN EDUCATION

This issue is dealt with elsewhere in the present volume; see above, pp. 185-189.

(2) LITERACY

There is general agreement that the 'liquidation of illiteracy' has been one of the major successes of the Soviet system. We have already seen the advance from the low level of 1914 to an average of 81 per cent literate by 1939. By the 1950's the Soviet authorities were claiming that literacy was virtually universal in the country as a whole, and that even in such places as Uzbekistan it was well over 90 per cent. Once again, some caution has to be exercised. Soviet officials usually claim that the test of literacy is to be able 'to read easily *Pravda* and *Izvestiya*'.[8] Anyone at all familiar with those newspapers, which are not exactly brilliant in typographical lay-out or vivid in style, may feel somewhat sceptical about this. As is so often the case, it is very difficult to check; the American observer, George Counts, estimates illiteracy as between 5 and 10 per cent.[9] There are probably some old people still completely illiterate, and others who must be reckoned functionally illiterate, especially by the rather daunting standards officially insisted upon. But whatever the niceties, there is little doubt about the main point; illiteracy is now extremely rare in the Soviet Union, and, in the circumstances, the odd doubtful 5 per cent is of relatively little consequence. Most developing countries would be delighted with a level of illiteracy much higher than Counts' figure. For all practical purposes, the country with a pre-revolutionary illiteracy rate of nearly 70 per cent is now a literate nation.

It is questionable, however, that the methods used to achieve this are quite relevant to the position in the developing countries. Many of these have been rather disappointed with the results of adult literacy campaigns, which proved so successful in the USSR in the 1920's. Two factors, however, made a considerable difference in the Soviet case. Firstly, these campaigns were conducted in a revolutionary situation, which not only provided a favourable social atmosphere but made it possible to mobilise the necessary resources, personal and material; this is not the case in most of the developing countries at present.

Secondly, the drive for literacy was part of a full-scale overhaul of society, changing not only the social and political structure but the occupational patterns as well; people had to be able to read in order to be accessible to propaganda by newspaper, poster and pamphlet and, in increasing numbers, in order to do their jobs effectively. Thus the attack on illiteracy was accompanied by a vast increase in the supply of reading matter, in a situation where literacy was becoming for more people not merely available but necessary for many aspects of their daily lives. Literacy is achieved, it seems, not merely by teaching people to read and write but by keeping them at it; this is not the case in most of the developing countries either. This should change with the development of industrial economies; meanwhile, there is little evidence from the Soviet experience that literacy campaigns can, of themselves, solve the problem—they have to be part of a wider and more complex process that *demands* literacy as well as *offering* it.

(3) WOMEN AND GIRLS IN EDUCATION

According to the Constitution, women have equal rights with men in every aspect of life, education included.[10] Constitutional provisions are, notoriously, often more a matter of rhetoric than effective guarantees of anything; but even if they are taken at face value, there remain difficulties of policy as well as practice. How far, for instance, should the differences between the sexes determine the course of their education? Does the principle of equality require the *same* or 'separate but equal' schooling? Soviet policy has switched twice on this issue. In the post-revolutionary period, naturally, segregation of the sexes was too closely associated with the discriminatory ways of the old regime, and was accordingly abolished. In Stalin's time, however, especially during the 1940's, many features of the Tsarist régime came back into favour, from military epaulettes and examination marking-schemes to broader issues like foreign policy. Single-sex education was one of these; after some rather perfunctory press discussion, segregation was re-introduced in the schools in 1943. In fact, this decision was implemented only in the towns; things were difficult enough in the countryside (of which more later) without making matters worse by trying to run two parallel school systems. In 1953, after more press discussion, the decision was reversed and co-education re-introduced. This is the position at present throughout the system, including the boarding schools.[11]

It would be unrealistic to claim that girls and women now enjoy complete equality in education; there is still, as elsewhere, a preponderance of men in senior positions. In the teaching profession, for instance, women make up 71 per cent of the total —87 per cent of the primary and 75 per cent of the secondary teachers. Yet in spite of this overwhelming female domination of the profession, it is not reflected in the numbers holding senior posts. Only primary school headships go mainly to women (78 per cent in 1968/9); the proportion of women holding headships of eight-year and complete secondary schools is only 26 and 23 per cent respectively.[12] They do rather better with deputy headships, but still not in proportion to their numbers in the teaching force at large. They are still, of course, a good deal better placed than their counterparts in many other countries, and the position has improved very slightly over the past few years, but it is clear that equality of opportunity is not yet complete.

On the other hand, note must be taken of the extent to which women pursue higher education and other post-secondary courses. At university and college level, they make up 47 per cent of the total number of students. In some fields, notably education, they are in the majority. This is far from unusual; more unexpectedly, they are in a majority in medicine, and make up over a third of the total in engineering and allied subjects, a field commonly regarded in many other countries as a masculine preserve. In secondary specialised institutions (schools providing 3-4 year courses for 15-year-olds or two-year courses for those who have completed secondary school), an over-all majority of the students are now women—overwhelmingly so in medical courses (for nurses and medical assistants), economics and law, and teaching; more noteworthy, perhaps, is the high proportion of women students in engineering and agriculture. (For details, see Table 2.[13]) Secondary specialised courses are of a lower standard than those in higher institutions, and the fact that women are in a majority at this level and a minority at the higher level does suggest, once again, that their

TABLE 2

Women in Higher and Secondary Specialised Education: Percentage of Total Number of Students, 1960-9

	1960/1	1966/7	1967/8	1968/9
Higher education of whom:	43	45	46	47
engineering, construction, transport	30	32	34	35
agriculture	27	26	27	27
economics and law	49	57	58	59
medicine, P.E., sport	56	55	54	55
education and art	63	65	65	65
Secondary specialised education of whom:	47	51	52	54
engineering, construction, transport	33	37	39	41
agriculture	38	35	35	36
economics and law	75	81	81	83
medicine, P.E., sport	84	88	88	88
education and art	76	81	81	81

position falls short of complete equality. But only just; they make up about half of the entire student body, and if they are disproportionately concentrated at the lower levels, this is only to a slight degree—their representation at the upper levels remains, by international standards, high.

Much of this, of course, is a logical outcome of the general assumption that everyone must work, married women and mothers not excepted. There is considerable social pressure; the widespread system of creches, kindergartens and maternity leave on full pay make it more feasible; and in any case the structure of wages and salaries appears to be based on the assumption that *both* parents in any family are employed. It would be an over-statement to say that conflict between marriage and a career never arises; there are difficulties, especially in view of the widespread reluctance of Soviet husbands to take on a share of domestic tasks, a matter of common complaint in the press. But these are annoyances rather than severe obstacles; the fact remains that women are expected to work and study on the same footing as their menfolk, and to a considerable extent that is what they manage to do. Nor can this be attributed to the heady atmosphere of a revolutionary situation; there is ample and growing evidence that the revolutionary dynamic of Soviet society has long since run out of steam. But the position of women, and their participation in advanced education, continues to improve; in the last decade, the proportion of women in secondary specialised and higher education has shown a slight but definite increase.

(4) EDUCATION IN REMOTE AND RURAL AREAS

One of the most intractable of Soviet educational problems lies in the countryside. The population pattern of the USSR is now more like that of the western than the developing countries; after decades of industrialisation, just over half now live in towns. The Soviet Union, with its strong industrial base, is in a much better position than the developing countries to deal with the problems of rural education, and indeed there have been considerable advances, even in the remoter parts. But there is still a long way to go before children in the countryside have anything like as good a chance as those in the towns. For all the official pronouncements about equality for all children, there are in practice wide discrepancies in the accessibility of schooling standards of teaching and attainment, and opportunities for further study. Many factors affect a child's educational chances, but the greatest single division between haves and have nots is between town and country.

The supply of teachers is one indication of this. Over the country as a whole, dilution is still something of a problem. All teachers of classes v (age 11) and over are supposed to hold higher educational qualifications, either from university or college; actually 71 per cent do. (Of the remainder, 18·2 per cent have qualifications now obsolete, which still leaves 10·8 per cent seriously under-qualified, though it is worth pointing out that this is a substantial improvement even on the 1965 position.)[14] But in many rural areas the position is a good deal worse than this; in the Omsk *oblast'*, for instance, only 35 per cent of the teachers had the requisite qualifications in 1967, while in many of the remote areas the proportion was lower still.[15] Even the under-qualified teachers are in shorter supply in the countryside in general and in the remote areas in particular.

Other shortages, such as building materials and school equipment, add to the difficulties; since they are generally due to faulty distribution rather than absolute shortage, the rural areas inevitably come off worse. The existence of a large number of small scattered schools makes it even harder to maintain standards; even if the staff can be found for them, one teacher may have to profess an unrealistically wide range of subjects. There are exceptions, but on the whole there is general agreement that standards of instruction are lower in the countryside. So, unsurprisingly, are the levels of aspiration. The 1966 plans for numbers of pupils going on to the ninth form (at the end of the compulsory eight-year school) were not met in the predominantly rural areas. In the Karelian and Udmurt republics, and in the Perm and Volgograd *oblasti*, for example, just over half the eighth-form leavers went on to the ninth,[16] while in the Yaroslavl and Vladimir *oblasti* the figure was not much over a quarter.[17] (By way of comparison, the national average in the same year was 64 per cent.) Even in 1969, when the *total* number of pupils was nearly equal (22·7 million in towns, 22·4 million in the country) the discrepancies were still obvious; while rural children outnumbered urban children by nearly a million in the primary classes, the position was reversed at the later stages—2·6 million in classes IX-XI in urban schools as against 1·9 million in rural schools.[18] (For details, see Table 3.) Not all of this is attributed to lack of facilities; there have been reports that the pessimism of the teachers produces indifference among the pupils, which in turn convinces the teachers that their task is hopeless and that 'the children just don't want to learn'[19]—a vicious circle to which many rural areas are especially prone.

Attempts have been made to deal with this by (among other things) putting pressure on more teachers to work in rural areas. Salary differentials favouring urban teachers were abolished in 1964, with little apparent effect. The local authorities in the countryside are supposed to provide teachers with free

TABLE 3

The Rural Problem: Pupils at Different Levels of General School in Urban and Rural Areas, in millions, 1940-69

	1940/1	1950/1	1960/1	1966/7	1967/8	1968/9
Total pupils in general schools	34·8	33·3	33·4	43·5	44·5	45·1
of whom:						
urban	10·8	11·8	16·1	21·8	22·4	22·7
rural	24·0	21·5	17·3	21·7	22·1	22·4
Pupils in classes I-IV	21·4	19·7	18·6	20·5	20·9	21·1
of whom:						
urban	5·4	6·8	8·4	9·7	9·9	10·1
rural	16·0	13·5	10·8	10·8	11·0	11·0
Pupils in classes V-VIII	11·9	12·8	13·2	18·5	18·9	19·2
of whom:						
urban	4·6	5·1	6·7	9·4	9·7	9·8
rural	7·3	7·7	6·5	9·1	9·2	9·4
Pupils in classes IX-XI	1·2	0·7	1·5	4·2	4·4	4·5
of whom:						
urban	0·7	0·4	0·9	2·5	2·6	2·6
rural	0·5	0·3	0·6	1·7	1·8	1·9

housing, heat and light, and a plot of land for their own use; but none of this seems to compensate for being cut off from the amenities of city life, and in any case there are frequent complaints that these requirements are inadequately met.[20] There is a system of extra payments for remote areas, whereby one can add 50 per cent to one's salary by working in such places as Kamchatka or the Far North, but this also seems relatively ineffective.

When all else fails, the authorities may use their powers to direct graduates anywhere in the country for up to three years. But there are ways of avoiding this, and the system of assignment, which gives graduates at the top of the pass list first choice of available jobs, ensures that the rural schools get the more mediocre graduates. Further, not all of those who go where they are sent stay for the full term of three years, and even those who do complete their term move back to town as soon as possible afterwards. All this makes it inevitable that even when the schools can be staffed with qualified teachers, the rural ones have to make do with the least able *and* put up with an unhealthily high turnover rate. The effects on standards and morale are clear enough; and in view of the failure even of coercive powers to deal with the problem, one can only assume that it will remain until living standards and amenities in the villages can be raised to something nearer the level enjoyed by the towns—an economic rather than an educational problem.

The trouble is partly geographical; the sheer size of the country, and the distribution of population outside the main urban centres, put formidable obstacles in the way of providing as wide a range of courses in the country as in the town schools. The amalgamation of small schools into larger units can help, of course, and there have been moves to use boarding schools— until recently mainly urban institutions—for this purpose.[21] Unfortunately, this is an extremely expensive solution; apart from the high capital outlay, a place in a boarding school costs over seven times as much to maintain as one in a day school.[22] With over 22 million pupils in rural schools, it is hardly conceivable that the country could afford to provide boarding education for even a majority of them, let alone all. It is, however, intended that boarding schools will be used to alleviate the problem to some extent, and a start has been made.

The size of the country also makes it difficult to enforce decisions far from the main centres. Formally, the central authorities are in a position to control almost everything that happens throughout the system right down to classroom level, but in practice their effectiveness is limited by difficulties of communication, under-staffing in the inspectorate, and a good deal of bureaucratic muddle. Sometimes little harm is done; indeed, this situation can sometimes make room in the system for rather more flexibility than the machinery would seem to allow. More usually, however, the effects seem to be negative. Even eight-year schooling, made officially compulsory in 1958, is still not fully effective in some areas, and although the recent description of this as 'one of the most important state problems'[23] may be rather over-drawn, it is true that there is some leakage from the system at about the age of 14.[24] Again, there are instances of school buildings, recorded as complete in the official returns, having to function for some time without adequate lighting, plumbing or equipment because of bottlenecks in supplies.[25] Distance also makes it more difficult to improve teaching methods; much attention has been given to this in recent years, but putting improvements into effect, relatively easy at the centre, becomes increasingly uncertain the farther one goes from the major towns. Even existing schemes may be hard to enforce; teacher-training institutions, for example, work to an extremely thorough and elaborate programme for the students' school practice. In many cases, however, it is not fully observed, and in some instances we are told that it has been 'abolished in practice'.[26] For all the power of the central authorities, the brute facts of geography make their effective use difficult in the extreme—not an encouraging precedent for countries lacking such machinery but beset by similar problems on an even greater scale.

(5) EDUCATION FOR WORK

In the early post-revolutionary period, the Soviet authorities made strenuous attempts to prevent the development of mass general education from merely expanding a white-collar élite, unfitted by their schooling for any kind of technical or manual work—a problem which many of the developing countries know only too well. On the contrary, there was an attempt, through the setting up of the 'Unified Labour School', to ensure that the education of Soviet youth would be polytechnical as well as general; boys and girls were to become acquainted, in theory and practice, with the fundamental principles, processes and materials of industrial and agricultural production as part of their normal educational experience. This was a much more ambitious concept than the mere addition to the curriculum of an element of vocational or technical training. According to Lenin's wife, Nadezhda Krupskaya:

> Polytechnism is not a separate teaching subject, but should permeate every discipline, be reflected in the choice of subject-matter, whether physics or chemistry, natural science or social science. These disciplines must be linked with each other, with practical activity and especially with labour instruction. Only thus can labour and instruction be given a polytechnical character.[27]

This policy was tried out effectively during the 1920's, but was not a great success, partly because the practical details were insufficiently worked out, partly due to a lack of adequate facilities for practical training. Inevitably, a reaction set in, and polytechnical education (along with a great deal of progressive educational practice which had been in vogue during this period) was swept away in the return to more formal content and methods at the beginning of the Stalin era. The general schools became, and remained, overwhelmingly academic in character.

But schools of this type had traditionally been geared to preparing students for higher education and the professions, and it was clear by the 1950's that the very successes in expanding secondary education were giving rise to other problems. As Khrushchov said when proposing educational reforms in 1958:

> We are striving to have our entire youth, millions of boys and girls, go through the ten-year secondary school. Naturally enough, they cannot all be absorbed in the colleges. . . . In recent years, in view of the growing numbers passing out of the ten-year schools, a smaller proportion of boys

and girls enter college. The greater part of them . . . turn out to be quite unprepared for life and do not know in which direction to turn. . . . Owing to the fact that the secondary school is divorced from life, these boys and girls have absolutely no knowledge of production, and society does not know how best to utilise these young and vigorous people. . . . This state of affairs can hardly be considered right.[28]

Khrushchov, however, was concerned with broader issues than log-jams at college entrance level or preparation for a wider range of occupations; he wanted to change the attitudes of the rising generation towards manual work, which many of them, taking the cue from their parents (who were frequently involved in it themselves), despised as *chornaya rabota* (dirty, literally black, work). This was regarded as not only socially unfortunate but politically unacceptable:

We still have a sharp distinction drawn between mental and manual labour. . . . This is fundamentally wrong and runs counter to our teachings and aspirations. Some [boys and girls who have finished secondary school] even consider work beneath their dignity. . . . If a boy or girl does not study well, the parents . . . will frighten him by saying that . . . he will have to work as a common labourer. Physical work becomes a thing to frighten children with. . . . Such views are an insult to the working people of socialist society.

Such an incorrect situation . . . can no longer be tolerated. . . . It must be constantly inculcated in the young people that . . . work is a vital necessity for every Soviet person.[29]

As he summed up in one of the pithy expressions of which he was so fond, 'Learning and labour go together', a rhyming jingle in Russian (*uchenie i trud—vmeste idut*).

Accordingly, the 1958 'Law on strengthening the links of the school with life and further developing the system of public education in the USSR' made provision for the extension of polytechnical activities of all kinds. Greater emphasis was laid on production practice outside the school—senior pupils in secondary schools were required to spend one third of their curricular time working in factories or on farms; although the objective was not primarily vocational, they could pick up a trade qualification in this way. Earlier policies of aiming for full-time general secondary schooling for all were dropped, greater stress being placed on secondary vocational, trade or part-time general courses. Partly as a means of providing the extra time needed for polytechnical and labour training, the length of the course in the compulsory basic school was increased from seven years to eight, and the complete general school course from ten years to eleven. This expanded educational system, closely linked at every stage with the realities of productive work, was to be the principal means of creating the 'new Soviet man'.

It was not long, however, before it became clear that things were going wrong. Even before the two-year transition period was over, complaints began to be heard, and by 1964 the need was obviously felt for governmental action. In August of that year the Central Committee of the Communist Party and the Council of Ministers passed a resolution 'On the change of the period of instruction in secondary general labour polytechnical schools with production training'.[30] (Since Khrushchov did not fall from power until October, this can hardly be attributed to a change of régime.) While the basic school kept the eight-year course, the recently added eleventh year was removed, and the time for polytechnical subjects was cut; in particular, production practice in factories and on farms was reduced from a third to a quarter of total curricular time in the senior classes, and it was made clear that further changes were on the way.

Apart from the possibility that the extra eleventh year had been proving something of a strain on the country's resources, the main reason for the changes appears to have been a widespread failure in the arrangements for production practice:

The necessary procedure has not been introduced everywhere. . . . There has been a lack of clarity in the planning of production training. Many programmes were needlessly overloaded with material not clearly necessary . . . which artificially prolonged production training. . . . All this caused serious discontent among pupils and parents, and teachers as well.[31]

All too often, in fact, little more had been done than make the pupils spend the appropriate amount of time in whatever kind of industrial enterprise happened to be at hand, whether or not there were adequate (or any) training facilities. Where there was room for the pupils, with training workshops and trained instructors, the system worked tolerably well, but otherwise the pupils spent most of their time doing dull and repetitive jobs, watching the back of someone's neck while crowding round the occasional demonstration on the machines, or simply getting in the way. Nobody—pupils, parents, teachers, workers or managers—could raise much enthusiasm for the system in practice, whatever its merits may have been in theory. Educationally and industrially, it was proving wasteful and ineffective in most cases. It was rationalisation that the 1964 measures demanded, however, not abolition:

> Education in and for work has become the sacred watchword of the Soviet school.... This change in no way means a return to the old ten-year school, a repudiation of production training. Every teacher, every worker in public education, must realise, and persistently explain to the pupils and the people that the new ten-year school is a labour school, a polytechnical school, providing production training for its pupils.[32]

In practice, however, the actual changes brought about in the school syllabuses on work-training (as in other things) were obviously short-term expedients, cutting and patching the existing plans; this, and a clear note of uncertainty running through most of the official pronouncements[33] at the time, made it clear that more changes were to follow. For the moment, the Academy of Pedagogic Sciences of the RSFSR continued to work out more stable programmes, while practically every area of the educational system, including the Academy itself, was subjected to searching and often searing criticism in the Press.[34]

Towards the end of 1966 came another resolution of the Party Central Committee and the Council of Ministers, entitled 'On measures to improve the work of the secondary general educational school', laying down the guidelines for educational development during the next five-year plan.[35] The most important decision was to aim for universal secondary education to be established 'substantially' throughout the country by 1970. More specifically, as the Minister of Education explained:

By 1970, 75 per cent of those leaving the eight-year school will go into the senior classes. The rest will study in professional schools (*tekhnikumy*), shift schools for working youth and other educational institutions.[36]

This marks an obvious swing away from the position held by Khrushchov; the emphasis is now on full-time general secondary education, with part-time, trade and other vocational courses playing a relatively minor role. There is also a move away from production training of the kind envisaged in the 1958 Law. Practice of the old type, with a vocational bias, is no longer general in secondary schools, except where factory or farm conditions favour its being done properly. This seems to apply to only a minority; according to the Minister, 'About a third of all secondary schools have decided to continue with production training. . . . Let them work out their experience.'[37] For most, however, the old type of practice has gone. 'Life', says the Minister, 'has confirmed the profundity of the Leninist idea of a polytechnical *but not vocational* general educational school.'[38]

But this does not mean the abolition of polytechnical and labour training. 'The school must not build a fence around its activities',[39] hence the need for familiarity with the various forms of production in the area. 'The school must not rear *byeloruchki* [white-handed ones]',[40] hence the desirability of direct experience of work, although this is now more likely to take place in a school workshop than in a factory. Vocational training is replaced by vocational guidance from about the age of 14, with the aim of 'giving the youngsters experience of *various* jobs, and their significance to the economy, and help towards an informed choice of future vocation'.[41]

It is recognised that there are still considerable problems. 'For the Soviet school to be truly polytechnical, a great deal of work still needs to be done. We must construct courses in the theoretical disciplines. . . . Introducing pupils to the laws of nature, teachers of physics, biology and other subjects can show . . . how they relate to production.'[42] A good deal of work is going on now in this field, in an attempt to relate polytechnical studies to the more theoretical side, much as

R   249

Krupskaya demanded in the 1920's. Although some vocational training for adolescents still goes on (in trade schools), there has been a tendency to emphasise vocational training for those who have completed the ten-year school; during the school course itself, the aim of polytechnical education, 'deeper than before', is to give 'a general understanding of production'.[43] In an age of rapid technological change, this makes sense; there is not much point in concentrating on specific vocational training for youngsters of secondary school age when the jobs they train for may well have ceased to exist in twenty or even ten years. Whether these changes in polytechnical education will have the desired social effect is another matter; it is probably too early to try to judge anything as long-term as that. What has become clear enough in the decade since Khrushchov's reforms got under way is that the rather crude additive approach—putting youngsters at a bench or behind a tractor and waiting for their attitudes towards labour to change——does not work, and may even be counter-productive. If a *meaningful* programme of polytechnical education can be devised, however, this will obviously be of considerable interest to the developing countries.

(6) SCIENCE AND TECHNOLOGY

While polytechnical education has had its ups and downs, the parallel policy of emphasising science and technology has been pursued much more consistently since the Revolution, and can be seen at every level of the Soviet educational system. One of the best-known examples, perhaps, is the group of special secondary schools founded in the early 1960's for children highly gifted in mathematics and the natural sciences. Rather too much has been made of these schools, inside the USSR and out. For one thing, there are too few of them to have much impact on the system as a whole; and for another, it is what happens to children in the ordinary schools, not to a handful of specialists, that is really significant here.

The Soviet ten-year general school, which takes pupils from

the age of seven to seventeen, does in fact show considerable scientific bias. All children study mathematics throughout, while the secondary course includes physics, chemistry, biology and astronomy, as well as the usual technical subjects. There are minor variation from one republic to another, but in general mathematics and science subjects take up just over 40 per cent of the total time over the ten-year course. This, it must be stressed, is for the entire age group. The organisation of Soviet schools is comprehensive to a more extreme degree than anything existing (or, indeed, advocated) in the West; it permits neither 'streaming' nor any other kind of ability grouping, nor separation of children into 'sides' emphasising science or the humanities. In the senior forms, *extra* time of up to four hours a week is allocated for optional or elective subjects, but that is all. There is no way of avoiding this fairly heavy dose of science nor, conversely, for the scientifically inclined to concentrate on them. The curriculum has been designed as a culturally balanced diet of science and humanities for everyone; concessions to differences of taste and appetite are relatively recent and, so far at any rate, slight. For details, see Table 4.[44]

At the higher educational level, however, there is much more intensive specialisation by American or even Scottish, but not English, standards. In the universities and colleges a student normally specialises for five, or in some cases four, years. The bulk of this time is spent on one subject *area*, such as Russian language and literature, mathematics, metallurgy or mining. These are fairly wide areas, comprising a variety of course offerings, and account for about 60-70 per cent of total curricular time. The remainder is devoted to ancillary courses—political subjects, foreign languages, physical education, optional subjects and, in teacher-training institutes *and* in the universities, courses in pedagogy, psychology and teaching method.

A clear majority of students specialise on the scientific or technological side, though precise figures are hard to come by. In 1968/9, for instance, there were nearly 4½ million students in higher institutes; of these, 52·5 per cent were following courses with a technological bent—engineering, construction, agriculture, transport and communications. Since those studying science do so at the universities, and since the figures for these are not normally differentiated from the university enrolments as a whole, one can only say that the scientific bias,

TABLE 4

Ten-year School Curriculum (Project, 1965)

Periods per week in classes:

Subject	I	II	III	IV	V	VI	VII	VIII	IX	X
Russian language	12/10	10	10	7	5	3	3	2	—	—
Literature	—	—	—	3	2	2	2	3/4	3	3
Mathematics	6	6	6	6	6	6	6	6	6	5
History	—	—	—	2	2	2	2	3	5/4	3
Social study	—	—	—	—	—	—	—	—	—	2
Nature study	0/2	2	2	2	—	—	—	—	—	—
Geography	—	—	—	—	2	3	2	2	2	—
Biology	—	—	—	—	2	2	2	2	—	2
Physics	—	—	—	—	—	2	2	3/2	5	5
Astronomy	—	—	—	—	—	—	—	—	—	1
Chemistry	—	—	—	—	—	—	2	2	3/4	3
Technical drawing	—	—	—	—	—	1	1	1	—	—
Foreign language	—	—	—	—	5	4	4	2	2	2
Art	1	1	1	1	1	1	1	—	—	—
Music	1	1	1	1	1	1	1	1	—	—
Physical education	2	2	2	2	2	2	2	2	2	2
Labour training	2	2	2	3	3	3	2	2	4	4
Total	24	24	24	27	31	32	32	32	32	32
Options	—	—	—	2	2	2	2	4	4	4

This curriculum was worked out by the Academy of Pedagogic Sciences in 1965; the curricula actually put into effect vary in detail from this one, but are based on it. Entries such as 3/4 indicate 3 periods a week in the first half-year, 4 in the second.

theoretical and applied, is even greater than the figure suggests. In the secondary specialised schools (which provide professionally oriented courses for 15-19-year olds) this bias is even more obvious. Out of over 4¼ million students enrolled in 1968/9, no less than 68·5 per cent were following technical or technological courses.[45]

The figures do not tell the whole story, but they do illustrate current policies and attitudes. The prestige of science, and especially *applied* science, is high. An engineer, for example, enjoys much more esteem than a lawyer or medical practitioner —an esteem reflected in the competition for admission to the appropriate courses and in the salary that the successful graduate can command. It is hardly surprising that a régime based, however remotely, on Marxist principles should emphasise the natural sciences and their application in practice—science is seen as the key to understanding reality, applied science or technology as the means of transforming it. Principles, however, are notoriously difficult to translate into policy, let alone practice; in the USSR, other factors favoured the development of a scientific emphasis in education. The eminently practical preferences of Peter the Great certainly played their part; so, paradoxically, did Russia's relatively late start, which ensured that the dominant ideas to which the infant system was exposed were eighteenth-century enlightenment and nineteenth-century ideas of progress, more encouraging to the growth of scientific studies than a longer but weightier tradition firmly anchored in mediaeval law or theology. This, of course, is an over-simplification—Byzantine obscurantism had a frequently stultifying effect before the Revolution as had Stalinist bureaucracy after it. Nevertheless, the fact that Moscow University was founded by a chemist, Mikhail Lomonosov, indicates the kind of tradition that had been developing; so, perhaps, does the fact that he was also a poet.

If the factors contributing to the current emphasis on science are mixed, so are the results. There have been many complaints that the enormous energy put into scientific research and the training of technologists has not had quite the expected effects on the economy, agriculture being the most conspicuous and constant failure. On the whole, however, the policy of stressing science and technology has paid off; industrialisation, and hence the establishment of Soviet society, would hardly have been possible otherwise. (Lenin put the point succinctly when he defined communism as Soviet power plus the electrification of the whole country.) Obviously, training scientists has not been enough in itself; it has had to be accompanied by the training of supporting forces of technicians and skilled personnel at intermediate and lower levels—which has important implications for any country determining educational priorities.

(7) SOCIO-POLITICAL EDUCATION

Mention has already been made of political courses in institutions of higher education. These are only one example of the political and social commitment of the educational system, which many, following the example of Lenin himself, would regard as its most important function. From the orthodox point of view, the issue is simple—education must serve society by training the rising generation not only in the necessary skills and knowledge, but in the required attitudes as well. This, of course, is common in principle to all societies; where the Soviet system differs from most is in the single-mindedness with which this aim is pursued and the directness with which it is spelled out. For example:

Upbringing must inculcate in the school-children a love of knowledge and of work, and respect for people who work; it must shape the communist world outlook of the pupils and rear them in the spirit of communist morality and boundless loyalty to the country and the people, and in the spirit of proletarian internationalism.[46]

Apart from specifically political courses, such as those in colleges and final-year classes in secondary schools, practically the whole work of the system is geared to this end. The curriculum is used as a vehicle for political values, discipline and moral education are socially (and hence politically) based, while the activities and organisation of the youth movement and other extra-curricular bodies convey a political message at different levels and in various ways, from direct exhortation to constant exposure to loyalty symbols such as the red flag or picture of Lenin—functionally, the Soviet equivalent of Old Glory, the crucifix or the Annigoni portrait in the classroom.

The effectiveness of all this is uncertain, but it does seem that for all the talk of 'the communist world outlook' of the pupils and 'the spirit of proletarian internationalism', Soviet patriotism has a greater role to play. Ever since the 1940's when Stalin discovered the strength of its appeal, 'patriotism' and all its trappings have been acceptable in the USSR; and although it is officially distinguished from negative phenomena such as nationalism or, worse, 'Great Russian chauvinism', the difference in practice is not always clear.

Obviously, the question of the suitability of political education of the Soviet type does not arise in the developing countries; even those with left-wing governments, communist or otherwise, prefer to handle this side of education in very much their own way. That the most successful part of Soviet political education has been in reinforcing national feeling (to some extent on a Soviet rather than merely Russian basis), rather than conveying an understanding of Marxist theory, may be of some interest to many developing countries, also consisting of diverse ethnic and linguistic groups and searching hard for ways of instilling a sense of national identity to combat built-in centrifugal tendencies. The use of an educational system as a means of doing this has obvious attractions. But there are difficulties. In the first place, certain national groups in the USSR are probably still disaffected in spite of strenuous attempts to put across a sense of Soviet nationality in the last decades; conversely, Russian chauvinism is still alive and, from time to time, kicking. As far as one can tell, therefore, the success of this constant effort in socio-political education is limited at best. Further, what success *can* be claimed depends on having a mass system to work with—no government can use the schools to foster a sense of nationhood in an entire generation if most of them have little or no contact with the schools, and if it is not done with the entire generation then all that has been achieved has been further fragmentation. At a time when countries from India to Nigeria are in danger of falling apart, this is one factor to add to the already complicated matter of deciding educational priorities in the midst of a general shortage of resources.

CONCLUSION

It does appear, then, that much of the Soviet experience in nation-building is not specifically relevant to the situation in most developing countries. As has been observed, Russia at the time of the Revolution was considerably richer and more advanced educationally than most developing countries are now, and thus had at the same time less leeway to make up and more resources to do it with. Things were helped, too, by the existence of a revolutionary situation. This does not apply in most developing countries; and in those where it does, poverty, and often political differences, make the adoption of Soviet solutions unlikely. It is worth noting also that in several of the problems most acute in the Third World—rural education, say, or the training and supply of teachers—even the much wealthier Soviet Union has not, as yet, managed to find a long-term solution.

But in spite of the differences and the failures, the success of the USSR in creating what is by any standards an educated nation is instructive. It has been shown possible, even under conditions of financial stringency and much worse, to maintain a consistently high priority for education at all levels, from kindergarten to university and, with a few lapses, comprehensive mass education at that. The achievements in extra-scholastic, adult, evening and shift class and other forms of part-time education should be particularly useful, in view both of scarcity of resources in many countries (full-time courses are, after all, more expensive) and the growing need for periodic re-training in more and more fields. While it would be ludicrous to claim that there have been no problems in the maintenance of standards, it is still true that many of the choicer élitist myths, still current in this country and fostered in former colonies, have been effectively exploded in the USSR some time ago.

Finally, there is the use of the educational system as a major instrument of deliberate social change. It is not, of course, the only one; but it is hard to imagine the elimination of illiteracy, the radical change in the position of women, or the advance of industrialisation, to take but a few at random, having happened by any other means. Nor has this promotion of change been confined to manpower deployment, the development of science and technology, the useful in the most obvious and narrow sense; the Soviet educational system, at the cost of considerable diversion of resources, has consistently made it a major objective to transform general culture from a minority prerogative to a popular possession. Hence the 'balanced diet' of school courses, the general element even in the more specialised higher courses, the insistence on all-round development as an appropriate educational aim for the farmer or the lathe-operator no less than for the teacher or the physician. That there are frequent failures goes without saying, but to a surprising degree the policy does seem to work, whether we judge by the popularity of opera or poetry-readings, or by the fury any Russian will show if accused of being *nekul'turnyi*—uncultured. This fundamental commitment to an idea of the 'quality of life' underlies the more immediate concerns with production, technique and even social engineering, and the host of failures, distortions and downright betrayals should not obscure it. The defects of the system are clear enough; the final impression, however, is the magnitude of achievements in the face of great odds, and the stubborn survival of the conviction that through education it is still possible to improve man and the society in which he lives.

NOTES AND REFERENCES

1 Hans, N., *The Russian Tradition in Education* (Routledge and Kegan Paul, London, 1963).
2 Medlin, K. and Cave, W., 'Uzbekistan: Research on Socio-Cultural Change' *Research News* (Ann Arbor, 1964), xv, 3.
3 ibid., and Grant, N., *Soviet Education* (Penguin, 1968).
4 ibid.
5 Estimate from Newth, J. A., Glasgow University Institute of Soviet and East European Studies.
6 Notably Khrushchov's postponement of universal full-time secondary schooling in 1958, when the shortage had reached the late teenage point.

7 *Narodnoe Khozyaistvo SSSR v 1968 godu: Statisticheskii Ezhegodnik* (Statistika, Moscow, 1969), p. 669.

8 Oral communication.

9 Counts, G., *The Challenge of Soviet Education* (McGraw-Hill, 1957).

10 *Constitution of the USSR*, article 122.

11 According to the director of one Moscow boarding school, keeping the sexes together is *especially* important in boarding schools.

12 *Narodnoe Khozyaistvo SSSR 1968*, p. 674.

13 ibid., p. 693.

14 ibid.; *Nar. Khoz. 1965*.

15 Pilipovskii, Ya., Sel'skii uchitel'—problemy, suzhdeniya. *Uchitel'skaya gazeta*, 25 May 1967.

16 Prokofiev, M. A., 'Segodnya i zavtra nashei shkoly' *Pravda*, 12 December 1966.

17 V devyatyi klass. *Uchitel'skaya gazeta*, 15 April 1967.

18 *Nar. Khoz. 1968*.

19 Zalivadnyi, V., 'Na puti iz vos'mogo v devyatyi' *Uch. gaz.*, 22 July 1967.

20 Sledovat' dobrym primeram. *Uch. gaz.*, 17 March 1967.

21 K vseobshchemu srednemu. *Uch. gaz.*, 17 March 1967.

22 Noah, H., *Financing Soviet Schools* (Columbia, 1967), pp. 105-9.

23 Zaitsev, A., 'Vazhnaya zadacha' in *Narodnoe obrazovanie*, 8, 1966, p. 9.

24 *Nar. Khoz. 1968*.

25 Kuznechenkov, M., 'Odnogo optimizma malo . . .' *Uch. gaz.*, 1 July 1967.

26 Kakoi dolzhna byt' pedagogicheskaya praktika? *Uch. gaz.*, 1 April 1956.

27 Shapovalenko, S. G. (ed.), *Polytechnical Education in the USSR* (UNESCO, 1963), p. 43.

28 Khrushchov, N. S., *Proposals to Reform Soviet Education* (Soviet Booklet No. 42, October 1958).

29 ibid.

30 V TsK KPSS i Sovete Ministrov SSSR: Ob izmenenii sroka obucheniya v srednikh obshcheobrazovatel'nykh trudovykh politekhnicheskikh shkolakh s proizvodstvennym obucheniem. *Sovietskaya Rossiya*, 13 August 1964.

31 Desyatiletnyaya, trudovaya, politekhenichskaya. *Uch. gaz.*, 15 August 1964.

32 ibid.

33 Novyi uchebnyi god: kakim on budet v shkole? *Sovietskaya Rossiya*, 13 August 1964. Chto novogo v shkole? *Sovietskaya Rossiya*, 25 August 1964.

34 Deistvovat' edinym frontom. *Uch. gaz.*, 3 July 1965.

35 V TsK KPSS i Sovete Ministrov SSSR: O merakh dal'neishego uluchsheniya raboty srednei obshcheobrazovatel'noi shkoly. *Pravda*, 19 November 1966.

36 Prokofiev, M. A., Vuzy-shkole. *Vestnik vysshei shkoly*, 9, 1966, p. 7.
37 Prokofiev, M. A., 'Segodnya i zavtra nashei shkoly' *Pravda*, 12 December 1966.
38 Prokofiev, M. A., 'K novomu pod'emu sovietskoi shkoly' *Uch. gaz.*, 26 November 1966.
39 ibid.
40 ibid.
41 Ivanovich, K. and Epstein, D., 'Znaniya, politekhnizm trud' *Uch. gaz.*, 20 May 1967.
42 Prokofiev, M. A., *Pravda*, 12 December 1966.
43 Ivanovich, K. and Epstein, D., op. cit.
44 Akademiya pedagogicheskikh nauk RSFSR: *Obshchaya ob'yasnitel'naya zapiska k pererabotannym proektam uchebnogo plana i programm srednei shkoly*, pp. 15-16 (Moscow, 1965).
45 *Nar. Khoz. 1968.*
46 *Bringing the Soviet Schools Still Closer to Life* (Soviet Booklet No. 44, December 1958: English version of the 1958 Theses of the Central Committee of the CPSU and the Council of Ministers of the USSR).

INDEX